Leading Progress, given the COVID-19 crisis, is a timely reminder of the profound importance of having and maintaining a professional public service. This is a history of a union and more. Important questions of capacity, professional autonomy, and democratization of administration are raised throughout—and, crucially, the relationship of professional workers to the state as employer and the broader labour movement and working class.

BRYAN EVANS, Professor in the Department of Politics and Public Administration, Ryerson University

The many characters, communities, and causes that *Leading Progress* captures accurately depict the heart and soul of all unions, past and present. With density now greatest in the public sector, the value of professional associations has never been more important.

DAVE BULMER, President, AMAPCEO – Ontario's Professional Employees

In a crisis, the value of Canada's professional public service is suddenly obvious to everyone. But in "normal" times, whether they know it or not, Canadians owe a debt of gratitude to the dedicated men and women who ensure the safety of our food and the health of our environment. I'm delighted we now have a rich history of PIPSC's remarkable story.

HASSAN YUSSUFF, President of the Canadian Labour Congress

Jason Russell's stirring and comprehensive history of the first century of PIPSC's innovative organizing among public professionals tells a marvelous story about the power of unionism—not just to lift the standards of work, but to build a stronger economy and society.

JIM STANFORD, Economist and Director, Centre for Future Work

A clear, thorough study of a large, important group of Canadian public-sector workers—the professionals—who were historically cautious unionists more inclined to collaboration than confrontation, until neoliberal governments disrupted their working lives. Jason Russell has made excellent use of the substantial archival record, but even more impressively, he has woven in the voices of a large number of union members he interviewed. A useful addition to the shelf of modern labour history.

CRAIG HERON, Professor Emeritus, Department of History, York University

In *Leading Progress*, Jason Russell has accomplished a rare feat. He has written a book that is at once an incisive overview of labour and working-class history, as well as a detailed institutional biography that vividly captures the birth and transformation of the PIPSC from one of reluctant unionism to being at the centre of many of today's most pressing struggles for social and economic justice.

CARLO FANELLI, Assistant Professor and Coordinator of Work and Labour Studies, York University

Leading Progress

LEADING PROGRESS

The Professional Institute of the Public Service of Canada 1920–2020

Jason Russell

BETWEEN THE LINES
Toronto

Leading Progress
© 2020 Jason Russell

First published in 2020 by
Between the Lines
401 Richmond Street West
Studio 281
Toronto, Ontario M5V 3A8
Canada
1-800-718-7201
www.btlbooks.com

Cataloguing in Publication information available from Library and Archives Canada
ISBN 9781771134781

Text design by David Vereschagin, Quadrat Communications
Cover design by DEEVE

Printed in Canada

The publication of this book was made possible because of financial support from the Professional Institute of the Public Service of Canada.

We acknowledge for their financial support of our publishing activities: the Government of Canada; the Canada Council for the Arts; and the Government of Ontario through the Ontario Arts Council, the Ontario Book Publishers Tax Credit program, and Ontario Creates.

Table of Contents

Illustrations

Figures

Table

Acknowledgements

This book was made possible through the efforts of people within the Professional Institute of the Public Service of Canada and beyond. It began in 2016 as part of wider one-hundredth-anniversary planning when the union formed an internal editorial committee, comprising Steve Hindle, Bob McIntosh, Brian Beaven, and Laureen Allan, to identify an author to write it. That committee later supplied comments on the book's various chapters and final manuscript and otherwise helped clarify aspects of the union's history. Laureen Allan deserves particular recognition for making this book possible, especially because of her work arranging interviews and then transcribing interview recordings. Other PIPSC staff helped make the book possible including Linda Gauthier, Mathieu Gorman, Marielle Nadon, Linda Martel, Tania Talbot, and Alain Daoust. Joseph Tohill edited the English manuscript, and Hélène Poulin of PIPSC's staff translated it into French. (Hélène thanks her colleagues Vicken Avrikian, Pascal Roseau, and Christian Poulin for helping make that possible.) The book's design was the work of David Vereschagin.

President's Message

Leading Progress is the story of the Professional Institute of the Public Service of Canada (PIPSC). This history commemorates the one hundredth anniversary of the founding of PIPSC and honours those individuals whose vision, time, and efforts have led one hundred years of progress for Canadians and produced a century of results for workers.

We have come a long way since 6 February 1920, when a group of public service employees assembled for their first meeting. Their purpose was to promote the welfare of their members, maintain high professional standards, and enhance the usefulness of the public service to Canadians.

We are defenders of Canada's world-class public service, a public service that acts on the basis of evidence with the sole purpose of protecting the public good. Canadians need and deserve public services with the resources and personnel to maintain and improve the quality of life throughout our vast country. This is why PIPSC protects the integrity of public service professionals who are the champions that safeguard the social, economic, and environmental wellbeing of Canada and Canadians.

PIPSC has been a leader in advocating for social and economic justice that benefits all. Our efforts have not always been immediately successful, but the foresight and tenacity of our members have led progress and produced results, even if, in some cases, it has taken many years.

I applaud the diversity of PIPSC members and staff whose dedication created and nurtured our dynamic organization. Our diversity is our strength, and—united—we are better together.

I am honoured to serve as PIPSC president, especially as we celebrate one hundred years of results. I am proud of the progress we have made, and I am confident that we will continue to lead progress over the next hundred years.

Debi Daviau
President
The Professional Institute of the Public Service of Canada

Foreword

With the completion of this new work and its companion volume, *Serving the State*, we now have a definitive account of the first one hundred years of our collective history. As we mark this impressive milestone—PIPSC's one hundredth anniversary—it is only fitting that we look back over this period, and especially the last fifty years, to discern patterns that help us understand who we have become as an organization of employee advocates. While the most significant event in our history is likely the change from professional association to bargaining agent, this new book demonstrates that we have been on a steady evolution toward our current status as a member-focused, evidence-based organization that embraces both unionization and the best attributes of professional associations.

The defining factor in this evolution is undoubtedly leadership. The Professional Institute has never been the largest union in the federal public sector, but sustained leadership and vision have enabled us to exert influence well beyond our size. The success of the Institute, as chronicled in this book, has occurred in areas as diverse as collective bargaining, government relations, and community goodwill. Leadership by elected members and dedicated staff is evident within PIPSC, among our sister unions, in the corridors of political power, and within our community of allies and friends. Leadership in all our endeavours has become our brand—an important part of our DNA as a union dedicated to the wellbeing of both our members and Canadian society. "Building community to act collectively to improve our members' lives" is our statement of purpose. This book amply demonstrates that we have lived up to this purpose over the last one hundred years. We have every reason to believe that over the next one hundred years we will build on our rich history.

Edward Gillis
Chief Operating Officer and Executive Secretary
The Professional Institute of the Public Service of Canada

Introduction

O ver the past forty years, a wide range of historians has examined the history of organized labour in Canada. Since labour history emerged in Canada as a vibrant sub-field of social history in the late 1970s, labour historians have emphasized writing history from the point of view of workers. They have thought about how workers organize to form new unions, pursue change through collective bargaining and advocacy beyond the workplace, resist job loss, engage in political action, and otherwise try to make better lives for themselves and their families.

This book is a history of the Professional Institute of the Public Service of Canada (PIPSC). A union founded in 1920 as a professional association, it now represents 60,000 public sector workers employed in a wide array of jobs in Canadian federal government departments and agencies, as well as some provincial and territorial jurisdictions. The book addresses three basic questions about PIPSC: What is it? What does it do? And how has it shaped its members lives and been altered by them? It also explores several sub-issues linked to these overall questions, including the circumstances in which PIPSC was founded, its relations with the government as employer, and changes in its membership and leadership, its internal organizational structure and governance, and its advocacy and collective bargaining.

PIPSC's leadership commissioned this volume to mark the organization's one-hundredth anniversary. Principally intended for past, current, and future PIPSC members, the book is also intended to be accessible to a wider reading audience, to those with an interest in organized labour or the public sector. This is a story about public sector union activists in an important workers' organization that helped shape the lives of everyday citizens, and activists' voices are often, eloquently, and forcefully heard. It is not meant to be a hagiography—nobody in PIPSC was interested in viewing themselves through rose-coloured glasses. Instead, it contributes to existing research on labour in Canada by presenting a balanced analysis of what this important public sector workers' organization did over a hundred-year period. While the book is not structured around a comprehensive theoretical framework, it does consider the changes in workers' lives over time and how they dealt with those changes. Historical materialism thus shapes the overall narrative.

PIPSC in Labour and Working-Class History   Unions have been the subject of historical inquiry in Canada since Eugene Forsey's magnum opus on trade unions in nineteenth-century Canada and Bryan Palmer and Greg Kealey's study of the Knights of Labour in Ontario appeared in 1982. The existing research tends to focus on private sector unions, especially those in manufacturing, rather than those in the public sector. Industrial workers and their unions are the focus of Sam Gindin's history of the Canadian Auto Workers, David Soebel and Susan Meurer's history of Inglis, Jamie Swift's work on the Communication, Energy, and Paperworkers, and Wayne Roberts's book on the Energy and Chemical Workers Union. Service-sector workers take centre stage in Eileen Sufrin's research on worker militancy at the Eaton's department store chain and Julia Smith's recent dissertation on union organizing in banks.[1] The broader working-class experience is the subject of a considerable literature exemplified by the work of Craig Heron.[2]

Public sector workers' organizations are comparatively understudied in Canada. Recent studies have explored the overall public sector union experience in Canada, but studies of specific unions, such as Stephanie Ross's dissertation on the founding of the Canadian Union of Public Employees (CUPE), are rare.[3] Studies of public sector unions in the United States include books on the American Federation of Government Employees, the American Federation of Teachers and the National Education Association, and the American Federation of State, County, and Municipal Employees. But American public sector unions are also underrepresented in American labour historiography, especially considering their centrality to the American labour movement.[4]

Because of its focus on a single, significant public sector union, this book helps to fill a void in the existing literature on the history of workers' organizations not only in Canada but also in North America more broadly. The fact that PIPSC members are professional workers also enhances this book's contribution to work on the history of unions in North America because people employed in professional occupations have received less scholarly attention than workers in other job classifications.

Researching PIPSC   Research and writing the history of any organization requires time and access to primary sources. The writing of this book was constrained by when PIPSC commissioned it to commemorate the organization's one-hundredth anniversary. Work on the book began in the summer of 2017, but it had to be completed by the end of 2019 to allow time for translation and printing in 2020.

An overabundance of research sources made writing the book possible but also resulted in the challenge of deciding what to include and emphasize. *Leading Progress* draws on extensive archival material deposited by PIPSC at Library and Archives Canada or held at its National Office, both located in Ottawa, Ontario. The book also relies heavily on oral history interviews. Dozens of current and past PIPSC members from across Canada readily agreed to sit for interviews, and the book incorporates as much content from each interviewee as was practicable. Oral interviews not only yield general recollections of past work and union experience but also reveal significant insights not found in documents. The interviews referenced here very much fall into the latter category as they describe PIPSC in a way that documents alone could not do. The availability of such varied research sources has tremendously helped the writing of PIPSC's history. The objective with all of the sources used was to try to ensure that the diversity of the PIPSC membership experience was presented regardless of where people were employed in the public service, where they lived in Canada, the official language that they spoke, or what they did for a living.

Organization   This narrative is divided into six chapters, organized chronologically around common topics and themes, including leadership and staff, governance, collective bargaining, the union in politics and the community, and the experience of being a union member. The book places more emphasis on the decades since 1970, as it is a sequel of sorts to *Serving the State*, the book PIPSC commissioned that year to mark the organization's fiftieth anniversary. That volume extensively covered aspects of PIPSC's progress from 1920 to 1970.

The first chapter of this book describes the period covered in *Serving the State*. Yet in contrast to the earlier work's emphasis on internal governance issues, chapter 1 describes the socio-economic and political conditions in which PIPSC was founded, how the organization progressed through the 1920s and into the World War II years, and how it became a union with the introduction of public sector collective bargaining legislation in the late 1960s.[5]

Begun as a professional association in a period when worker militancy was suppressed in Canada, PIPSC was part of a wider effort to professionalize the public service, eliminate cronyism, and promote the principal of hiring based on merit. From 1920 to the late 1960s, PIPSC members viewed themselves as professionals, members of an employee association. As Canada grew and became more industrialized and prosperous, PIPSC changed along with the country. In its early decades, the organization was made up of white, male, anglophone professionals, a reality that reflected who the employer hired at the time. The composition of the Institute altered after World War II as more women entered the public service. Public policies like official bilingualism and multiculturalism shaped PIPSC. More francophones joined in the 1960s, and in the following decades its membership reflected Canada's changing demographics, becoming more diverse and including more new Canadians from a wide variety of countries.

In the late 1960s, as PIPSC changed from an association to a union, its members continued to try collectively to better their own lives and those of the people they served. Much of PIPSC's organizational identity was formed well before the introduction of the Public Service Staff Relations Act (PSSRA) in 1967, which allowed the unionization of public employees. That law was rooted in discussions of the nature of public service employment relations that began decades earlier, but its passage still had a profound impact on PIPSC and how its members viewed themselves. Much of the change in perception that occurred related to the idea of public service professionalism. PIPSC members have historically had much higher levels of educational attainment than what is found in wider Canadian society. Past and present members use the term "PIPSC" interchangeably with "Institute" when describing the organization, but "union" is used with far less frequency—even fifty years after the introduction of formal collective bargaining through the PSSRA. (All three terms will be used interchangeably in this narrative.) The second chapter covers the 1970s. This was a transformative decade for PIPSC, during which its members adapted to the benefits and limitations of collective bargaining and public sector workers suffered from the imposition of wage and price controls. PIPSC grew during the 1970s, and that growth led to difficult internal discussions about the organization's structure and governance. Chapter 3 describes the 1980s, during which PIPSC began to experience greater demographic change as the first baby boomers began to move into leadership roles. PIPSC had already elected its first woman president in the 1960s, and the 1980s brought more women into elected positions. Political changes during that decade also affected PIPSC. Canada elected its first majority Progressive Conservative government since John Diefenbaker had been prime minister in the early 1960s. Attitudes about the role of government began to change with the emergence of neoliberalism, a political and economic ideology that advocated policies such as diminishing the role of the state, deregulating business, pursuing free trade agreements, and weakening social safety nets. Canadian public employees felt its influence.

The fourth chapter focuses on the 1990s, when governments implemented neoliberal fiscal austerity policies that adversely affected PIPSC members. During this period, the organization developed a greater public profile, brought in new members, became more complex, and dealt with internal conflict. Chapter 5 covers the difficult period that followed in the 2000s. The election of a new Conservative government—the party had pointedly dropped the prefix *Progressive*—brought open hostility from that government toward public service workers. Yet the Institute continued to make gains through collective bargaining. PIPSC elected its third woman president, and there was more generational change as younger workers joined the union and baby boomers retired. The final chapter chronicles the 2010s. Many of the issues that had concerned PIPSC in preceding decades remained the same—wages and benefits, changes in job requirements, and government policy toward public servants, for example—but the organization and its members had learned how to handle them better. The return of a Liberal government in 2015 marked another significant political change. PIPSC elected its fourth woman president, and as a new generation of activists became involved, the organization took stock of its first hundred years.

The story told in these chapters is a complex one that highlights the achievements of and the challenges faced by the Institute and its members during PIPSC's first century. During that time, PIPSC evolved to become a union that engages in collective bargaining and advocacy beyond the workplace. Its origins as a professional association have shaped the Institute's evolution in ways that have made it different from other public sector unions: it remains organized on occupational lines rather than by department or agency; it avows non-partisanship, even as it has become more politically engaged; and it takes a more collaborative approach to labour-management relations and collective bargaining than most of its counterparts. As it has from the beginning, PIPSC represents public servants across Canada, though its members are concentrated in major urban centres. Half of PIPSC's members are located in Canada's National Capital Region, with Toronto having the second-largest number and

Montreal and Vancouver vying for the third-highest concentration. As they have for a century, PIPSC members continue to influence the lives of Canadian citizens, even if Canadians remain unaware of that fact.

Chapter 1

Starting as Professionals, 1920-69

To understand how the Professional Institute of the Public Service of Canada (PIPSC) now operates as an advocacy organization for its members, we need to look back to the formation of the early Canadian civil service. The context for the Institute's development can be traced back to the late nineteenth century, indeed almost to Confederation in 1867. PIPSC originated shortly after the end of World War I. This was a key period in Canadian history as organized labour overall was under attack and in decline. Several important trends that appeared in Canada from just before the turn of the twentieth century to the 1920s fundamentally shaped how the Institute would develop and how its leaders and members would view themselves into the post–World War II years. This chapter discusses how PIPSC emerged and changed along with Canada during its first fifty years, when major external and internal influences shaped the Institute.

This chapter differs from those that follow as it covers a much longer time period. And because the Institute did not engage in collective bargaining until the very end of this period, it says much less about negotiations with the employer than later chapters. This chapter focuses on who joined the Institute, what it was like to a be a member, and the agenda its members pursued. It incorporates substantial archival material held at Library and Archives Canada but makes much less use of oral history than later chapters. From its founding to the late 1960s when the introduction of labour legislation turned PIPSC from a professional association into a union, PIPSC evolved along with the country and the federal government. Yet even as its members experienced significant change, there was remarkable continuity in the Institute's activities. The Institute's fundamental ethos was formed during its first half century, and, as later chapters will show, that ethos endured beyond 1970.

Forming a Civil Service   The nineteenth-century origins of the Canadian civil service might not seem immediately germane to the formation of the Institute in 1920. Yet there is a direct progression from the establishment of the Confederation-era civil service to PIPSC's development in the years immediately following World War I. The need for a permanent structure to implement government policy in the pre-Confederation period—namely, a civil service—was noted as early as the late 1830s by John Lambton, the first Earl of Durham. Lambton authored what became popularly known as the Durham Report in the aftermath of the 1837 rebellions in Upper and Lower Canada, and he noted that the lack of a civil service contributed to governance problems in the two colonies.[1]

Canada achieved Confederation in 1867, and the first Civil Service Act was passed the following year. That act divided the civil service into two groups: the departmental staff based in Ottawa, known as the inside service, and the outside service comprising people who worked across the country. Yet the act failed to address patronage and cronyism problems that pre-dated Confederation. The so-called spoils system that prevailed in Canada, as well as in the United Kingdom and United States, meant that whichever party formed the government had the right to replace civil servants as it thought necessary.[2]

The obvious problem of governments appointing their allies rather than people who were qualified for civil service roles led to reform efforts in all three countries. Canada's next Civil Service Act of 1882 introduced entrance exams, which had first been used in the United Kingdom. The problem was that these exams were not especially difficult, setting a low bar for prospective appointees. The late nineteenth-century federal government, which was dominated by the Conservative Party during the crucial years after Confederation, recognized that attracting qualified people to the civil service required offering inducements that could not be readily found in the private sector. Since government could not necessarily afford to pay wages as high as those paid by firms, it offered other benefits, such as pensions, first offered with passage of the Superannuation Act of 1870.[3]

Recognizing the need for further study of the civil service, the government of Liberal prime minister Wilfrid Laurier established the Civil Service Commission in 1908. The Canadian state had steadily formed new administrative entities to run the country from 1867 onward, and managing the growing civil service had become part of that process. The Treasury Board, an entity that would loom large in the history of PIPSC, had been created on 2 July 1867, along with other original government departments and functions, including Agriculture, Finance, Justice, the Post Office, the Privy Council Office, Public Works, and the Secretary of State. The Department of Labour was added in 1909. PIPSC members would eventually work in all of these various departments or in successor organizations. The basic structure of the Canadian civil service was in place by the end of the first decade of the twentieth century, but major change occurred during the four-year period beginning in 1914.

World War I, the Workers' Revolt, and Whitleyism   When PIPSC was founded in 1920, Canada had just emerged from World War I (1914–18). The experience of four years of global conflict transformed the country. Most importantly for organized labour, the early 1920s marked the end of the Workers' Revolt, a period of labour unrest across many of the victorious allied powers and an era most commonly associated in Canada with the Winnipeg General Strike of 1919. Canadian schoolchildren do not learn much labour history, but that landmark strike is one event that elementary and secondary school history classes cover. Yet the Workers' Revolt involved far more than just one strike in Winnipeg, even though that was a key event in Canadian history. As Craig Heron writes, "between 1917 and 1925 working-class defiance swelled up in industrial centres across the country." Strikes erupted across Canada and the United States, led by union leaders with radical goals. The 1917 Russian Revolution caused governments across Europe and in North America to fear that revolution was at hand. This was certainly true among the victorious allied powers such as Britain, where the Glasgow General Strike of 1919 sowed fear of revolution.[5]

Worker militancy in Canada right after World War I can be attributed to some fundamental factors. The country that experienced the Workers' Revolt differed markedly from pre-war Canada. Nobody then had paid personal income tax, although provinces and municipalities began trying to collect estate and corporate taxes in 1900. The country's major companies had been concentrated in industries like railroads, banking, and insurance. Yet by 1918 wartime production had increased and diversified Canada's industrial capacity. The country had produced over a billion dollars' worth of munitions for the British imperial war effort, and 62,000 Canadians had died fighting in Western Europe. Income tax, initially introduced as a wartime measure, became permanent.[6] The war fostered enormous economic expansion in Canada, and though prosperity was unevenly shared, the experience of the war transformed people's expectations about the quality of their lives. Workers and their unions had little interest in returning to the pre-war status quo, and the Russian Revolution captured the imagination of many left-wing labour activists. If it happened in Russia, then it could happen in other countries.

In Canada and elsewhere, the state and business violently opposed workers' new militancy. The Winnipeg General Strike affords the most obvious insights into what happened to workers. It pitted the Winnipeg Building Trades Council and Metal Trades Council, the two bodies representing workers, against the Citizens' Committee of One Thousand, which represented the city's employers. The strike grew to involve 30,000 workers, including federal public sector postal workers. Striking workers maintained essential services in Winnipeg, but the federal government intervened, and strike leaders were arrested and convicted of sedition. Across Canada, authorities used similar sanctions to end strikes, sending a clear message: workers and their organizations could operate only within very limited legal parameters in post–World War I Canada. This knowledge, no doubt, weighed on the minds of those thinking about forming an association to represent civil servants.[7]

The Workers' Revolt period set the boundaries of industrial legality up to World War II. Industrial legality broadly means what the state deems permissible in workplace relations. Under the system of "industrial voluntarism" that then prevailed in Canada, the state, business, and labour participated as partners to deal with work and employment issues. However, labour was at best a junior partner, with the state and business wielding far more power and workers lacking basic collective bargaining rights. Additionally, what was legal for Canadian workers to do in terms of their resistance to employers and the state had been shaped by the experience of conflict in industrial workplaces, making the applicability of the boundaries of industrial legality and industrial voluntarism to the public sector an open question. The precarious legality in which unions operated following the Workers' Revolt was nothing new. Throughout the nineteenth century, unions had existed in a precarious legal environment. Passage of the 1872 Trade Union Act had made unions legal in Canada, but they remained constrained in many other ways.

Whether workers fell under federal or provincial jurisdiction further complicated the state's role in setting the limits of industrial legality. The events of 1919 showed the federal government's clear willingness to intervene in labour disputes across the country, regardless of jurisdiction. The matter of jurisdiction over labour and employment matters was decided in 1925 by the Judicial Committee of the Privy Council through the *Snider* decision.[8] That case held that labour and employment matters were under provincial authority. But people employed by the federal public service would obviously fall under federal legislation.

Even so, Canada was unique in the early twentieth century as it had a leading public figure who was keenly interested in workplace relations and how to keep them peaceful. William Lyon Mackenzie King, who would later become Canada's longest-serving prime minister, was the country's first industrial relations expert. An associate of the Rockefeller family, he helped develop the Colorado Industrial Plan in response to the Ludlow Massacre that occurred during a strike at a Rockefeller-owned mine in the United States. He abhorred social conflict and expounded his ideas for workplace partnership and the resolution of industrial disputes in his 1918 book, *Industry and Humanity*.[9] The fact that King was open to employees being partners in organizations was important because, even though the Workers' Revolt was suppressed in Canada, he would be the country's prime minister for most of the first thirty years of the Institute's existence.

Nineteen eighteen was an important year leading up to the formation of the Institute because it also marked the introduction of another civil service act. Prime Minister Robert Borden, who had advocated for further civil service reforms since 1914, was committed to appointment by merit, an end to the abuses of patronage, and a return to superannuation. (Superannuation, or civil service pensions, had been repealed in 1898, and Borden was particularly critical of that decision.) At that time, the federal government employed slightly over 47,000 civil servants, the largest number working on railways and canals. Just under 4,300 were employed in the inside service based in Ottawa.[10] The 1918 Civil Service Act aimed to end partisan political involvement, enshrine merit-based selection and promotion, and further professionalize the civil service.

A key development that emerged in the United Kingdom towards the end of World War I—the Whitley Council—profoundly influenced Canadian civil service employment relations in the postwar years. Understandably, given Canada's origins as a British colony, the organization of Britain's civil service had profoundly influenced the shape and purpose of its Canadian counterpart. The Whitley Council, named for British member of Parliament John Henry Whitley, emerged from the British government's efforts to find new methods of handling industrial disputes and blunting labour militancy and racialism, especially the Shop Stewards Movement, during World War I. Whitley, a Liberal and a businessman, called for a "New Liberalism." The Whitley Committee on Relations between Employers and Employed was created in 1916 to consider how to deal not only with wartime militancy but also to establish conditions that would stay in place after the war. His committee produced reports in 1917 and 1918 that made key recommendations, including the creation of Joint Industrial Councils (JICs) to govern employment relations in key industries.[11] Those councils, which became known as "works councils," provided forums for management and labour to meet to negotiate workers' terms of employment. Whitley's recommendations on workplace relations significantly shaped civil service employment relations into the late 1960s not only in Britain but also at the federal level in Canada.

Founding PIPSC   The founding of PIPSC in 1920 was influenced by two key factors that would long remain at the centre of policy discussions in the Institute: pensions (superannuation) and job classification. By 1920, the size and complexity of the civil service surpassed the workforce of the largest private sector employers. That year, the Civil Service Commission, unable to handle the extraordinarily difficult task of managing the rising number of job classifications for the country's civil servants, resorted to hiring American consulting firm Arthur Young and Company to devise a system.[12] The American federal civil service had already successfully devised a classification system, and the Civil Service Commission obviously reasoned that the same could be done in Canada. Civil servants across Canada were invited to submit information cards describing their duties in as much detail as they wished. In the end, the consultant's recommendations produced widespread disapproval and a lack of consensus on how to create a classification system encompassing the entire federal civil service. In contrast to the job classification issue, superannuation was dealt with more satisfactorily, but with the understanding that the government would have sole discretion over the terms of pension plans. A new superannuation act was passed in 1924.[13] The Institute approved of the concept of public pensions, but its activism in the 1920s and 1930s was more genteel than militant. The 1920s Institute was part social club, part advocacy organization. Members were concerned with pay and pensions in the first two decades of the Institute's existence, but they were also preoccupied with maintaining professional occupational standards. At this time, PIPSC was a professional organization and acted like one.

The fact that professional employees in the federal civil service wanted to establish an organization to represent their interests was not unusual in Canada during the late nineteenth and early twentieth centuries. Other professional associations formed during this period included the Canadian Medical Association (1867) and the Association of Professional Engineers of Ontario (1922).[14] The idea of forming the Institute had been proposed first by John Challies, a member of the Engineering Institute of Canada. Already a Civil Service Association had been formed in Ottawa, but there was widespread feeling among professional employees that it did not adequately represent their interests. Civil servants in pro-

J. B. Challies, Founder of the Professional Institute

Figure 1-1: PIPSC founder J. B. Challies. *PIPSC photo database.*

fessional classifications were also aware of the British Professional Institute of Civil Servants and felt it appropriate to found a Canadian equivalent.[15]

The Whitley Council model and the British Professional Institute of Civil Servants shaped the form of Canada's postwar civil service, but so too did the Canadian government's strong interest in increasing Canada's independence from Britain. An expanding Canadian civil service was needed to help the country shake off its pre–World War I status as a British dominion and assume international status as a country equal to others. Prime Minister Robert Borden felt that having professional civil servants strengthened Canada's role at the Versailles Peace Conference. Greater autonomy from Britain was supported by O. D. Skelton and many of the other "Ottawa Men," as historian J. L. Granatstein describes them, who created Canada's civil service at its senior levels during the interwar years.[16]

As a workers' organization, PIPSC was, from the beginning, unique for a key reason: the education level of its members. Earning a university degree was an extraordinary accomplishment at the time; only 4,007 bachelor's degrees were awarded in Canada the year that PIPSC was founded. (That number would grow to slightly over 17,000 by 1950.) PIPSC members all had either degrees or professional qualifications. And, in the 1920s and 1930s, they were overwhelmingly anglophone men who led middle-class lifestyles. This meant that their view of themselves was markedly different from that of people who joined other workers' organizations. PIPSC members were not like workers who toiled in manufacturing or service-industry jobs. Working in a professional occupation in the pre–World War II civil service came with status similar to management in private industry.[17]

From the start, the Institute strongly emphasized maintaining professional standards and ongoing education for its members. The first resolution passed at the 1920 annual general meeting related to helping civil servants who had not begun or completed their university degrees. Directly tying the Institute's policy position to the greater welfare of the country, the resolution, proposed by future PIPSC president K. M. Cameron, noted that such members were "handicapped" in their career progression and so could not provide the public with the best possible level of service. This was an early example of the Institute's tactic, evident in its annual general meeting documents and other position papers, of linking the interests of its members to those of the Canadians they served.[18]

The professional employees who formed the Institute's membership in the early 1920s were part of an organization that had the approval of government (in the sense that Robert Borden, among others, wanted a professional civil service). Yet they were also critical of government policy as it pertained to them. The government's approach to civil service reorganization, especially its hiring of outside consultants, attracted particular scorn. The Institute's position on such an issue might well have been predicted by the government. Institute members held professional designations and exclusive educational credentials by 1920s standards, and so they felt they could ably undertake any necessary reorganization of the civil service, especially since they made up so much of it. The decision to hire an American rather than a British consulting firm was also at odds with the general pattern of British influence in the shaping of Canada's civil service.

The influence of British civil service practice was keenly felt and welcomed in Ottawa in the 1920s, yet government policy-makers looked south to the United States to supply recommendations that would shape civil service policy. Even though Britain in the 1920s had management consultants and organizations like the Tavistock Institute that specialized in employment policy, the government hired a Chicago firm instead. In response, the Institute's 1922 annual general meeting passed a resolution appointing a committee "to prepare a memorandum deprecating the employment of the Chicago firm Griffenhagen and Associates for the purpose of reorganizing the civil service of Canada and requesting that the contract with the firm be cancelled."[19] The use of external consultants continued to vex the Institute from the 1920s to the 1940s, routinely reappearing to raise its ire.

PIPSC in the Community to World War II

The government may have found the Institute's criticism of reorganization annoying, but it nonetheless valued the Institute's public advocacy role on behalf of the civil service. During the interwar years, the Institute became both a local Ottawa institution and a national organization—one that enjoyed a public respectability and stature that other professional associations and unions would surely have envied. The Ottawa-centred nature of PIPSC's membership was determined by the structure of the civil service. From 1920, the Institute's members were based mainly in Ottawa, and that situation persisted into the war years. Yet the Institute was also able to project a national voice that few other worker organizations in Canada could rival. The federal government helped the Institute project that voice by giving it privileged access to the newest form of mass communication: radio.

The Institute's radio presence enabled it to educate Canadian citizens about the roles performed by the country's professional civil service. Beginning in 1925, the country's first national radio network, operated by the Canadian National Railway, invited Institute members to present talks on a range of issues pertaining to their specific expertise, and these were broadcast by local stations across the country. Such talks, no longer than fifteen minutes, had to be approved by the members' government departments and delivered preferably (though not always) by those who wrote them. PIPSC showed great interest in seeing a publicly owned radio service expanded across the country. In 1928, when the Liberal government of William Lyon Mackenzie King set up the Royal Commission on Radio Broadcasting, or Aird Commission, the Institute submitted a brief supporting the creation of a national public-radio network.[20]

Radio talks were a major undertaking in the 1930s, with twenty-five of them delivered in 1933 alone. Clearly intended to have wide, non-partisan appeal, the talks covered such topics as tourists and national parks, income tax laws, plant breeding, art and life, and scientific and professional work under the government of the Dominion of Canada. Broadcast from 7:30 to 7:45 p.m. on Tuesdays, they allowed Canadian families, who had finished dinner earlier in the evening and were perhaps going to listen to a radio drama at 8 p.m., to first spend a few minutes learning about the valuable role that the federal government and its professional workers played in their daily lives. The relatively benign nature of the radio talks may have bored some listeners, and the discussion topics seem at odds with social and economic conditions of the Great Depression, which gripped Canada in the 1930s. But the talks were undoubtedly meant to help reassure people that government was functioning well at a time when the economy most certainly was not.[21]

The Institute appeared, too, in Canada's national print media, attracting national press coverage from the time of its founding. A *Globe and Mail* article described a speech given by a University of Toronto professor at the Institute's 1921 annual general meeting (AGM), for example, and a 1925 article in the *Christian Science Monitor* discussed a McGill University professor's speech to the thousand people who attended that year's AGM in Ottawa. The Institute's priorities also garnered attention in print, such as a 1922 *Globe and Mail* article that explained PIPSC's requests for wage increases.[22] The media portrayed the Institute as a professional organization, a responsible part of the civil service that made reasonable demands of government. Because it was not perceived as a workers' organization, even though it acted like one in advocating for pensions and salary increases, for example, the Institute escaped the scorn that the media in the 1920s often heaped upon other workers' organizations in Canada.

PIPSC emerged largely unscathed from the economic turmoil of the 1930s. The 1935 AGM minutes reflected a growing organization with an accomplished and occupationally diverse membership. That year, a member named Diamond Jenness, an ethnologist at the National Museum of Canada, was awarded an honourary doctorate by the University of New Zealand. That sort of distinction was not unusual, as another member, Arthur Gibson, who worked as an entomologist at the Department of Agriculture, was awarded an honourary Doctor of Laws degree by Queen's University in Kingston. As Canada headed into the Second World War, such members meant the Institute was well prepared to assist the Canadian government in the war effort.[23]

World War II, The National Joint Council, and Collective Bargaining

The Institute's records, both internal and at Library and Archives Canada, do not go into detail about World War II (1939–45), but that conflict's lasting impact is still evident. The war years further professionalized the Canadian federal public service. The Institute's relations with the government changed, and new labour relations practices were introduced in the private sector that would later have a lasting impact on public sector labour relations. PIPSC was one of several federal employee associations that coordinated their efforts to pursue common policy objectives, such as superannuation.

The year 1944 was important in Canadian labour and employment history. The country had again engaged in full war mobilization, unemployment was virtually eliminated, and organized labour expanded. Canada had long been home to unions affiliated with the American Federation of Labour (AFL), and the Congress of Industrial Organizations (CIO) had arrived in the country to support striking auto workers during a 1937 strike at General Motors in Oshawa, Ontario. The CIO, founded in 1935, was a more militant competitor of the AFL, and it was CIO unions, like the United Auto Workers and the United Steelworkers of America, that grew the most during the war years. The influence of American labour organizations grew to such an extent that, during the first two decades following World War II, most unionized private sector workers in Canada belonged to American-based international unions.

In 1944, Canadian workers forced a reluctant Prime Minister Macken-zie King and his wartime Liberal government to recognize the right to col-lective bargaining. Nearly a decade earlier in the United States, the National Labour Relations Act (1935), or Wagner Act, had extended the right to collect-ive bargaining to American workers. A key part of President Franklin Delano Roosevelt's New Deal—a series of innovative economic and social programs and regulations passed to combat the Great Depression—the Wagner Act was intended to ensure labour peace and give workers a voice in their places of employment. The Wagner Act, along with the Railway Labour Relations Act (passed in 1926 and amended in 1936 to apply to airline workers), asserted national government jurisdiction over private sector workers in the United States, and public sector workers would eventually fall under a combination of state and federal laws, depending on whether they were employed by local, state, or federal governments.

In contrast, most unionized workers in Canada fell under provincial labour and employment law, as confirmed by the 1925 *Snider* decision (issued by the Judicial Committee of the Privy Council, Canada's highest court at the time), unless they worked in certain federally regulated industries. Canadian federal labour and employment law governed workplace relations for only a minority of workers. This gave King an excuse not to copy the American example of enshrining the right to collective bargaining in Canadian law. King approved of voluntarist methods of resolving disputes, as he had outlined in *Industry and Humanity*, and he was also widely known to be aghast at many of the New Deal policies enacted by Franklin Delano Roosevelt. He was, in many ways, the polar opposite of the American president. Whereas Roosevelt was tre-mendously at ease communicating with the public and press, Canadian news-paper reporters came up with a telling rhyme to describe the country's prime minister: "William Lyon Mackenzie King, never tells us a goddamn thing."[24]

By 1944, surging support for social democracy accompanied by a wave of wartime strikes pushed King, ever cautious and suspicious of social unrest, to enact some progressive social policies of his own. In 1942, a Co-Operative Commonwealth Federation (CCF) candidate had defeated the Progressive Conservative Party leader and former prime minister, Arthur Meighen, in a by-election in the riding of York South, and by the following year the CCF led the Liberals and Conservatives in a public opinion poll. In 1944, the CCF formed the government in Saskatchewan. There was also considerable labour-management conflict during the war, including a major strike by gold miners at Kirkland Lake, Ontario, in 1941. In response to the labour unrest, King's cabinet introduced Privy Council Order 1003 (PC 1003), which extended Wagner-style collective bargaining to Canadian private sector workers and established the template on which postwar provincial and federal labour relations acts would be based. Organized labour gained considerable legitimacy through the introduction of legal collective bargaining, though often at the expense of labour radicalism.[25]

For federal civil servants in Canada, the Whitley model of labour relations had been accepted policy since World War I, and it was strengthened in 1944 when the National Joint Council (NJC) was founded. A clear manifestation of Whitley's sector-wide bargaining model and the main structure through which the various federal civil service associations would cooperate, the NJC became a critical part of federal labour relations in Canada, even though its existence and purpose would remain largely unknown to the Canadian public. The NJC's first major policy positions were requests for the government to pass new superannuation and civil service acts, which the government did in 1946. Throughout the 1950s, the NJC addressed concerns pertaining to working conditions. The civil service expanded during those years, but there were also concerns among employees that long-serving civil servants lacked sufficient access to promotional opportunities. Involvement in the NJC provided one avenue for advancement in the public service, though more senior people were also involved. For instance, Hugh Keenleyside, who enjoyed a well-regarded career as both a senior bureaucrat and diplomat, chaired an NJC committee in the late 1940s.[26]

During the 1950s, the associations that belonged to the NJC began to grapple with the prospect of engaging in formal collective bargaining with the federal government. The popular perception in Canadian history is often that collective bargaining rights were extended to public employees as a result of a wildcat postal workers' strike in 1965.[27] In fact, the idea of formalizing employee representation was already under consideration in the 1950s. The

Institute played an active role in those discussions, with PIPSC president Frances Goodspeed and executive director Leslie Barnes calling for greater use of the Whitley model and not necessarily for a Wagner-based system.[28] However, by 1963 the federal government had established the Preparatory Committee on Collective Bargaining chaired by Arnold Heeney, formerly the clerk of the Privy Council and subsequently the chair of the Civil Service Commission. The various public sector employee associations, including the Institute, formed a Staff Side Conference for Collective Bargaining.[29] The Heeney Report marked a step toward a bargaining model that incorporated significant aspects of the private sector labour relations system into the public sector, and it led to landmark labour legislation in 1967: Bill C-170, the Public Service Staff Relations Act (PSSRA).

The PSSRA has received less attention from labour historians than preceding laws like the 1948 Industrial Relations Disputes Investigations Act, PC 1003, the 1907 Industrial Disputes Investigations Act devised by Mackenzie King, or the 1872 Trade Unions Act. Yet its importance is equal to any of those earlier laws; the PSSRA set the stage for Canada's labour movement to become concentrated in the public rather than private sector. The PSSRA permitted federal public sector workers to bargain collectively and even to strike in certain instances. As Ian MacMillan suggests, this was a remarkable change of policy from both the Liberal and Progressive Conservative parties.[30]

Organizing federal civil servants changed as a result of the PSSRA. Geographic dispersal of people across the country made organizing difficult, as did the sheer size of the civil service. There were seven hundred job classifications and 1,700 grades of employees in the federal public service just prior to the passage of the PSSRA. While passage of the PSSRA did not immediately alter the Institute, it led to a merger of the other two main employee associations—the Civil Service Federation and the Civil Service Association—to create the Public Service Alliance of Canada (PSAC) in November 1966, just as the PSSRA was about to be enacted.[31]

The PSSRA did two things usually associated with labour relations acts: it created a mechanism for workers to form unions of their own choosing, and it provided a dispute-resolution system to resolve impasses in collective bargaining and disagreements over the administration of collective agreements. That second feature was embodied in the Public Service Staff Relations Board (PSSRB). The formation of the board further illustrated the far more rapid nature of public sector unionization in Canada compared with the patterns found in the private sector. Unions such as those affiliated with the Congress of Industrial Organizations had only gradually earned legal legitimacy and the right to collective bargaining because of strike action and pressure on governments and employers. Passage of the PSSRA transformed public sector unions from comparatively small-scale voluntary employee associations to large unions that would eclipse what existed in the private sector.

The PSSRA set up two processes for resolving a bargaining table impasse—conciliation with the right to strike or, alternatively, compulsory binding arbitration—and gave the choice of which method to access to the employees' bargaining agents. But this important choice had to be made prior to the commencement of a round of collective bargaining. Of the two options, the first gave unions a wider scope in bargaining because the Conciliation Board had greater discretion to mediate a settlement on any matter covered by a collective agreement. A union that opted for compulsory binding arbitration, as the Institute did in the early rounds of collective bargaining, faced the more limited jurisdiction of an Arbitration Tribunal, which could only rule on disputed matters listed in the act.

Regardless of which option was selected, the scope of bargaining was also limited by existing legislation covering staffing and related matters (the Public Service Employment Act) and pensions (the Public Service Superannuation Act) and by managerial prerogatives. If the decision was to opt for conciliation with the right to strike, the employer had the right to name employee groups that could not, for reasons of public safety and security related to their normal duties, participate in strike action. While the unions could dispute such designations and appeal to the PSSRB for a decision, the employer could (and did) use its wide prerogative over the assignment and definition of duties to undermine the effectiveness of potential strikes by exempting large numbers of employees. Unlike typical Wagner-inspired labour legislation, however, the PSSRA did not give the employer the right to lock out workers.

Under the new legislation, the PSSRB quickly grew into a significant adjudicating body. It dealt with disputes arising from interpretations of collective agreements or from penalties imposed as disciplinary measures (up to and including termination of employment). An adjudicator appointed by the PSSRB conducted a hearing and issued a binding decision to resolve the dispute. Yet the board was not a forum where workers could go to air their complaints with a steward in tow. The PSSRA and the board took disputes to a level that often required unions to employ experts and legal counsel to resolve labour relations issues. The alienation among unionized workers caused by such labour relations processes, which elevated disputes out of the workplace and out of the hands of workers themselves, is a familiar theme in labour and working-class history. The board's Pay Research Bureau was also mandated to "obtain information on rates of pay, employee earnings, conditions of employment and related practices prevailing both inside and outside the Public Service to meet the needs of the parties to bargaining, or in the case of occupational groups where no bargaining agent is certified, as may be requested by the employer." That was a striking level of responsibility, considering that comparable provincial labour boards did not gather compensation and other employment information on behalf of corporations or unions.[32]

Some private sector unions initially opposed the PSSRA. The Canadian Labour Congress and the two postal workers' unions thought it afforded bargaining rights inferior to those found in the Wagner-inspired Industrial Relations and Disputes Investigations Act of 1948 (IRDIA), which covered private sector workers. They argued that the government should simply update the IRDIA to cover the public sector. Unions especially opposed the act's provisions for compulsory arbitration.[33]

PIPSC was less vocal than other workers' organizations. The April 1967 edition of the PIPSC *Journal* included key language from the new act and declared that "the era of the 'consultative process' [had given] way to the 'collective bargaining' age."[34] The Institute's leadership, like that of every civil service employee organization, may not have fully recognized what the PSSRA would bring, but momentous change had arrived. Some public sector workers, like those in the postal service, fully embraced unionization. But accepting collective bargaining was a more intellectually difficult process for PIPSC members. Since 1920 they had viewed themselves as professional employees rather than wage workers, but their association now had to grapple with the idea of being a labour organization as much as a professional association. The dissonance caused by this shift would loom large in the Institute's collective consciousness well into its future. Yet as PIPSC member Patrick Kinnear recalled pragmatically, the introduction of the PSSRA meant "we got paid more money."[35]

Leadership and Membership

Although the Institute was initially run entirely by volunteer labour, the growing size and complexity of the Institute's work on behalf of members led to the hiring of paid staff, which by the 1960s had expanded beyond the three-person shop of the immediate post-WWII years. None of the elected positions were paid, and the executive director, the top staff job in PIPSC, played a significant role in running the organization, including in policy-making. Although PIPSC's leaders throughout the Institute's first half century were overwhelming middle-class, anglophone men, this had begun to change by the 1960s. Women, especially, gradually entered leadership roles, and in 1961 Frances Goodspeed became the first woman elected president. The popular perception within the Canadian labour movement is that Grace Hartman became the first woman to lead a major North American union when she was elected president of the Canadian Union of Public Employees (CUPE) in 1975. In fact, PIPSC president Frances Goodspeed more likely deserves to be recognized as the first woman to lead a major workers' organization, as her PIPSC presidency predated Hartman's by fourteen years.[36] The Institute was a trailblazer in the Canadian labour movement due to the important role women played in leadership positions.

While, as earlier noted, much of this chapter is based on archival sources, the recollections of PIPSC's members like Patrick Kinnear reveal much about what PIPSC was like, both as a member organization and as an employer, prior to the passage of the PSSRA. Their memories of PIPSC when it was principally a voluntary membership organization reveal how rapidly the PSSRA and the advent of formal unionization transformed the Institute.

Lorraine Neville was a long-serving member of the Institute's staff who started in the mailroom and concluded her career as executive secretary. Before working for PIPSC, she had not worked in the public service:

> No, that was my first job. ... I came here to the Institute to stuff envelopes. They had a big mailing to go out, and they asked me to do that. So, I did, ... and then I just stayed. It was a one-room shop—it was in the machine room. It wasn't on the main level of the building on Bronson—you know 786 Bronson, which had just opened. And I was downstairs in a back room by myself, stuffing envelopes, running the Xerox machine and an old Gestetner machine, and I stayed on.

Neville's recollections show the Institute as having a relatively basic organization with some unusual management practices and operating on a shoe-string budget.

> So, I read everything that came in, and everything that went out of the PIPSC office came through me too. So, I became very familiar with all the members of the Board of Directors. ... There were twenty-five members

Figure 1-2: PIPSC office at 786 Bronson Road, 1964-89. *PIPSC photo database.*

on the board at that time. I think the first president I knew was Frances Goodspeed. ... There was a general manager named Hector LaRue who had a very unusual idea of how to run the office. When I went upstairs to visit the staff—and it was a staff of ten—to talk to the people, you [had to] pick up a red chair. I remember this very distinctly—this was his rule. And you brought the chair to the person you wanted to talk to, [to] his desk, and sat down to give them whatever information. ... Usually I was just delivering mail, so I thought it was kind of silly. I guess I was a little brash—maybe a lot—and I told Hector this was wasting my time—picking up a chair to deliver mail—and he agreed. And I said, "Fine," and we proceeded [without the red chair] through the years.

Neville had a wry way of remembering her interaction with Hector LaRue, and that approach to her job surely served her well in such a clearly hierarchical organizational structure.

Her work was often routine, part of continuing efforts to get members to pay their dues. Prior to 1967, the Institute's funding rested on voluntary payment of membership fees. Automatic dues deductions mandated by the Rand Formula only applied when the first collective agreements came into force. (The Rand Formula, well known in Canadian labour history, resulted from an arbitration ruling issued in 1946 by Supreme Court Justice Ivan Rand to end a strike at a Ford Motor Company plant in Windsor, Ontario. It required workers covered by a collective bargaining contract to pay dues regardless of whether they were members of the union.)

> And through that first period of time of my employment, we were ... becoming a bargaining agent. Before that, the Institute was the Professional Institute. I think we had about 2,500 members. And how they paid their dues [before unionization] was very interesting. As I said, I received everything. They could pay with postage stamps—which we needed because we didn't have a machine. We didn't have the finances to have a stamping machine, so we had to use stamps. And then we would register the money in the ledger—which I did [as] I was receiving everything coming into the building. So, this was an intriguing time. And I think it was in 1966 that I had to go to the Executive Committee of the Institute because they had a mailing that was going to go out monthly, and I had to lick all these stamps—2,500 [of them]. And I asked the Executive Committee if I could buy a sponge because the stamps were getting to me. And I went to the Executive Committee—I think they were kind to hear me. I didn't get my six dollars for the sponges. So, I went and bought the sponges myself and I was able to do the mailings every month.

The introduction of the PSSRA had an immediate effect on the Institute's internal operations:

> So ... we were now going [to be] a bargaining agent. And the government had decided to structure bargaining groups using BUD codes, ... a Bargaining Unit Designation number. And I proposed to Lou Mosley [the office administrator] or Jim Mazerall, who was the executive secretary of the Institute at that time, that the Institute change its complete system of membership numbers to [match the government's] designation. In other words, if you were an actuary, the BUD code for that was 201. So, the first two numbers of a membership number would say where you lived—00 was Ottawa, 01 was Newfoundland—and you would go through the different provinces. The next three numbers would be the BUD codes for the bargaining units or groups in the government—201 being actuary, 204 would be auditing, 208 would be economics. So, we used the government codes. And the last four would be the individual number of each Institute member.

Changing membership numbers was just one task that had to be completed after passage of the PSSRA. Other changes facing the Institute were not so routine. As Neville remembered, the Institute's staff were skilled negotiators, but they also came from backgrounds steeped in the Whitley Council model:

> I guess it was in about 1967 and Leslie Barnes was the executive secretary [the top staff position in PIPSC]. He hired people from England—Ken Phythian, Ken Strike, Tony Agius [among others]—who were already involved in bargaining in Europe, who had distinct experience—the Whitley Committee was one. So they came to us with experience to deal with the new bargaining relationship and the PSSRB. The Institute became well known for arbitration cases. We were exceptionally good at arbitration through that period of time—through the 1960s, 1970s, and into the 1980s.

Barnes, a former PIPSC president who had joined the Institute's staff in the mid-1960s, and Frances Goodspeed had filed the early 1960s PIPSC position paper advocating for continuation of the Whitley Council model and questioning collective bargaining.

The hiring of people from the United Kingdom was noteworthy. PIPSC was an outlier in late 1960s Canada in having people from Britain in prominent positions on its staff, though as Neville noted they were skilled at dealing with the employer. The interest that staff from Britain showed in the Whitley model was anomalous within the context of 1960s Canadian labour relations. The Second World War had accelerated the process of drawing Canada into the American economic sphere and moving the country away from Britain. The influence of Americans was especially pronounced in the Canadian labour movement, which was dominated by American-based international unions. During the 1960s, the Canadian labour movement grew increasingly nationalistic. Union locals that were part of large American-based organizations were growing restive because they felt that their voices were not being heard. The Canadian Union of Public Employees, which would eventually become the country's largest union, was founded in 1963 as a Canadian-run organization.

The shift to collective bargaining also had a profound impact on how members viewed themselves, challenging their long-held view of PIPSC as a professional organization, not a union. Neville commented on the shift in perception:

> The Institute's approach to collective bargaining changed over time. ...
> Through education, the negotiators we had here at the Institute had to
> change the philosophy of people that would never think of striking—ever.
> Research scientists, the NRC—you know, there's no way these people are
> ever going out on strike. There was an influx of negotiators from the prov-
> ince of Quebec. So, having that influence come into the Institute from a
> province where strikes by professionals had occurred changed the Insti-
> tute in this way.

The shift toward unionization obviously meant adopting some, if not all, of
the usual practices of a labour organization operating under collective bargaining laws. A strike or lockout is often viewed in industrial relations as a
failure of the dispute-resolution process, so, in theory, getting to that point
in bargaining should be avoided at all costs. In practice, unions go on strike
and employers engage in lockouts. However, many of the Institute's members
were not ready to accept the need to strike.[37]

Lorraine Neville's comments on the way in which the Institute was run in
the 1960s and how it changed after the introduction of the PSSRA were echoed
by Dr. Ed Napke, an elected official for several years who held several positions on the Institute's board and chaired the Medicine Group. When asked
what the Institute was like in the 1960s, he replied, "It was an amateur crowd":

> I'm serious. They knew nothing about—well, there were too many Brits that
> were in, running it like a British setup. They didn't understand that this is
> Canada. Leslie Barnes—he was the executive director—he thought every-
> thing would go through him. There was some type of board and they would
> all rubber stamp things. ... Leslie Barnes was executive director of the Insti-
> tute just at the cusp of when the Institute became a bargaining agent. And
> Ken Pythian was one of the first negotiators. Leslie Barnes was an advisor
> to the Board [of Directors]. But I didn't like that because I was responsible
> for the board. If there was a court action, Leslie Barnes would have nothing
> to do with appearing before the [PSSRB] or the court. We were the board;
> we had to act like responsible individuals—warning the board.

Napke obviously had a less positive opinion than Neville of staff members like
Barnes and Phythian, and his concerns appear to have been principally rooted
in organizational governance. His indignation about there having been "too
many Brits" also suggests at least some feelings of Canadian nationalism.

Napke's own views on unionization reflected the ambivalence felt by many PIPSC members for whom the transition to unionized workers challenged their professional identities. For Napke, professional identity took precedence over collective action though unionization:

> Well, they [PIPSC's leadership] got tied up with a lot of committees and stuff. And they forgot what their responsibilities were. You know, we're professionals. Live up to it. There's a code of ethics for each of the professional groups. Live up to your code. During the last part [of the transition to being a union], it became about dollars and cents. And I said, "No. This [PIPSC] is not about dollars and cents. It's way above that. We will guarantee that for you."

This problem of how to reconcile being a professional employee with being a union member was one of the unexpected consequences of the start of formal collective bargaining.[38]

While PIPSC members themselves often struggled with how unionization was challenging their identity as professional civil servants, the Liberal government of Lester Pearson, which brought in the PSSRA, clearly felt extending collective bargaining rights to federal public sector workers was a good public-policy idea, even if it did not give public employees the exact same rights as their private sector peers. The Pearson government spent the mid-1960s in a minority position, largely propped up by the New Democratic Party. The PSSRA was part of a wider social democratic public-policy agenda, within which public sector unionization was overshadowed by nation-building, welfare-state policies like the Canada Pension Plan and universal health care.

The Pearson government did not see the Institute as an adversary, nor had any of its predecessors. From its inception, PIPSC had concerned itself with practical matters like superannuation and taken a more cooperative approach to its advocacy on behalf of its members than most unions. The federal government was not inclined to accept overtly partisan or militant behaviour among public servants. This was especially the case in the early Cold War period following the Second World War, when the Red Scare saw the loyalty of federal civil servants carefully scrutinized. The 1945 defection of Igor Gouzenko, a cipher clerk at the Soviet embassy in Ottawa, had revealed that his country had recruited spies among Canada's public servants and was doing the same thing in other western countries. This had led the Liberal government to form the secretive Kellock-Taschereau Commission in 1946 to ferret out communist moles and sympathizers within government.[39]

Acting on the commission's report, the government had implemented security screening of civil servants, conducted by the RCMP, and increased surveillance by that police service of suspected communist activities, not only in the public service but in civil society in general.[40] Canadians from student activists to trade union leaders would, in subsequent years, find their activities had been documented in RCMP files. PIPSC had never been particularly militant in comparison to other workers' organizations, especially militant unions like the United Electrical Workers, which had a large contingent of communist members. But it was probably more militant than other professional associations, like the Professional Engineers of Ontario or any of the law societies across the country. And the circumstances of the Cold War certainly encouraged PIPSC leaders, like Frances Goodspeed and Leslie Barnes, as well as rank-and-file members across the public service, to keep their advocacy efforts focused on practical matters, such as superannuation, rather than something more contentious, like the campaigns for nuclear disarmament pursued by other unions in the 1960s.

Reviewing the career trajectory of PIPSC's first female president, Frances Goodspeed, helps illustrate the collaborative relationship between PIPSC and the government in its role as employer. She left the Institute after serving as president to become director of operations at the government's Pay Research Bureau. At that time, Goodspeed was one of twenty-eight women in executive roles in the federal public service. In addition to her obvious qualifications, she was not likely to have been considered confrontational or radical. She was

Figure 1-3: The 1959–60 PIPSC National Board of Directors. Frances Goodspeed is in the second row, third from the left. *PIPSC photo database.*

also continuing a tradition established much earlier by people like Hugh Keen-leyside who had moved from membership or leadership roles in PIPSC into high positions in the public service. Her promotion showed that, pre-PSSRA, the Institute was viewed as more of a complement to the civil service and occasional partner to the government rather than an adversary.[41]

Ready for the 1970s   The 1960s ended with PIPSC being a much differ-ent organization than it was in 1920. The somewhat genteel professional association that had emerged during the Workers' Revolt years had become subject to collective bargaining conventions by 1967. Sig-nificantly, much of the change that PIPSC experienced was externally imposed rather than initiated from within. The Whitley model adopted by the Cana-dian government in the interwar years was a form of union substitution, intended to satiate any potential worker demands for more militant forms of organizational representation. Yet PIPSC was not merely a creation of the Borden government, which had favoured the creation of employee associa-tions as part of the Whitley model. Instead, PIPSC's formation resulted from the efforts of people like John Challies, and its founding was part of a wider effort by Canadians working in professions to advocate on behalf of them-selves. PIPSC members wanted a distinct collective voice, but they were not inclined to engage in radical workplace activity. The Whitley model had defi-nite appeal for them.

During the Institute's first fifty years, its membership differed greatly from other employee associations in Canada. Mostly notably, its members were far better educated than the average Canadian worker. PIPSC's homoge-neity reflected the demographics of the public service. And they had a woman president—Frances Goodspeed—at a time when women were confined gen-erally to low-paid, non-professional occupations. PIPSC members were mostly located in Ottawa but were increasingly employed across the country. Firm believers in professionalism and their status within the federal government, they were a highly accomplished group of people who enjoyed a public profile across the country and the respect of the governments that PIPSC interacted with from the 1920s to the 1960s. Internal PIPSC communications reveal no worries that either Conservative or Liberal governments were ever interested in diluting the Institute's professional standards.

Moving to a collective bargaining relationship recalibrated relations between PIPSC and the government because, even though the collective bar-gaining process is meant to resolve conflict, it is still inherently adversarial.

The Institute's leadership had not actively campaigned for collective bargaining and had even showed a continued preference for the Whitley model into the early 1960s. Yet when PIPSC members found themselves covered by the PSSRA, their leaders considered it a historic moment. The PSSRA would bring major benefits for all public sector workers, but, as the next chapter will show, it triggered changes in PIPSC that its leaders and members were not entirely ready for. The Whitley model would gradually be diminished, while collective bargaining became the Institute's central activity.

The Institute's members and leaders witnessed enormous change in Canada between the 1920s and 1960s. PIPSC was founded when the country was just getting over World War I, and it would endure the Great Depression and World War II, then participate in postwar socio-economic expansion. The increased size of the public service between the 1940s and 1960s ensured that PIPSC members were going to be more central to the lives of Canadians than they had been in the past, and unionization accentuated that fact. Canada had just over 47,000 federal public servants in 1920, just under 116,000 in 1945, and nearly 233,000 in 1969, an enormous increase over a forty-nine-year period. Did the Institute go from being a group of amateurs to a more professional organization, as Dr. Ed Napke suggested? Its leaders and members already were professionals in their fields, but the nature of their voluntary organization limited what they could collectively accomplish. The Institute entered the 1970s poised for growth and change, but the circumstances that confronted PIPSC and the responses of its members during that decade would be very different from those experienced during the first half century of its existence.[42]

Chapter 2

We Are a Union, What Do We Do Now? 1970-79

The 1970s was a crucial decade in modern Canadian history and a decade of expansion and re-evaluation for PIPSC. The Institute continued to evolve, adapting to changes in the Canadian government and public service. PIPSC adopted specific ideas about how it would function as a union, which meant it did not always act in the same fashion as other unions, and the decisions it made in the 1970s would guide the Institute into the next decade. This chapter will discuss who belonged to and led PIPSC in the 1970s, how collective bargaining took place, and what policy positions the Institute adopted. And it will explore the collective agreements reached and cases brought before the Public Service Staff Relations Board (PSSRB). PIPSC made considerable progress in the 1970s but took a different path than it had in preceding decades.

The 1970s was a decade of considerable change in the Canadian labour movement, particularly for public sector workers. The passage of the Public Service Staff Relations Act (PSSRA) in 1967 led to an overall increase in public sector unionization across the country, and the nature of the public sector workforce began to change considerably as women increasingly entered the labour market. The PSSRA had a profound impact on the size of PIPSC's membership and the manner in which the Institute engaged in collective bargaining. The postwar economic boom, which had featured developments such as the standard employment relationship (SER), wage increases that met or exceeded the rate of inflation, and the influx of millions of new workers, came to an end in the mid-1970s. Workers from the baby boom generation were entering full-time employment by the early 1970s, and their arrival marked the start of considerable generational change in Canada's public and private sector workforces.[1]

Changes in the nature of the labour market were part of much wider changes in Canadian society, and PIPSC's trajectory during this time occasionally reflected broader social and political trends. As well as experiencing a postwar baby boom, Canada had also enjoyed an increase in immigration from the late 1940s onward. Whereas Europe had long been a source of immigrants to the country, by the 1970s immigrants from Asia were an increasing proportion of those seeking new lives in Canada. Immigration, which has historically shaped Canadian society and been linked inextricably to work and employment, eventually changed PIPSC's membership as well.

Canada was governed by Liberal governments at the federal level for virtually all of the 1970s, with the exception of Joe Clark's short-lived Progressive Conservative government in 1979–80. Federal-provincial relations were complex during the decade, especially as a result of the election of Quebec's first Parti Québécois government in 1976. Neoliberal political thought began to appear in the 1970s, most notably with the election of Margaret Thatcher in the United Kingdom in 1978. That political view emphasized shrinking government, privatizing services, and otherwise diminishing the role of government in society. In the United States, a federal labour law reform act failed in 1977 amid rising right-wing attacks on unions. Neoliberalism did not yet influence public policy in Canada in the 1970s, and governments at the federal and provincial levels still pursued interventionist economic policies. This was an era of Canadian economic nationalism, and the state still played a significant role in the economy through existing crown corporations, including Atomic Energy Canada Limited, Air Canada, and the Canadian Broadcasting Corporation, and newly created ones like Via Rail, Petro Canada, and the Canadian Development Corporation. The Liberal government also implemented other social and economic changes that would affect PIPSC, including Canada's conversion from imperial to metric measurement.

Labour relations between the Liberal government and public employees were often contentious in the 1970s. The Liberal government of Pierre Trudeau imposed wage controls on public sector unions between 1975 and 1978. Public sector workers were at the forefront of a national day of protest on 14 October 1976, the closest that Canada has ever come to a national general strike.

Leadership   PIPSC's leadership during the 1970s was largely made up of long-service members, the vast majority of them men. The size of the Institute's organizational chart altered somewhat during the 1970s as well. The Institute began the decade led by a president, four vice presidents, six Ottawa directors, and ten regional directors. As professional employees, they reflected the employment backgrounds of the Institute's membership. Ken J. Harwood, who had been with the public service since 1958 and was employed in the Dominion Bureau of Statistics, was president in 1970. Harwood had a bachelor's degree, presumably in a field related to statistics, and had been involved in several internal Institute committees. Only one woman, Edweena Mair, occupied a vice president role in 1970. Mair, who held a bachelor of science degree, was director of dietary services in the Department of Veterans Affairs and served on several internal PIPSC committees. A second woman, Pamela Poole, was a registered nurse employed in the Department of National Health and Welfare, an Ottawa-area PIPSC director, and a member of the Institute's board, having risen to that position after a relatively short tenure in the public service of only five years.[2]

Most of the other members of the Board of Directors had been in the public service for at least ten years. Indeed one, C.E. Hoganson, had joined PIPSC in 1947. Most members of the Institute's board had backgrounds similar to Harwood's. The board was overwhelmingly made up of anglophone members, with the exception of the two representatives from Quebec. Most possessed at least one degree, and five held PhDs. The board members also came from a wide range of departments, including Foreign Affairs, Audit, Veterinary Services, Scientific Research, and Engineering and Land Survey, though science and math disciplines predominated overall. Apart from the substantial role of economists, none of the board members had a background in the humanities or social sciences.[3]

Until 1975, all of the Institute's elected officers were unpaid volunteers, but in that year the position of PIPSC president became a paid one; the staff executive director role was eliminated, with the president now fulfilling many of its functions. Chesley Lockhart was elected as the first paid president in 1975. He served until the end of 1979 and was succeeded by Jack Donegani. Turning the office of president into a paid, full-time position transformed the post into a highly attractive career goal for union activists that equaled well-paid professional public service positions.

By the mid-1970s, the leadership was changing in other ways, with younger members becoming involved on the board. J. E. Maloney, for example, had joined in the early 1970s. Representatives still came predominantly from science occupations such as professionals in the Scientific Research Group and Computer Systems. Only one out of twenty-one board members, A. Doris, was a woman, and like Edweena Mair she came from nursing. The addition of one francophone board member from the Ottawa area improved francophone representation slightly, but there was no evident ethnic diversity.[4] However, as figure 2-1 shows, women could still be objectified in the Institute's internal discourse.

The influx of baby boomers and women into PIPSC was more fully reflected in the membership of the 1979 board. It comprised twenty-four members, including two people of colour and three women, one of whom, Iris L. Craig, was a vice president.[5] The Institute's publications no longer included biographies of each board member, but younger faces were more common than they were in the middle of the decade. The inclusion of more young members on the board surely influenced collective bargaining objectives.

Figure 2-1: A PIPSC cartoon from the October 1977 issue of the *Journal of the Professional Institute* depicting an idealized vision of labour relations between PIPSC (represented by the seated figures labelled "P.I." and "staff side") and the Treasury Board Secretariat ("T.B."). The caption reads, "Contract Language 1, Article 1.01. The purpose of this Agreement is to maintain harmonious and mutually beneficial relationships between the Employer, the employees, and the Institute." By today's standards, the depiction of smoking, drinking, and a nude woman emerging from a cake as the social lubricants facilitating harmonious relations seems incredibly dated (not to mention sexist). *PIPSC Storage Room.*

Staff   During the 1970s, PIPSC's staff was much smaller than it would be in later years. Staff members unionized by forming the Professional Institute Staff Association (PISA). Relations between leadership and staff were generally good during the decade, with the exception of a short staff strike in 1979. Lorraine Neville led PISA at that time and commented:

> In 1979, we were at the bargaining table with the Board of Directors. … We had settled the issues on the table, and it had all to do with the pension plan. … We had finished negotiations. We went to lunch. We came back from lunch. And [PIPSC negotiator] Carmel Casper says to us, "Everything is off the table."
>
> And we said, "What did she have for lunch? I mean, what happened?" And [referring to the pre-lunch agreement] she says, "No. No. We can't do that."
>
> And I said, "But you agreed before lunch. We could have signed then. But we all agreed that we'd go to lunch." I said, "What happened?" She wouldn't talk at all. She was actually in tears. And we said, "Okay. Fine." So, I left that meeting.
>
> Ken Strike was the negotiator for PISA. I left the meeting and went downstairs to the [staff in the] membership section. That is where I started. Most of the people there knew me quite well, and I said, "if you walk out with me now, all those officers upstairs will come out."
>
> And they said, "Are you sure?" And I said, "I'll promise you this. Ken Gibson [a PIPSC official] told me to come down and see if you would strike. He said if I get you out—if you'll come with me—he'll get the officers." … So, we went outside and went on strike. And the rest of the officers came out. At the time, the Institute [staff] had, I think, maybe three people that couldn't strike [due to managerial exclusions under the Ontario Labour Relations Act]. That was all.
>
> So, we all went outside. Then most of the people came back to my house and we made up signs and everything else. We were getting ready for the next day and to advise people. Our biggest problem with our strike was we had members—one drove a Mercedes, another one had a Corvette, another one had a big huge Buick. One walked the picket line with a sable coat—a lot of heavy stuff there.
>
> And we were there, and we were out for a total of nine hours—two hours one day, and then seven hours the next day. The Canadian Union of Postal Workers stopped their mail truck. Then people from the Russian

embassy came with cameras. We had to get some people off the picket line—especially [the person] in her full-length sable coat—and those cars belonging to people who were working with us. It did not look very good. And we were out the next day. And they [management] called us in, and they settled.[6]

Membership   During this period, PIPSC represented a remarkable range of professional workers who, in 1970, were divided into forty occupational groups, each with its own local executive committee. (See appendices.) The Institute also had branch representatives, including boards with chairs, in thirty-eight communities across the country.[7] Although the Institute's members were primarily concentrated in Ottawa, they also lived in all parts of the country. The wide range of agencies in which PIPSC members were employed raised significant challenges for the Institute, which had to understand the mission, organization, funding structure, and management of each agency. The Institute also had to be familiar with the job requirements, including professional credentials, specific to the many roles its members filled in those agencies.

By the 1970s, many PIPSC members had been with the public service for decades. The Institute's internal publications were replete with career summaries of members like E. J. Doyle who were clearly devoted to their occupations and who had spent their entire working lives in jobs that were largely invisible to, but nonetheless highly important to the welfare of, the Canadian public. Doyle had been a PIPSC member since 1947. Born in a small Ontario town in 1905, he had served in the Royal Canadian Air Force during World War II, received a master of science degree from the University of Wisconsin in 1947, and begun his career with the public service in the Ottawa Seed Research Laboratory. By 1970, he was part of the Institute's Chemistry Group and represented Canada several times at meetings of the International Seed Testing Association.[8]

From the late 1960s on, the Institute had access to steady revenues because unionization meant it benefitted from the automatic dues check-off established by the Rand Formula. Because not everyone who paid dues actually signed a membership card, the Institute conducted outreach to anyone who was paying dues but had not yet formally joined. Disinterest in joining among non-members was attributed to some basic factors, including lack of knowledge of the Institute and how it benefitted members, lack of personal contact with members of the Institute, and apathy or antipathy to the idea of a unionized professional organization.[9]

The Institute's leadership made an effort to engage non-members so that "they would be able to obtain the advice, views, and support of their colleagues in their Group and in the Institute." The Institute presented itself to potential signees as a professional advocacy organization that offered a list of benefits and services to potential members, including assistance on appeals and grievances, newsletters from their group, the Institute's monthly magazine, and information and advice on financial matters, group insurance, and charter vacation flights.[10] Economic considerations were of paramount concern to members, but the Institute also provided members with a voice, which was crucial since workers primarily join unions because they feel undervalued and silenced by their employers.

The centrality of the Institute's ethos of professionalism continued to be evident throughout its communications. For instance, a 1970 profile of PIPSC Senior Research Officer A. J. "Tony" Agius illustrated the importance of professionalism to the Institute. Agius was quoted in *Professional Public Service*:

> In our collective bargaining research, we are trying to go beyond the parameters of employer-employee relations for professionals in the public service, as found in the textbook labour relations model. ... Things are different here. If the membership were not first and foremost professional public servants, then the Institute would be like any other union, but fortunately we are lucky enough to have some of the top brains of the country helping to serve their colleagues. ... In or out of the collective bargaining arena the Institute's position has always been objective and, consequently, I feel strongly that "what's good for the Institute is good for the country at large."[11]

Agius was clearly thinking of former General Motors CEO Charles Wilson's widely known and often misquoted statement to a congressional hearing in 1953: "I thought what was good for our country was good for General Motors, and vice versa."[12] The belief that the interests of the country and the Institute were aligned similarly informed Agius's view of the role that PIPSC played within Canadian public life.

Efforts to foster professionalism among the Institute's members were frequently evident in membership publications. For instance, the *Professional Public Service* featured lists of recommended scholarly publications.[13] The Institute's leadership also sought to portray an image of professionalism through financial and administrative competence. Detailed financial statements audited by an external accounting firm were published every year, and they generally showed an organization in good financial health. The automatic dues check-off that came with unionization brought a substantial increase in revenues. PIPSC had revenues of $762,144 in 1970, a 34 percent increase over 1969.[14] The Institute also had fixed assets worth $319,425 in 1970, an increase of 12 percent over the previous year.[15] The Institute's financial statements reassured current and potential members that it was being professionally led.

The positive image of the Institute as a well-managed, professional organization that was presented in the Institute's internal communications in the early 1970s masked a certain degree of dissent and discord within the leadership and over PIPSC's political orientation. That orientation does not overtly appear in publications and other internal documents up to the 1970s for a basic reason: The Institute viewed itself as a non-partisan entity.

The commitment of PIPSC leaders to this outlook manifested itself very clearly in an episode involving Executive Director R. Val Scott. Although the exact reasons for Scott's eventual removal from what was then PIPSC's top staff position are unclear, and none of the details appeared in the Institute's communications to its members. Yet Scott clearly ran into internal opposition when he tried to push PIPSC in a more political direction. In 1974, while he was still under probation in his role as executive director, Scott violated PIPSC's unwritten policy on non-political alignment when he attended a New Democratic Party meeting. He soon faced a coordinated effort by PIPSC board members to remove him. The Institute's elected leaders accused Scott of procedural violations and attempting to remove confidential documents from PIPSC's office. Ontario Region Director H. S. Weiler requested that a commission of inquiry be established to look into Scott's activities, and others pushed to have the locks changed in the Institute's office so that Scott would not have access.[16] This episode reveals a key fact about the Institute: its leaders had clear ideas about what it existed to do. They saw PIPSC's members as professionals within the public service, and they expected that people hired to work for them would align with long-standing values rather than attempt to change the organization's direction.

Scott may not have lasted long, but he still contributed to an effort that would have a major impact on PIPSC: the implementation of the McGill committee's report. PIPSC's leadership had commissioned the report, written in 1972 by a collection of academic experts on institutional collective bargaining, in light of the passage of the PSSRA. The committee was led by Frances Bairstow, a faculty member at the Industrial Relations Centre at McGill University, with assistance from colleagues at other institutions: Archie Kleingartner (University of California, Los Angeles), Hélène LeBel (University of Montreal), and Brian Downie (Queen's University). Everyone but LeBel, a law professor, was in the industrial relations field and had considerable experience in it. Bairstow was American, although she taught at McGill, and was likely the most senior member of the group. She also worked as an arbitrator; indeed she continued to hear cases until the age of ninety. Kleingartner went on to specialize in human resource management, and Downie became a specialist in dispute resolution.[17] Notably, but not surprisingly, PIPSC chose to reach out to advisors from academia rather than from the labour movement for advice on how to reorganize in response to the changes wrought by the PSSRA. PIPSC's members were themselves professionals, the vast majority of whom possessed at least some post-secondary credentials, and the Institute's leaders clearly reasoned that hiring academic professionals was the most appropriate way to assess their future direction.

In 1973, PIPSC distributed *Rebuilding the Professional Institute*, a two-part document based on the McGill committee's report, and its recommendations were also shared in condensed form in a dedicated issue of the *Journal of the Professional Institute*. R. Val Scott, then still the Institute's executive director, argued vigorously in favour of reorganizing PIPSC to improve communication with and services to Institute members. His preface to the first volume of *Rebuilding the Professional Institute* was highly critical of PIPSC leaders' paternalistic way of treating members:

> Frequently in the past, the Institute leadership has been accused of not keeping the members abreast of what is happening, what policies are being discussed, what proposals are being made to the employer on their behalf. Too often, the members have been presented with a fait accompli, which, however well intentioned, contravenes the true spirit of democracy in an organization where every individual is entitled to some input before the fact.[18]

This was a politically fraught way to frame the introduction of a reorganization plan, implying that there were problems with the way in which the Institute had been run up to that point. It was perhaps no surprise that some within PIPSC did not want to see Scott continue as executive director.

In contrast to *Rebuilding the Professional Institute*'s desire to break with past practice in terms of PIPSC's relations with its members, the report recommended continuing the Institute's traditional collegial approach to relations with the employer. The concept of corporate humanism was central to *Rebuilding the Professional Institute*. Although the document did not clearly define the concept, earlier planning documents did:

> Corporate Humanism rejects the traditional adversary approach to industrial relations, so that the current prevailing emphasis on conflict and the assumption that there is a fundamental difference between the interests of the employee and those of the employer are superseded by a truly democratic relationship, not only at the bargaining table, but also at the workplace. Abandonment of the adversary relationship should in turn remove or at least greatly reduce employee alienation and the subordination of individualism which exist all too often at present.

Despite the fact that the Institute's labour relations were now conducted under the Wagner-based system that formed the basis of the PSSRA, Scott and the other authors of *Rebuilding the Professional Institute* believed the Institute should adhere to elements of the old Whitley model. They believed that management preferred a non-confrontational approach and that adopting one would lead to PIPSC having a role in planning and decision-making within the various agencies in which its members worked. Perhaps most importantly, they continued to believe that this was the method of labour relations best suited to a professional workforce.[19]

This was a remarkable position to take in 1973, as this was a period of greater conflict between unions and employers in both the public and private sectors. PIPSC stood out for its move to adopt non-confrontational labour relations practices at a time when most other Canadian unions were becoming more militant. Other public service unions had highly adversarial relationships with employers. The Canadian Union of Postal Workers clashed frequently with the post office, which was not yet a crown corporation, and postal-worker conflicts received considerable media attention.[20] Still others like the Canadian Union of Public Employees and the Public Service Alliance of Canada engaged in struggles with public sector employers.[21] And, as previously noted, the Canadian labour movement engaged in the closest thing to a general strike that the country has had on 14 October 1976 when there was a national day of protest over wage and price controls.[22] The public sector strikes involving other unions make clear that the Government of Canada's managers had no aversion to conflict.

The actual practice of collective bargaining soon put PIPSC's non-confrontational approach to the test. The Institute quickly realized that a bargaining strategy based on corporate humanism was not going to work and never officially adopted it. PIPSC still tried to be non-confrontational, but events in the decades that followed would further challenge this approach, ultimately leading the union to abandon it.

Governance   PIPSC continued to operate within a well-established internal governance structure during the 1970s, though the new formal collective bargaining environment imposed by the PSSRA led the Institute to reconsider its governance. Many of the changes it made resulted from the McGill Report. A comparison of the Institute's by-laws in 1966 and 1978 reveals significant differences.[23] The earlier by-laws had already undergone some revision in anticipation of the Institute's prospective role as a bargaining agent, and by 1978 the by-laws codified the changes in the structure and decision-making machinery of the Institute. Events during this twelve-year period caused a re-invention of the Institute, a process not without tensions. Whereas PIPSC had previously been a comparatively small, collegial organization made up of professionals who joined voluntarily, the association was now a full-fledged union that grew quickly with the inclusion of new bargaining units. PIPSC collected more dues because of the PSSRA, but increased costs led to financial challenges and internal conflicts over finances and governance issues.

The changes in governance during the 1970s reflected a fundamental change in PIPSC's basic purpose. In 1966, PIPSC's by-laws contained only a short statement asserting that the Institute's purpose was "to enhance the usefulness of the Public Service of Canada, to maintain high professional standards and to promote the welfare of its members." By 1978 organizational objectives had been recast into six sub-sections highlighting various activities that supported the Institute's "fundamental purpose"—namely, to "serve the welfare of its members through effective collective bargaining with their employers."[24]

A comparison of by-laws also reveals major changes in membership. In 1966 people could become members only if they met certain criteria. They had to be already employed in "position[s] subject to the Public Service Superannuation Act"; "be employed in a professional capacity or directing professional work"; and either "possess educational qualifications attained through graduation from a university or college of recognized standing" or "hold membership in a recognized professional association." Prospective members had to apply and be accepted based on an assessment of these criteria completed under the authority of the Board of Directors. Although these requirements had been modified over time, they essentially dated back to the Institute's founding. Another three categories of membership had also emerged over the years to deal with special circumstances: life memberships, limited to a maximum of one hundred, could be granted by the board for "outstanding service to the Institute"; emeritus membership could be granted to members upon their retirement from the public service; and emeritus life memberships could be granted to any life member who left the employ of the Public Service.

The new collective bargaining framework led to the creation of two new membership classifications: affiliate and associate. Affiliate membership enabled those whose positions denied them access to collective bargaining (that is, members who took up encumbered or "excluded" positions outside of the scope of the bargaining unit) to retain their membership, albeit without the right to vote or hold elected office. Associate was reserved for those employed in bargaining units "for which the Institute wishes to seek or maintain certification" but who did not meet the criteria for membership listed above. (People working in a job category represented by PIPSC now paid compulsory dues, but they still did not automatically become members.)[25]

The 1978 version of the by-laws listed five categories of membership: regular, affiliate, life, honorary, and emeritus. Life and honorary memberships could be extended to individuals to recognize outstanding service. The limit on the number of life memberships was lifted, and an honorary membership could be granted to any person who had not been a member. Emeritus status applied to retired regular members who no longer required "continuing services from the Institute" but who wished to remain members. The definitions of and process for entry into these last three categories of membership were entirely within the authority of the Institute.[26]

PIPSC's membership growth in the wake of the PSSRA meant more revenue from dues, but this was more than offset by the much higher operating costs involved in bargaining on behalf of and having to represent a growing number of members. By the end of 1972, this situation reached a climax under incumbent president Kenneth Harwood, a member of the Economics, Sociology and Statistics (ES) Group. The previous year, an appeal to the annual general meeting for a dues increase to cover rising costs had fallen short, with the meeting approving only 20 percent of the requested increase. Finances became so stretched that the chair of the finance committee of the Board of Directors (and future PIPSC president), Don Buchanan, declared that the Institute faced a "crisis situation," and cuts to expenditures were forecast. In this charged atmosphere, the Institute's *Journal* described the 1972 AGM "as a raucous affair not ending until after midnight ... where the rulings of President Harwood were challenged and some pointed comments were made about the Board." The debate was further polarized by the view that "a vote against this fee increase would be a vote of non-confidence in the Board and the senior paid staff."[27] The membership's rejection of the proposed fee increase led Harwood to resign shortly after.

Such disputes over finances were reflective of larger struggles over governance, especially regarding the powers of the elected and non-elected board officials. The 1966 by-laws assigned responsibility for all executive functions of the Institute to the Board of Directors, which was "responsible to the membership through the Annual Meeting, the Biennial Convention, or any Special General Meeting." The board was responsible for the "representation of professional public servants in dealing with their employer" and had the power to "appoint agents to act on its behalf in matters pertaining to collective bargaining," to ratify collective agreements, and represent the Institute at arbitration proceedings.

The board's sweeping power over the Institute's conduct throughout the collective bargaining process was tempered by a caveat that the board would take no action on behalf of any specific group that was expressly "contrary to that Group's previously declared wishes." A similar proviso also declared that "the Board shall take no action which might adversely affect a specific region without prior consultation with that region," except at the board's semi-annual meeting or in cases of emergency. In short, the board possessed enormous power, controlling all the executive functions of the organization, with an accounting provided only at the annual or any special general meetings or biennial conventions. Constituent bodies served in an advisory capacity to assist the board in the exercise of its authority.[28]

Although the size and geographic constituencies represented on the board did not change over the twelve-year period in question, by 1978, as a result of the recommendations of the McGill Report and internal struggles over finances and accountability, the board saw its power curbed, and new rules governed the election of its members. Under that year's by-laws the board retained residual executive authority, but its power was now explicitly

made subject to "these By-laws and policy decisions of General Meetings."
The omnibus authority to represent "professional public servants" had been
deleted, though the board's power over collective bargaining remained a notable exception. However, the board could not enter into collective agreements
without a recommendation to do so by the relevant executive of the group
covered by a given agreement. In the event of a dispute between the group
executive and the board, the by-laws gave the board the authority to hold a
vote of the registered members of the group on the issue in question. This
meant that control over collective bargaining was now shared between group
executives and the board, with membership referenda ultimately settling
any disputes.[29]

The process that governed the election of board members also changed
in the 1970s, shaped by recommendations in the McGill Report. The twenty-
five-member board of 1966 included three ex-officio positions: the immediate
past president in the first year following his or her term of office; the executive director, then the most senior staff position; and the national joint council representative, a person appointed by the board. In 1966, only delegates
to the annual general meeting were eligible to cast ballots for the election
of officers and directors of the board. Ballots could be cast either by mail
received in advance of the AGM or in person at the meeting. The size of each
branch or group determined, according to a formula, the number of delegates
each could elect. A branch or group with between ten and nineteen "paid up"
members in good standing received one delegate, while a maximum of five
delegates was assigned to any branch or group with 160 or more "paid up"
members in good standing. Delegates also had to live in the National Capital
Region, creating a curious situation in which a delegate living in Ottawa had
the responsibility to represent colleagues, for example, resident in Winnipeg.
In addition, the 1966 by-laws provided for an Advisory Council to the board,
which had been a feature of the Institute's governance structure for at least
a dozen years. The council consisted of representatives from each group and
branch, the numbers of which were determined by the same formula used to
determine the number of delegates to the annual or special general meetings.
This meant that advisory council attendees, too, had to reside in the National
Capital Region.[30]

By 1978 the system of election by delegates was replaced with a more
democratic system of universal suffrage, granting all members the right to vote
for the candidate of their choice for president and vice presidents. Members
within each region also had the right to cast a ballot for the election of their

respective regional director. The Advisory Council had also been replaced with a dual structure of regional councils, one for each of the five recognized regions outside the National Capital Region, and a Negotiating Council situated in Ottawa. Regional councils consisted of one representative from each branch or, in consideration that all members may not be assigned to a branch, in a ratio of one representative for each one hundred members resident in the region, plus two additional members. Hence, a region with two thousand members could send twenty-two representatives to regional council meetings. Although not an obligation, the by-laws did refer to two members of the Institute's Board of Directors from each region serving as the chair and vice chair of each of the regional councils. The by-laws also provided for regional negotiating councils made up "of one representative from each bargaining unit for which the Institute is the certified bargaining agent."[31]

The Negotiating Council, comprising one councillor from each group, was given the job of designing overall strategies and policies for the Institute's approach to the bargaining table and developing negotiating proposals to serve as ideal models for its constituent groups. The Negotiating Council was tied into the Board of Directors by the Collective Negotiations Panel, a board committee struck to coordinate implementation of negotiation council initiatives. The panel was chaired by the president and comprised one of the vice presidents, three directors from the National Capital Region, and two directors from the other regions. The by-laws established an expectation that the model proposals and strategies for collective bargaining would be forwarded to regional negotiating councils for their consideration. In addition to the Collective Negotiations Panel, the by-laws also established another board committee known as the Member Services Panel, which initiated and coordinated inter-group meetings "of general matters of interest to members" and fulfilled planning needs for "the recruitment and training of Stewards."[32]

The introduction of a paid president position and the elimination of the executive director position also followed from the McGill Report and represented a marked change in how the Institute was led. The members of the McGill Committee were aware that they were suggesting major changes to the Institute's structure and operations, but their recommendations also enabled the Institute to better deal with the complexities of collective bargaining in the public sector. Hours of deliberations and debate by representatives throughout the organization led to decisions at successive general meetings to adopt and solidify these changes. By 1978, the by-laws established that a full-time, paid president would be elected by a mail-in ballot of the general membership.

From an unpaid role limited to presiding over meetings of the board, executive committee, Advisory Council, and general membership meetings, the president had become the senior paid official, employed directly by the membership, and PIPSC's chief executive, incorporating duties formerly handled by the executive director.[33]

Despite the leadership's best efforts to improve governance to meet the challenges of being a union, PIPSC's growing pains led to more than just the resignation of the occasional elected official like Ken Harwood. By the early 1970s, a growing, discontented faction within the ES Group to which Harwood belonged was intent on leaving the Institute. To that end, the dissidents, led by some current and former elected representatives of the ES Group, formed a new Economists, Sociologists, and Statisticians Association (ESSA). The rise of ESSA was a troubling development because, by 1974, the ES Group was the second-largest group within the Institute, representing over 2,100 dues-payers, and it supplied many of the Institute's activists. As one concerned PIPSC member noted in a letter published in the PIPSC *Journal*: "The efforts of a substantial number of members of the ES Group to separate is interesting in view of the fact that this group has provided us with our present president and two of his immediate predecessors, 50 percent of the members of the Executive Committee and 23 percent of the members of the Board, all from 10 percent of the total membership of the Institute."[34]

What started out as protest against Institute priorities and management of resources soon gathered its own momentum, and ESSA set a course for decertification. The first and most compelling argument marshalled by the protestors centred on the cost of membership fees for a group overwhelmingly located in Ottawa. The ES Group did not use regional offices and did not require a regional structure to represent its members. Their second grievance was the lack of group autonomy within PIPSC. Why support a structure, they asked, that was empowered to override the will of a consensus of ES group members?

Following procedures established by the PSSRB, ESSA filed a displacement (or decertification) application, and eventually a vote was held over a period of weeks in the fall of 1974. The results were 1,024 for ESSA and 394 for PIPSC, clearly exceeding the PSSRB threshold of 50 percent plus one. After some delays sorting out which employees warranted exclusion from the bargaining unit because of the managerial and confidential nature of their duties, the PSSRB upheld the displacement application, and the ES Group left the Institute in 1975. During the separation process, the Institute continued to negotiate the renewal of the ES group collective agreement, reaching a tentative settlement that its members voted to accept.

The departure of the ES Group represented a significant loss of members, talent, and revenue, but over time the Institute adjusted to compensate for the loss. The impact on morale within the organization was another matter. On one hand, the most overt malcontents were gone, thereby facilitating greater internal harmony. On the other hand, the very existence of ESSA provided an alternative to the Institute, especially for the larger Institute groups. Finding a path to restore confidence in the Institute as the vehicle to best serve members' interests would remain a challenge, and other groups would follow the ES Group out of PIPSC later in the decade.

Employers and Collective Bargaining

The abrupt advent of collective bargaining in the public sector contrasted the experience in the private sector. The Wagner-based labour relations system in Canada had first come to the private sector with the introduction of Privy Council Order 1003 in 1944 during the Second World War, and the Industrial Relations Disputes Investigations Act (IRDIA), passed in 1948, had further codified and expanded the terms of the wartime order. By 1950, the provinces had also passed versions of the IRDIA, and over the next twenty years the collective bargaining system in the private sector had gradually evolved. The Canadian public service had the whole process thrust upon it much more rapidly with the passage of the Public Services Staff Relations Act (PSSRA) in 1967, and by 1970 the adjudicating body established by the act—the PSSRB (Public Services Staff Relations Board)—was labouring to keep abreast of public sector developments. The 1970 PSSRB report revealed the scale of federal public sector union growth in just three years—114 new bargaining units certified, including 198,000 employees. The largest bargaining unit had ten thousand members, while the smallest—a unit from the National Research Council—had only nine.[35] All of this meant that an enormous amount of activity—from establishing a legal collective bargaining framework to actually using it—happened in a very short span of time. And the situation would only become more complex over time.

The PSSRA may have turned PIPSC into a union and given federal public sector workers a right to collective bargaining, but it did not give away the government's vast prerogatives as an employer. Collective bargaining in the public sector was (and is) markedly different than in the private sector because the state has a power that no corporation ever could. In addition to possessing all the prerogatives conferred upon employers by common law, the state also has the power to change the legislation that regulates employment—that is, to change the rules of the game. This fundamental difference complicates public sector collective bargaining. For instance, governments can force its own striking workers back to their jobs with legislation. The Canadian government has legislated postal workers back to work during strikes and even, in a recent case, before they actually went out on strike.[36] The state can also designate public sector workers as essential and thus prohibit them from going on strike, forcing them to rely on binding arbitration. The government in the 1970s preferred arbitration over conciliation to resolve disputes.

The growing number of workers represented by PIPSC after the introduction of the PSSRA also added to the complexity of the collective bargaining process. The question PIPSC had faced since the 1920s persisted into the era of formalized collective bargaining: Was the Institute dealing with a single employer that presented itself as many employers or with many employers that collectively formed a whole? PIPSC seems to have adopted both views during the 1970s. The Institute lobbied government as its collective employer, but it also had to conduct almost continuous negotiations with the Treasury Board Secretariat and various separate employers. This was further complicated by the fact that PIPSC members were organized by occupation rather than by workplace. In fact, PIPSC was really dealing with one employer, as the government ultimately funded all the agencies and departments in which its members worked. This meant that the Institute might have been able to achieve clear bargaining patterns across the public service. But in the 1970s, PIPSC did not conclude such a master collective agreement with the Canadian government.

Focusing on achieving such an agreement is a model of collective bargaining favoured by many other public sector unions, like the Canadian Union of Public Employees (CUPE), as well as by industrial unions, which like to establish benchmarks for bargaining with all employers in an industry. One way of doing this is to have master bargaining agreements that cover all workers employed by an organization regardless of the location in which they work. Examples of such agreements today include those that the Power Workers' Union (a CUPE affiliate) has with Ontario Power Generation or Unifor has with General Motors of Canada. These agreements often contain sub-agreements that pertain to specific work locations. In the case of General Motors, local agreements govern labour relations in the assembly and component plants operated by the company. Unions also sometimes conclude separate sub-agreements for skilled and semi-skilled workers. Concluding master agreements enables a union to set terms common to every member and also helps prevent employers from "whipsawing" workers—that is, forcing them to compete against each other for work and investment.[37]

Despite the potential that existed for PIPSC to conclude a master collective agreement, it did not pursue one in the 1970s. Instead, it negotiated a wide range of agreements that shared considerable commonality. Examining the term of specific bargaining agreements, such as those covering the Medicine and Social Work Groups, helps assess whether PIPSC's negotiators were successful. The Institute concluded six medicine and five social work agreements between 1969 and 1979. Similar numbers of agreements were negotiated for the other PIPSC occupational groups as well.

The 1969 Medicine Group's collective agreement concluded between PIPSC and the Treasury Board of Canada and printed, like all PIPSC's agreements, in both French and English included thirty-two clauses and three appendices over eighty-eight pages, which was about the average size of collective agreements concluded across Canada in the late 1960s and early 1970s. The 1969 agreement contained mostly the type of standard content expected in a collective agreement, including clauses setting out management rights, recognition of the union, the rights of employees, and vacation days and statutory holidays. The short duration—only one year—was a distinguishing aspect of the agreement. Working under contracts of short duration means nearly constant bargaining for both union and management.[38]

The management rights clause was remarkably short. Similar clauses grew to great length and detail in the private sector as the postwar decades progressed, but the medicine agreement simply stated, "All the functions, rights, powers and authority which the Employer has not specifically abridged, modified or delegated by this agreement are recognized by the Institute as being retained by the employer." A private sector agreement would have also included language on hiring, firing, reclassifying, determining work processes and procedures, and so on. This agreement basically said that the employer—meaning the state—could do what it wanted unless otherwise stated.[39]

Another clause, common to PIPSC agreements but unknown to those negotiated in the private sector or even by other public sector unions, highlighted the sensitive nature of many PIPSC members' work and consequently gave the government additional power. The "state security" clause read:

Nothing in this agreement shall be construed to require the Employer to do or refrain from doing anything contrary to any instruction, direction, or

> regulations given or made by or on behalf of the Government of Canada in
> the interest of the safety or security of Canada or any state allied or asso-
> ciated with Canada.[40]

This was a broad way of saying that national security trumped collective bargaining, but it also left considerable room for interpreting what constituted
safety and security. The idea of agreeing to language giving employers such
broad discretion is usually anathema to unions, yet the government must have
persisted in its demands to ensure that matters of national security took precedence over anything in an employment relationship.

Other clauses, fairly routine by today's standards, were groundbreaking
in the social context of Canada in 1970. A lengthy clause covered bereave-
ment leave, for example, although it allowed only three days maximum for the
loss of an immediate family member. Other provisions gave women up to six
months of unpaid maternity leave and protections against termination during
their leave and male employees one day off for the birth of a child, and all
employees could get jury duty leave or personnel selection leave if they were
involved in a recruitment process for a job elsewhere in the public service.[41]

The Medicine Group's 1969 contract was typical of PIPSC agreements
in reflecting the Institute's interest in promoting professional development
among its members. It provided leaves to write exams or engage in training
and career development so that "each employee shall have the opportunity for
the exchange of knowledge and experience with his professional colleagues."
Employees on training or career development leaves were compensated at
usual rates.[42] The priority the Institute gave to such professionalism clauses
is evident in the fact that they were among the lengthiest in the agreement.

The medical workers' agreement also revealed the complexity of the
employee classifications that fell under a single agreement. It covered three
classifications of medical officers, with twenty step increases across them.
Medical Officer 1 had nine steps in it, for example, and annual rates of pay
in 1969 ranged from $11,085 for Medical Officer 1 at the first step to $22,521
for the final step in Medical Officer 3. This may seem fairly straightforward,
indeed fair, as the salary scale made provision for increases in seniority and
experience. The problem for PIPSC and the employer was the determination
of any additional criteria for and variables affecting movement along the salary scale, such as level of responsibility and physical location. The pay language stipulated that a person would advance a step every twelve months, but
the employer still had some discretion over movement. Additional pay scales

covered personnel in medical specialist classifications. This led to a further complication for PIPSC: how to explain to some members that they may not be entitled to the same level of pay as others in a seemingly similar classification. To further exacerbate the complexity of the pay scales, something called the "Senior Merit Pay Regulations" held sway over one level of the medical specialist classification and over non-excluded managers.[43]

The Social Work Group's 1970 agreement shared similarities with the one for medical personnel. It was also for a short duration and included forty-one clauses and some appendices.[44] The general provisions, such as management rights, found in the medical workers' agreement were also included in the social workers' contract, as were the provisions referring to professional obligations. Education, examination, and career development leave were included, although the language for these clauses was briefer than in the other agreement. Some clauses not found in the medicine agreement reflected concerns specific to work in the social work field. The agreement obligated the employer to provide, for example, access to social work publications needed by bargaining unit members, access to telephones, and employment references, if requested. The fact that something like phone access was guaranteed by the agreement suggests that Institute members had encountered access problems in the past. Another clause specifically described what constituted an illegal strike.[45]

The Social Work Group's contract laid out twenty-eight job classifications, considerably more than the three of the Medicine Group's agreement. Wages ranged from $6,869 per year for a Social Worker 1 to $14,304 for an Administrative Officer 6. Like the medical workers' agreement, the social workers' contract contained a clause pertaining to a "penological factor allowance" but included much more detail about how the clause would work.[46] A penological factor is essentially a way of calculating an allowance for additional risks arising from working in a federal correctional institution—in other words, danger pay. Neither the medicine nor social work agreements referred to overtime or seniority. The social workers' agreement also contained the state security clause, though it is difficult to imagine a situation in which a federal social worker (or a medical officer, for that matter) could damage relations with closely allied countries.

The most obvious thing about the early 1970s collective agreements between PIPSC and the Canadian federal government is that they reflected the fact that bargaining was enormously complicated. Collective bargaining can be an arcane, byzantine process that is the domain of practitioners with highly specialized knowledge and that can often cause rank-and-file union members to feel alienated. And despite appearing to provide clear language on crucial aspects of employment, the contracts involved enough ambiguity to lead to conflict. Fortunately, the PIPSC agreements included grievance procedures, and the PSSRB was in place to adjudicate disputes.

Despite—or perhaps because of—the complexity of bargaining and the collective agreement language, PIPSC members were not reticent about raising concerns over collective bargaining. Ed Napke was involved with medicine group bargaining for several years, and he kept detailed records pertaining to the 1970 agreement. The preparations that preceded bargaining for just this one group were comprehensive. Many of the members working in the Medicine Group were employed in remote parts of Canada and worked with First Nations populations. PIPSC actually located every member working in this group on a map. It also mapped out all the links between the Department of National Health and Welfare and universities with medical schools.[47]

The terms of the different agreements could lead to considerable internal deliberation not only on the union's side but also on the employer's. For instance, a confidential 1974 government communication revealed considerable management discussions over how and when psychiatrists should be compensated for on-call services. Although PIPSC clearly did not give short shrift to bargaining preparations, members still raised concerns. In one 1974 letter sent by a number of medicine group members to Napke, the members complained about insufficient wage increases in their latest agreement and advised Napke that the next agreement negotiated should be only one year in duration, in the hope that more frequent arbitration would lead to better economic outcomes.[48]

Politics and Community   The nature of the PSSRA meant that PIPSC would engage in collective bargaining in a different way than many other Canadian unions, but its political orientation was also markedly different. As previously noted, one executive director came under criticism for showing an overt political orientation. Even in its internal communications, the Institute avoided potentially partisan political or policy issues. Internal memoranda did not reference the major issues facing the Canadian labour movement, such as wage and price controls, which enraged most Canadian unions. PIPSC staff and officers also avoided discussion of other major events and public-policy challenges. For instance, the fact that a sovereignist government had been elected in Quebec did not, apparently, warrant any mention. The struggles waged by other Canadian unions were not discussed; indeed, there were few references to other public sector unions, like the Public Service Alliance of Canada.

Yet PIPSC's political sympathies can still be inferred from its actions, even if they were not overtly articulated. It might have seemed natural for PIPSC to have supported the New Democratic Party (NDP) and participate in allied labour federations such as the CLC (Canadian Labour Congress), as these were common policy positions in the Canadian labour movement at the time. The NDP strongly supported public sector bargaining rights, and its support for Lester Pearson's Liberal minority government had been key to passage of the PSSRA. Choosing to endorse or oppose any specific party would have put the Institute in a precarious position, depending on the outcome of federal elections, and the NDP did not form governments in the 1970s. PIPSC was also not the only Canadian union not to openly support the NDP or affili-ate with the CLC. For instance, building-trades unions had a long tradition of eschewing overt political affiliation, and other professional unions, like those representing teachers, were not affiliated with national and provincial labour federations during the 1970s. As the Institute's membership wrestled with changes brought by the PSSRA and McGill Report, adding CLC affiliation or appearing to support the NDP would have added to internal tensions.

Moreover, PIPSC clearly found dealing with Liberal governments compati-ble with its political orientation. By 1970, the Institute had been in existence for fifty years and had spent thirty-nine of them dealing with Liberal governments; by the end of the decade, it had been engaging with Liberal governments for almost forty-eight years. This situation was perhaps only replicated at the provincial level in Ontario and Alberta under those province's long-running Progressive Conservative regimes. PIPSC dealt with one employer, and that employer was run for decades by basically the same group of leaders. In short, PIPSC's rejection of overtly political policy positions in the 1970s rested on both principle and its level of comfort in dealing with the political status quo—at least as it applied to a Liberal government as its members' employer.

PIPSC in the Media

PIPSC, like most major Canadian unions, had an active media presence in the 1970s, with coverage centred in national media, such as the *Globe and Mail* newspaper. This marked a continuation of what the Institute had experienced during its first five decades. Media reports on PIPSC covered member concerns, changes in leader-ship, and, occasionally, policy differences within the Institute. For example,

PIPSC's internal discussions over official bilingualism sometimes spilled over into popular media discourse. A 1970 article in the *Globe and Mail* asked, "can two solitudes be avoided in the civil service?" Concerns about how government services would be offered in both official languages were raised by both the Public Service Alliance of Canada and PIPSC, with the Institute described as adopting a "wait and see" attitude to the creation of French language service units.[49]

The media also covered the Institute's position on collective bargaining matters, though PIPSC did not receive the same volume of coverage that larger private sector unions enjoyed. In part, this resulted from the fact that media outlets preferred to highlight the drama of labour disputes, like strikes and lockouts, rather than the complexities of collective bargaining. Coverage of potentially divisive policy issues such as official bilingualism drew PIPSC into the limelight because, unlike unions outside of the federal public service, its members were directly affected by this government policy. The Institute's frustration with the restraints imposed by the Public Service Staff Relations Act also appeared in media commentary. A 1971 report described how PIPSC proposed changes to bargaining rules in order to expand the range of topics that could be covered in negotiations. It was also uncommon in the mid-1970s to read media reports about large numbers of women workers engaging in collective bargaining, as was the case with the 1,600 nurses represented by the Institute who, as the *Globe* reported in 1975 rejected the government's wage proposal.[50]

The PIPSC Experience in the 1970s

PIPSC's members continued to be remarkably well educated by 1970s standards. Major policy efforts to improve access to post-secondary education, such as the emergence of community colleges across the country in the mid- to late 1960s, were beginning to increase the number of Canadians with a post-secondary education, but only a 18 percent of Canadians had a university degree in the 1970s. By contrast, virtually everyone in PIPSC had a post-secondary credential, if not two or three of them.

The recollections of people who belonged to the Institute in the 1970s reveal much about how membership changed during the first decade after passage of the PSSRA. Patrick Kinnear joined the public service in 1966, a year before the PSSRA was passed, and worked in Customs and Excise and Veterans Affairs. Reflecting on the PSSRA, he remarked, "Well in 1966–67, [with] the introduction of collective bargaining, firstly our salaries went up, then

[PIPSC] started becoming more of a union, you know, [leading to] grievances and better protection for employees."[51]

In contrast to PIPSC's official neutrality on issues of government policy affecting the Institute, the recollections of members like Kinnear make clear that individual PIPSC members often held strong opinions on government policies such as wage control and official bilingualism. On wage controls imposed on the federal public service by the Liberal government of Pierre Elliott Trudeau between 1982 and 1984, Kinnear commented:

> What's interesting about "six and five" [the legislated maximum wage increases permitted in two consecutive years] was that that's the biggest raise we ever got. It was pretty traumatic because when the inflation board came in with the six and five it was quite drastic, but what happened when they took six and five off [for private sector workers], they kept it for the public service. We were treated not as proper Canadians but as public servants separately.

On the government's official bilingualism policy, Kinnear said:

> That was good because it was how most of us felt. ... I mean we started to have a second official language. It's part of the government, and I know there was a lot of resentment at one time, but in the end it made sense. I thought it was a good idea because I spent part of my growing-up years in Quebec, then later moving to Ottawa, and it was an English town. I found that a little strange. I was quite pleased with official bilingualism.

The challenges that women faced in their workplaces in the 1970s was revealed by Lucienne Bahuaud, who was employed at Revenue Canada for almost thirty-four years, starting in the agency's Winnipeg office. She reflected on what it was like for a woman working in the Canada Revenue Agency in the 1970s and her experience leading an audit:

> Very, very few [women worked at the CRA] at the beginning. I remember when I went into the business area, I was the only woman there, and the rest were men. And I remember the first time I called a taxpayer to set up a meeting, an appointment, to go out and do it. And he said, and who are you calling [to make the appointment] for, and I said, I am—I'm the one who's going to be going out. And he was just taken aback.

Bahuaud eventually arranged for her audit team to meet with the man, who obviously found dealing with a female auditor such a novelty that he wanted to show her off to his friends. She describes the unusual incident:

> We had our initial meeting [with the taxpayer I was auditing], ... and I was going to be there for a week. And it was out of town, so our whole team was at the motel. And we went into the bar to relax. Next thing I know, here's my taxpayer coming into the bar with four of his buddies to introduce the woman that was auditing him. So that was interesting, but I think they got over it and companies got used to it [a women auditing them]. But yeah, I was the only female in Winnipeg in the business audit section initially, and then of course it increased.[52]

New Canadians also began to join the public service in increasing numbers in the 1970s, making PIPSC's membership more diverse than in preceding decades.[53] Randy Dhar, an architect employed by Public Works Canada for thirty-two years, discussed his experience of immigrating from India and joining the public service in the 1970s:

Figure 2-2: A PIPSC member working as a nurse at the Blood Indian Hospital in Cardston, Alberta, circa mid-1970s. *PIPSC Storage Room.*

I did my undergraduate work in architecture in India with a scholarship from the State Department of [the] USA. I came to the University of Illinois, and I did my master's degree there and worked for a while. And a condition of that scholarship was that I had to go back to India to serve [the] Indian government for at least three years, which I did. Then I got married, and then there was an opportunity for me to come back to North America, and my wife had never been outside India, so we accepted that and came to Saint John, New Brunswick.

Some positions [at Public Works] were for architects and some for engineers. We were called project managers, in charge of projects [ranging from] $500,000 renovations to $25 million major construction projects—buildings, [including the] grounds around [them] and so on. So, the total responsibility was given to us as project managers, and [we would use] either the in-house architect engineers who produced the drawings [to our] specifications and [the] tender documents, or we would hire private sector consultants who would be working under the direction of the project manager to produce the documents necessary to go [to] the marketplace to hire a contractor.

Dhar also described how he joined and became active in PIPSC:

In 1974-75, although I joined the public service … I didn't … know that I was not a member of PIPSC [until] somebody told me, "fill in this form and you become a member." My dues were being deducted from my salary and it so happened I saw that, and then I found there was no organized architecture group for PIPSC, and there was only one member of the staff who was looking after [us]. … There was a group called Architecture and Town Planning with a small number of members, so I took the initiative to offer my services, and then people said, you are welcome to provide these services and leadership.[54]

As the Institute's membership grew larger and more diversified, its paid staff also began to increase, largely as a result of the McGill Report's recommendations. Bob McIntosh joined the staff in 1973:

My first day of work at the Institute was May 14. That came about because I was working at the Department of Labour in a research assistant role, and basically that [kind of job] was available at the Institute. And at the time it was a little bit of a promotion pay-wise, and I took advantage of that. But I didn't know very much about PIPSC before that. It was actually one of the economists who mentioned, "Oh, I think PIPSC is hiring; you should go over there," because I was on a term [contract], you see.

So, that's how it started, and [I] went from there and got involved. I have a bachelor's degree from Trent University—in geography and statistics. But I think it was primarily my experience of Labour Canada—because we were doing support work on labour surveys—that attracted the interest of those at the time who hired me. I started out as an assistant research officer—basically providing support for collective bargaining—doing various surveys and analysis of pay data and various benefit data, and then working with a negotiator to present information to bargaining teams, to the employer, and to the third parties.

McIntosh also commented on tensions between veterans who wanted to maintain PIPSC's professional traditions and newer members who viewed unionization as a means to make gains for members:

The first thing that became obvious to me ... was the tension between the older members—[over] professionalism and the maintenance of professionalism and the interpretation of what that meant—and the more recent members. It was not necessarily an age issue because some of them were older when they came in. But they were new members, and they were looking for results. They would say, "We've joined this union, we want to behave like a union, and we want to see improvements in various issues that affect our members," including professional recognition.

And so, there was that kind of a dichotomy [between old and new members who were] trying to work together, to blend that [their different points of view] into a constructive way. For me, that's how I characterize the early seventies and mid-seventies—which led to some real vigorous debates and ultimately some decertifications. And then after we went through that [difficult] period of time, the late seventies, ... the momentum turned, and then we started to grow. We actually acquired some groups, and our membership in ... existing units was growing, too, with the gradual professionalization of the public service.[55]

Although Kinnear, Bahuaud, and Dhar all had differing roles and experiences on the job, some common themes characterize their recollections. They all found their work in the 1970s, either as PIPSC members or staff (in McIntosh's case), to be interesting, and they were affected by the challenges and changes PIPSC faced during the 1970s, including the introduction of official bilingualism, wage controls, and the entry of more women and new Canadians into the public service. They saw some challenges in their work but more often saw progress, covered by PIPSC collective agreements that improved on the pre-1967 working conditions of the Institute's members.

To the 1980s   PIPSC ended the 1970s in a markedly different situation than it had begun the decade. The PSSRA and the adoption of collective bargaining practices had changed the Institute, which faced an increasingly complex collective bargaining environment and the challenge of reconciling its members traditional identity as professionals with their new identity as unionized workers. The Institute grew larger and more diverse as more women and people of colour were hired into the public service, joined the Institute, and moved into leadership positions. As PIPSC's membership and financial resources expanded, it hired more staff on a permanent basis. The Institute made gains for its members under the PSSRA, making full use of the dispute-resolution mechanisms in the act. But frustration increased with the limits that the act imposed on collective bargaining—limits that meant that the Institute could not negotiate over the same range of issues that a private sector union could. Other government policies also had a profound impact on PIPSC members, particularly official bilingualism and wage control. Yet while other Canadian private and public sector unions waged public struggles against governments at all levels, PIPSC maintained a somewhat lower profile.

PIPSC was ready for the 1980s. Yet it would be a very different decade than the one that had just ended. The 1970s were a time when the Canadian state's expansion was still viewed favourably in popular and political discourse. Neoliberalism had not yet emerged in Canada as it was beginning to in the United States and United Kingdom, and Canada continued to have comparatively high union density. The 1980s would bring new challenges.

Chapter 3

Achieving Better Results for Members, 1980-89

The 1980s began for PIPSC much differently than the 1970s. Canada had experienced internal turmoil in 1970 because of the October Crisis, but the country's economy was still strong and government spending was growing. Ten years later, the country's economic prospects looked less promising. The Liberals were back in power with Pierre Elliot Trudeau, but the Progressive Conservatives would return to power in 1984 and not just as a brief break from the Liberals. The country experienced a short but severe recession from 1981 to 1982. The Constitution was repatriated from the United Kingdom in 1982 after protracted and contentious negotiations between the federal and provincial governments. That event would have a profound impact on the legal framework, including labour law, in which Canadians lived.

Canada's demographics, which were already changing by the end of the 1970s, further shifted during the new decade as a result of changing Canadian immigration policy in the 1970s. As the country became more diverse in the 1980s, so too did the public service. PIPSC grew during the 1980s, and its membership reflected the wider demographic trends found across the country. However, the issues that Institute members and leaders faced grew more complex. This chapter will describe those issues and how PIPSC responded and will draw even more than previous chapters on interviews with current and past PIPSC members. Their voices illustrate the experience of working in the public service and belonging to the Institute in the 1980s.

Leadership   The demographics of PIPSC's leadership continued to evolve as younger members became involved, the Second World War generation retired, and more women took on leadership roles in the organization. The pattern set during the previous decade, of the baby boom generation assuming positions of responsibility, accelerated in the 1980s. Images of PIPSC meetings show younger people becoming active members, including increasing numbers of women and people of colour. PIPSC elected its second female president, Iris Craig, in 1986.

The 1980s seemed like a promising decade to the Institute's leaders and members. Prior to Craig's election, the Institute was headed by Jack Donegani, only its second full-time, paid president, who was certainly a departure from some of the staider presidents who preceded him. Known for charting his own course, he concluded his time as president by dancing a waltz with his wife at a union banquet to Frank Sinatra's "My Way." In early 1980, the Institute's sixtieth anniversary, Donegani outlined the organization's priorities and issues: job security and retraining in the face of potential government cutbacks and layoffs; pensions; increased funding for programs; promotion of women members; collective bargaining rights, including the right to strike; and the political rights of public servants.

That list of priorities was revealing for several reasons. The Institute had clearly adjusted to working within a collective bargaining regime as a bargaining agent, though, as subsequent analysis will show, describing PIPSC as a union was still somewhat of a rhetorical leap for many of its members. Pushing for greater bargaining rights was always a priority for public sector union members, as was the right to strike. All unions across Canada were worried about maintaining pension plans during this period. Improving the ability of women to pursue promotion in the public service reflected gender change in the federal workforce and the growing influence of women in the Institute.[1] Nineteen eighty was also a federal election year, and members were encouraged to get to know something about the candidates in their ridings.

By 1980, the Institute's process for electing its own officers was much more inclusive and democratic than it had been a decade earlier, as members now voted directly for candidates. Running for national office required a candidate to gain support from and be attuned to issues and concerns raised by members across Canada and to avoid a reflex to concentrate on problems that seemed more immediate because they came from the membership in the National Capital Region. Elections also involved unofficial slates of candidates.

Figure 3-1: President Iris Craig (*right*) and Chief Statistician of Canada Ivan Fellegi (*left*) presenting the Professional Institute's Gold Medal award to Leroy Stone (*centre*). *PIPSC Storage Room, PIPSC Photo Albums, 1992–1997.*

Staff   Elected officials, like Donegani, eventually fulfilled their terms, and new officers assumed leadership roles. The union's full-time, paid staff provided continuity over time, generally staying with the organization once hired. During the 1980s, the supervision of PIPSC's staff was consolidated under a management committee that coordinated staff efforts to support Institute activities. Notably, the Institute drew a clearer line than many unions between elected positions and paid staff roles. By the 1980s, PIPSC no longer routinely recruited staff from the membership, as was common in private sector unions especially and as the organization had done in expanding the staff in the late 1960s. Staff members also did not run for elected leadership positions.[2]

Former PIPSC employees remembered dealing with challenging situations but consistently spoke positively about their years on staff. Lorraine Neville witnessed the expansion of the Institute's staff. Her reflections on the organization's leadership in the 1980s illustrate the key role that paid staff played in supporting the union's leaders. She spoke at length about President Iris Craig:

Before Iris became president, she was the chairman of the Finance Committee [a volunteer position] and thought she knew a lot about the organization. She was shocked when she became president that she didn't fully understand ... the financial practices ... whereby the former president, who had [a] public relations budget assigned to his office, opted [instead] to use funds from a regional office budget to pay for his public relations activities in the region. ... As the chair of the Finance Committee Iris said, "I didn't know he was spending money out of the regional budget." ... So, she had to grow into the position, understand bargaining strategies, and gradually learn the process of how the organization worked, even though she had been an active volunteer in the Institute for some time. ... She had to learn all that.

And I would think that the majority of the Institute members thought she did an exceptional job. She was even keeled and didn't lose sight of objectives. Under Iris's leadership new ... groups joined the Institute. ... She had other elements [tasks] that she had to do up on Parliament Hill, and she did those very well. She was trying to maintain the Institute's professionalism—maintain that structure—still doing briefs to Parliament, still making sure that we're talking [to] the right level [of government].

In the Institute's relationship with the government, staff like Neville played a key role, handling contacts with the ministries below the ministerial level. As Neville noted, "the president doesn't talk to deputy ministers. The staff do. The president talks to the ministers. Her [Craig's] predecessor, Jack Donegani, had made that clear so as not to diminish the presidency of the Institute."

As well as helping Craig understand the ins and outs of the union's day-to-day operations and assisting in the union's government relations, Neville also supported Craig through her first strike experience:

She was involved in the first major strikes undertaken by members. Actually, she had never been involved in a strike in her whole life and acknowledged to me that she didn't understand its implications for her as president. ... She did walk a strike line—her first one—on Riverside Drive [in Ottawa]. The CS [Computer Systems] Group was on strike. So, I drove her out there and gave her a picket sign. And she said, "What do I do?" And I said, "You just walk around with people and talk to them and you'll be fine."[3]

With the help of paid staff like Neville, Iris Craig fully adapted to the many functions of PIPSC's presidency.

Membership   Just as the image and reality of Canada as a nation overwhelmingly comprising peoples of British, French, or
Indigenous origins continued to change under the influence of official multiculturalism and the immigration reforms of the 1960s and 1970s, so too did
PIPSC. Many members now came to the public service with credentials earned
in other countries. Although PIPSC had now been a union for over a decade,
members still usually viewed themselves first as professional employees and
second as union members. By 1988, the Institute had 19,047 active and emeritus
members spread across employee groups that ranged in size from three members, in one of the nursing groups, to 3,029 in the Computer Systems Group.[4]

The Official Languages Act of September 1969, which had given French
and English equal status, had introduced bilingualism into the federal public service in the 1970s, and this continued to affect members in the 1980s.
Prior to the act's passage, apart from frontline federal services in the province
of Quebec, the federal public service operated with English as the language
of work. Designating positions as bilingual led to language training and the
application of a bilingual bonus in the 1970s, and such designations were gradually extended to most supervisory and executive positions. By the 1990s, civil
servants in these positions would require even higher functionality in both
official languages, directly affecting career mobility. Over time great progress
was made toward a bilingual workplace.[5]

Membership engagement is an issue for all unions, which ultimately
rely on a small core of dedicated activists to provide advocacy within them
and the broader community. Like other Canadian unions in the 1980s, PIPSC
actively encouraged women, young members, and people of colour to become
activists, and these efforts clearly bore some fruit, even if they did not always
work for other unions. PIPSC did not collect internal demographic information about its members, but it was managing to get a new generation of members involved. Images of PIPSC meetings in the 1980s show younger and more
diverse workers becoming active. Figure 3–2, taken at a 1986 meeting of the
Quebec Regional Council, reflects this demographic change.

Governance   The Institute continued to focus strongly on internal
governance in the 1980s, a continuation of how it had
operated since the 1920s. The Institute's ongoing evolution necessitated
changes in governance, and by-law discussions were often a main focus at
annual general meetings. Rank-and-file members of PIPSC might only have
been aware of such changes if they read the minutes of those meetings.

Figure 3-2: The Quebec Regional Council in 1986. *PIPSC Storage Room, Photo Album 1986.*

Dealing with governance issues had become a routine matter, with structures in place to handle the task. Questions such as how to determine committees of the executive board, the focus of one 1986 meeting of the Policy and Planning Committee, were not exactly compelling ones for an average union member, even if they were crucial to determining how the Institute's board would do its work.[6]

The challenge in administering a governance system, which was a key function of the PIPSC Board of Directors, was in trying to reconcile the wide range of opinions that often manifested themselves among members working across a geographically large country. Don Burns, a former board vice president, described the challenge of reconciling the interests of the National Capital Region with those of other parts of the country:

> I guess that's a bit of a rub for the people outside of the NCR. Because obviously with half the membership here they do dominate in a lot of ways the politics and what goes on. But I think within the Institute there is definitely a good recognition that not everyone is in the NCR, and the regions have a strong voice on the Board of Directors. It was clear through my experience with the Institute that you don't need to be a big group. You don't need to be part of the NCR. If you're a small group in a region

you're treated very similarly to a big group. We had members in the Yukon where their employer wanted to get rid of them—a very small group. And the Institute invested time and effort to make sure those members were represented. The Institute has a very strong national view of things.[7]

As PIPSC expanded, the board was an increasingly busy entity with a lot of work to complete on an annual basis. Blair Stannard, another former vice president and member of the CS Group, reflected on his experience as a volunteer member of the PIPSC board in the mid-1980s. His comments reveal how much of the routine governance work relied on the unpaid work of those in elected, volunteer positions:

> There was, basically, the running of the Institute. As vice president, I got a bunch of extra responsibilities. You have to appreciate that, at this time, vice presidents didn't get a salary. But the board, in their great generosity, gave us—I think it was at first—a $500 a year honorarium, which you then got a T4 for at the end of the year and paid half of it back in income tax. Then they very magnanimously increased it to $1,000 after we told them how many hundreds of hours we worked. ... The elected officials would go to the PIPSC office building on Bronson, in those days, and work at night or on the weekends. And in the beginning, they paid for their own meals when they did so. Finally, some of us who were involved said, "Well, if we're going to be here five nights in a row for meetings, then we are not going to settle for St. Hubert chicken or sandwiches five nights in a row." But again, the person who was the head of Finance was as careful with our money as he was with his own. We said, "Well, that's fine, but if you've got people who are not getting paid any salary or any honorarium, then you've got to do something."[8]

Stannard's comments show that being on the board was not simply a perquisite. It was a lot of work and could quickly encroach on a person's evenings and weekends.

Another major function of PIPSC's governance structure was overseeing the Institute's finances. In 1980, PIPSC had just over $1.8 million in assets and revenues of $2.4 million. Eight years later, both had more than doubled; assets had increased in value to $3.9 million and revenues to $5.9 million.[9] Audit statements produced by external auditor Price Waterhouse painted a picture of an organization in strong financial health. The statements also show that an effective governance and oversight function had become even more important because PIPSC had become such a large financial entity.

Employers and Collective Bargaining   The unique nature of collective bargaining in the federal public sector was increasingly evident in the 1980s. The federal public service was far larger in scope and reach than those found in any province or municipality in Canada, which meant collective bargaining was complex. Other unionized workers, especially those working in manufacturing, would have been surprised to learn that members of the Institute were organized along occupational lines rather than by government department. This was a long-standing practice confirmed by the Public Service Staff Relations Act, a practice that made it possible for the government to reorganize departments without disrupting the union's structure. Newly elected governments routinely reorganized government departments, which often involved shifting public servants from one department to another. Organizing workers on occupational lines facilitated such reorganizations by making it possible for employees to change departments without it affecting their union affiliation. Yet the fact that PIPSC members were organized principally by occupational grouping (and only then more loosely by department or agency) gave the Institute the structure of a craft union as much as one representing professional workers.

As it had since unionization, the Institute continued to try to avoid confrontation with the government, and the employer avoided deliberately provoking PIPSC into a militant response. The two sides attempted to find common ground on issues, especially through the establishment and use of joint labour-management committees. The issue of equal pay for work of equal value for women—commonly known as pay equity—was a major labour-management issue by the late 1980s and into the 1990s. The federal government formed a joint initiative with the public sector unions to determine how to implement pay equity. The preamble of the initial committee report discussed the complexity of the issue and the need for a common job evaluation plan to enable progress toward pay equity. (The report did not note that the wider issue of formalizing job classification had been ongoing since 1920.) The committee's work was enormously valuable to the public sector, especially at the federal level, leading to the implementation of greater pay equity. Collective bargaining continued to revolve around two key functions: negotiations and contract administration. Grievances and adjudications were central to the latter function.

Organizing   By the 1980s, the Canadian labour movement was well on its way to becoming a public sector movement. The slow but steady decline of private sector unionization that began in the 1960s became more pronounced. In 1984, slightly over 78 percent of public sector workers in Canada were unionized, while just over 38 percent of the overall non-agricultural workforce was organized into unions. Virtually everyone in the public service who could join a union belonged to one.[10] High public sector union density prevailed throughout the 1980s, and public sector unions became dominant players in the Canadian labour movement. The Canadian Union of Public Employees, for example, became the country's largest and most influential union. Other unions, like those in the postal service, waged high-profile strikes.

Like most unions, PIPSC did not devote nearly enough resources to organizing new members, even though organizing remained one of its a key functions, as it did for all unions. One of the main reasons that industrial unions made such huge gains from the mid-1930s to the 1940s was because they devoted considerable time and effort to signing up new members. They made less effort once they achieved legal collective bargaining and organized labour appeared to have secured a seemingly permanent, if less equal, seat at the bargaining table with government and business.

PIPSC's organizing efforts differed considerably from those of private sector unions. A union trying to organize a factory, for example, would first try to establish an internal organizing committee, then assign a full-time organizer to the task of signing up members in the hope of filing an application for certification with the labour board. PIPSC never had full-time organizers standing outside of government offices trying to get people to sign union cards. Instead, it relied more on attracting new members by word of mouth. While private sector employers virtually always mounted some form of resistance to an organizing campaign, the federal government's passage of the PSSRA meant that in the case of federal public servants their employer was encouraging them to organize.

Bob McIntosh confirmed that, despite its lack of proactive organizing drives, the Institute was looking to expand and bring in new members in the 1980s, including some who worked for provincial governments:

I'm pretty sure it was about that time—the early eighties—when the Institute received enquiries about membership from professionals in provincial jurisdictions. The first certifications outside federal jurisdiction covered agrologists and home economists in the New Brunswick public service in 1982. Shortly after, their colleagues in the Veterinarians Group and the Engineering and Land Survey Group also joined. A bargaining unit of professional engineers working for the province of Manitoba joined later. So, the Institute was looking outside of the federal sphere at other professionals who weren't represented, or who weren't happy. In some cases they were representing themselves and were looking to become part of a bigger union.

Some PIPSC members, like Neil Harden, who started working in the public service in 1976, spent considerable portions of their careers as provincial-government employees. The issues facing provincial and federal workers were not always the same, but Harden, for one, learned more about national PIPSC issues as a member of the union's advisory board.[11]

The transfer of veterans' hospitals and other health care facilities from federal to provincial jurisdiction contributed to PIPSC entry into provincial territory. Institute members in these institutions were typically absorbed into existing provincial unions, but in April 1983 nurses, dieticians, social workers, and pharmacists retained the Institute as their bargaining agent when Deer Lodge Centre was transferred to Manitoba's authority. Eventually physicians at Deer Lodge also organized into a bargaining unit within the Institute.[12]

However, some of the workers affected by the transfer of health care facilities to provincial and territorial governments were unable to keep their PIPSC affiliation. In the Northwest Territories, for example, the government refused to recognize PIPSC as the bargaining agent of health care workers now under its jurisdiction. PIPSC took the government to court, challenging the constitutionality of section 42(1) of the Northwest Territories' Public Service Act of 1974, which enabled the government to decide which unions or employee associations it would bargain with. However, in case of *Professional Institute of the Public Service of Canada v. Northwest Territories (Commissioner)*, the Supreme Court ruled against PIPSC in a four-to-three decision that placed limits on the right of public sector workers to choose their own bargaining agents.[13]

PIPSC also grew by bringing in members from other federal public sector unions. When federal public servants decided that they wanted to move from another union to PIPSC, it created an uproar. The motivation underlying the decision to move was conditioned by how people thought about their roles as public servants and how they related to other workers. The recollections of

Phil Jolie, a federal auditor, and Bob Luce, a full-time negotiator on the Institute's staff, illustrate how and why some workers decided to switch unions. Jolie described how he and his fellow auditors, who were originally members of the Public Service Alliance of Canada (PSAC), decided that they wanted to join PIPSC:

> I was an Auditor with the Department of National Revenue Canada, ... now the Canada Revenue Agency. I was a member of the AU [Auditing] Group. And in 1985, when I joined the department, and up until 1988 we were a part of the Public Service Alliance of Canada. I was never thrilled to be a member of a union at all. I was never involved in a union. In 1988, contract negotiations were not going well. The Alliance was being very political, taking political positions about the Mulroney government, and I thought—and my colleagues thought—that's not really what a union is supposed to do. It's supposed to go on with negotiations. And there was a meeting at PSAC to give us an update on the bargaining at the time. It was just before Easter weekend in April, I think, of '88, ... and it didn't go well.
>
> Ian [Rathwell] and I were walking. Ian is a friend of mine who joined the department at the same time I did, in '85. We both came to Ottawa a year or two later. He said, "It doesn't feel good. I wonder if people would want to get out of PSAC." So, we just took a blank piece of paper and put a heading on the top, "Would you want to get out of PSAC?" and "Phone Number." And we passed it around to some people, some AUs we knew at headquarters. And, we just got flooded with replies. People photocopied the page and sent it on to other people who gave it back to us. It was just a tidal wave. And we thought, there's something happening here.
>
> Well, Ian and I thought, we don't know anything about unions. We never had to before. So, we thought, we'd better find some backup here. So, we phoned up PIPSC and got Bob McIntosh. We just phoned up PIPSC— blind—on the phone. We said, "We're two AUs thinking of changing unions. What have you got?" We went over to the offices on Bronson in April or early May of '88 and had a conversation. And they gave us some explanations. [They said,] "you could form your own union, but if you want to consider joining the Institute, here are the application forms; here are some questions and answers; and if you want to talk to us again, feel free."
>
> We brought the blank application forms back to the office, and passed them out to people in headquarters. And because we were at headquarters

and were giving advice to people who had been performing work in district offices across the country—and some of our friends were traveling across the country—we gave them some application forms.

Well, "it" hit the fan. The Alliance found out we were doing this, and they were just outraged. But people were signing the forms and sending them back. And we were getting very, very, very—almost unanimous responses, saying: "Yes. Here's my form. Here's my dollar. Let's go."

Jolie went on to describe the responses from the employer and also from PSAC:

One of my friends was in Calgary, and he was passing the forms around. Well, it wasn't a job-related function, but he brought the forms with him and passed them around the office—team leaders were calling their staff in from the field to sign the forms—and they gave them back to them. And he got a call from his boss at headquarters, saying, "Quit doing that."

"What am I doing? I'm not doing anything."

"Whatever you're doing, quit it."

I got calls from my bosses saying, "Quit using the department phones for this. You can't use the department phones to do this proselytizing." But the responses kept coming in.

The Alliance sent its first letter out to people saying this was a full-blown raid: "It's terrible. And we're in the middle of contract negotiations now and we're in the retroactive period [when the previous contract had already ended]. And if you change unions, you'll lose the retroactivity."

Well, it dried it up immediately. No one wanted to sign forms anymore. We went to tell the Institute. We asked Bob McIntosh, "Well, is that right?" He said, "Of course not. It doesn't matter if you change bargaining agents." So, we arranged for the Institute to write a letter to me because people were tired of hearing from me because [of] who am I. They wanted to hear from the Institute. So, the Institute wrote a letter to me, and we copied it and sent it to everybody. So, the Institute wrote to me and answered all my questions, including retroactivity and so on.

We got contacts across the country, eventually got more than half the members to sign up, and, I think I got an official "babysitter" by July of that year. The Institute had assigned Bob Luce to look after us, and he looked after us from that point onwards, and that's how I got involved.

Bob Luce's memories of how the auditors moved to PIPSC add further insights into how PIPSC members thought about collective bargaining and what they wanted from a union:

I came from a labour relations background to the Institute and was essentially assigned—in addition to the "babysitter" role that Phil referred to—I was also the negotiator for the group and the official spokesperson, although the leadership of the group clearly came from the group. My role was really to convey their wishes both to the employer, but also, I think, which was interesting to some extent, I became the grease in the gears for the group to deal with the Institute because there needed to sometimes be some translation of what the group wanted and then some translation back [about] what the Institute expected. And so that was a role that I felt evolved for me, which probably became more and more true for other groups as they became more autonomous. There is a relationship between the group and the Institute, and vice versa. ...

One concern [that the auditors had] was how the Alliance was organized. The umbrella organization is the Alliance, and then the subcomponents are by department. So, all the PSAC employees of the Department of National Revenue belong to one component. And that component was the way the members related to PSAC. But in ... the Department of National Revenue, where most of the AUs [auditors] worked, ... the AUs were a minority of the members in the component. So, most of the people who worked for National Revenue were CRs [clerical and regulatory], or PMs [program management], or some other Alliance group.

The AUs didn't really feel they had a voice in the Alliance because they could be overwhelmed by the CRs and PMs. The AUs were more than represented in the steward function and employee-relations function, and in negotiations with management and on the subgroup executive, but that wasn't in their capacity as AUs. There was no one in the UTE [Union of Taxation Employees, part of PSAC] who really spoke for the AU group—that was one thing.

The auditors' impetus for changing unions was thus the same thing that led workers throughout the labour movement to switch organizations—namely, dissatisfaction with how the first union operated. In this case, the auditors felt that PSAC's organization on departmental lines didn't serve their needs.[14] The auditors found that structure to be unwieldy and a poor vehicle for making their voice heard, and they wanted more acceptable representation through some other organization.

The role of politics in shaping the decision to switch unions was an interesting aspect of this case and one that again highlights how different PIPSC's non-partisanship was from other public sector unions at the time. Electoral politics had divided Canadian and American unions in the past, though the debates usually focused on how far left a union should act when it came to supporting political parties. But switching to a union because it was *not* partisan was uncommon. The government's response to the switch from PSAC to PIPSC also differed from how private sector management would likely have acted. Corporate managers often try to exploit competition between unions, but federal public sector managers clearly saw a potential change as a major headache for them. Conflict between two unions in an environment with high union density had the potential to be enormously disruptive.

This discussion of bringing in members from other unions leads to the question of whether PIPSC was engaged in raiding. The term *raiding*, meaning actively trying to recruit members from other unions, did not loom large in the Institute's lexicon. Raiding was forbidden under Canadian Labour Congress rules (though PIPSC was not a CLC member), and provincial and federal labour laws also placed clear limits on when and how workers could switch unions. Despite the rules, charges of raiding were common when workers switched unions and sometimes attracted media attention, as the losing union was usually adept at appearing aggrieved. By the 1980s, changing unions became easier in the private section because many of the major unions were beginning to organize workers in industries outside of their traditional area of interest. The Canadian Auto Workers, for example, would eventually include people employed in everything from fishing to airlines. In the case of PIPSC and the auditors, it's clear that the institute did not actively solicit Phil Jolie and the others. The impetus to join PIPSC came from the auditors at Revenue Canada, not from PIPSC. Yet even though PIPSC's did not engage in active raiding of PSAC members, once they showed interest in switching the Institute did much to ease the process.[15]

Collective Agreements   Although PIPSC negotiated collective agreements with multiple management teams representing different ministries and departments within the federal government, the Treasury Board was the central player on the employer side, providing the mandate for all employer representatives. That department's innocuous-sounding name masks the enormous influence it wields over the public service. Former PIPSC president Steve Hindle commented on how this affected bargaining with the employer, observing:

> The way I'd characterize it, as a member, is that we have a group of members on our bargaining team with a professional negotiator. The professional negotiator is the spokesperson at the table. The decisions on what gets dropped, what gets changed, etc. are made outside of the face-to-face with the employer in the back rooms where the members take over. Our view of the employer side is that the management reps are there to fill the chairs and to provide a little bit of information to—in most cases—the treasury board negotiator, but the Treasury Board and the negotiator are the ones that make the decisions, not the management on the other side.

To draw a private sector comparison, the Treasury Board functioned as the labour relations representatives in a human resources department. They provided bargaining expertise to various negotiations and strove for consistency across collective agreements. Treasury Board representatives ensured that nobody from management said or did anything that might establish a difficult precedent.

Bob McIntosh added what he referred to as "a little caveat" to Hindle's characterization of the Treasury Board's role in bargaining:

> The negotiator on the employer's side at Treasury Board is handed a mandate from somewhere—"the ghosts," they say—and pretty much that person's hands are tied. So, they have to have a really unusual situation to get that mandate changed. It could be a strike or a serious recruitment problem for example. The policy probably comes from the minister, but also the Finance Department, as to what is the overall game plan within human resources in the public service in that particular round of bargaining.

Regarding approval of tentative collective agreements, Hindle added:

> Yes, they [the agreements] have to be agreed to by the Treasury Board—which is the treasury board minister in concert [with the federal cabinet]. And then an Order-in-Council would follow. The recommendation of the treasury board minister would be agreed to, so cabinet would have to say

yes. And on our side, tentative agreements are put to the full membership for a vote.

McIntosh and Hindle described what is considered a mature bargaining relationship in industrial relations circles. It was also complicated, with the role of the government as employer and legislator again fully evident. This complexity also manifested itself through the actual collective agreements.[16]

The nature of the 1980s collective agreements is on full display in those of the Computer Systems (CS) and Law Groups. The growth of the CS Group reflected the impact of computerization on the federal public service during the decade. Whereas Nursing had been a key group in the early 1970s, CS was well on its way to taking on that role by the end of the 1980s. The 1981 CS agreement was eighty pages in length and included standard collective agreement provisions such as management rights, rights of employees, and a grievance procedure. Several appendices described essential information, including salary scales. The agreement also included language on joint consultation and career development, the introduction of new technology that was substantially different from existing equipment, and national joint council agreements.

The last two clauses are particularly interesting because, by the early 1980s, Canadian unions were beginning to grapple with the problem of automation as a bargaining issue. No consensus existed on how to respond to the loss of jobs because of changes in technology, and organizing private sector workers in emerging occupations like information technology proved to be extremely difficult. The language agreed to in the contract was striking because employers elsewhere in Canada either refused to negotiate over technological change or agreed only to limited language on it. Yet PIPSC got the federal government to agree to an actual definition of technological change, fairly detailed language on how it would be implemented, and a process for protecting workers affected by it. The clause read:

> In this article, technological change means:
> a) The introduction by the Employer of equipment or material of a substantially different nature;
> b) A major change in the manner in which the Employee carries on his work;
> c) A major change in operations methods.
> Both parties recognize the overall advantages of technological change for the general improvements in the Computer Systems field. The

Employer agrees to provide the bargaining unit with as much advance notice as practicable but not less than ninety (90) days before the introduction of any major technological change which would result in significant changes in the employment status.

If, during the life of this agreement, it becomes likely that an employee will be in a surplus status, the Employer will notify the Institute forthwith and agrees to meet with the Institute within fifteen (15) days to discuss the matter and to inform the Institute of the extent of the Employer's manpower adjustment activity and progress being made on the resolution of the surplus employees' situation.

This language was particularly important for CS workers considering the accelerated influence of change in the information technology field.[17]

Although the Law Group's agreement was highly unusual, on one hand—few Canadian lawyers were unionized and most worked on a fee-for-service basis with no job security—it was, on the other hand, fairly standard for other PIPSC contracts of that era. Like the computer systems agreement, the 1981 law group agreement also included standard clauses like management rights, dues check-off, and a grievance procedure. It was shorter than the CS agreement, though, with a total length of slightly over twenty pages. It also included an unusual clause requiring the government to provide references to prospective employers:

Personal references shall be given to a prospective employer on application by such employer, indicating length of service, principal duties and responsibilities, and performance of such duties provided that the Employer may withhold such references until receipt of written authority from the employee or former employee.

This clause was quite remarkable because employees usually obtain references on an informal basis by asking someone who can provide glowing comments on past job performance. And generally, a human resources department will only confirm a current or former employee's dates of service. For a union to bargain inclusion of a clause on job references meant that this was an important issue to members of the Law Group, and it also showed the government was prepared for its lawyers to leave the organization. In contrast, a private sector employer would not show much interest in facilitating the voluntary departure of employees.[18]

Both the CS and law agreements illustrated the economic benefits of PIPSC membership. The 1981 agreement divided the CS Group into five classifications: from CS-1 to CS-5. The wage range was quite wide, with an entry-level CS-1 earning $14,920 per year and a top-rated CS-5 making $48,846. This led to an average of around $32,000 per year. The Law agreement divided lawyers into two classification levels—LA-1 and LA-2—and their salaries ranged from $16,613 for the first step in LA-1 to a maximum of $47,696 in the final step in LA-2, with an average salary of just over $32,000. The similar salary ranges of the two agreements suggests that the Institute and government were interested in keeping comparable professional groups closely aligned in terms of compensation. They also show that PIPSC bargained wages that supplied members with a much better standard of living than most Canadian workers, especially if the members were women. By comparison, the average male income in Canada in 1980 was $15,918 and the average female wage was $8,424.[19]

As outlined in chapter 1, the PSSRA provided two processes for the resolution of a bargaining-table impasse: binding arbitration or conciliation with the right to strike. The bargaining agent was required to register its choice of dispute resolution with the Public Service Staff Relations Board (PSSRB) before the commencement of collective bargaining, and that choice remained in effect for succeeding rounds of bargaining or until, at the start of a future round, the bargaining agent opted for the other method of dispute resolution. In 1980–81, of the thirty-one bargaining groups certified by PIPSC, nineteen opted for arbitration, and twelve opted for conciliation with the right to strike. (Six of the twelve PIPSC groups opting for conciliation had just switched to PIPSC that year.) The corresponding figures for PSAC are similar. Of fifty-seven certified groups, thirty-three opted for arbitration, and twenty-four for conciliation with the right to strike. By 1988–89, a smaller proportion of PIPSC groups were opting for arbitration. That year only twelve did so, even though the number of bargaining units had increased to thirty-eight, mostly through the government devolving parts of existing departments into new separate employers.[20]

Grievances and Dispute Resolution

In the 1980s, despite its preference for and history of cooperative relations with the employer, PIPSC exhibited militancy through frequent use of the formal dispute-resolution procedures established by the PSSRA. The act had established the PSSRB and given it power to adjudicate grievances involving interpretations of collective agreements. Such grievances could not be referred to adjudication without the approval of the bargaining agent, which gave unions control over which matters would be referred to a third party, the decisions of which could establish precedents shaping future cases. The PSSRB also decided grievances filed against employer-imposed disciplinary penalties, up to and including dismissal. In such cases, the griever did not need the approval of the bargaining agent and could either represent themselves or hire a representative. More typically, PIPSC (and other unions) provided representational services to members.

By the 1980s, the PIPSC grievance and PSSRB adjudication processes were well established and, on the surface, were comparable to those used by other unions. In practice, grievance and adjudication procedures were enormously complicated and could ultimately involve appearing before the PSSRB. The board dealt with matters of discipline and dismissal, but much of its work concerned matters of contractual and statutory interpretation. For example, PIPSC made three applications to the board in 1980 to challenge the employer's position that certain workers in the Law and Architecture and Town Planning Groups were excluded from PIPSC because they were employed in confidential roles; the board upheld the exclusions in only one case. PIPSC sought adjudication 1,176 times in the 1980–81 reporting year and 1,135 times in 1988–89.[21]

Politics and Community

While the Institute made full use of the PSSRB adjudication process during the 1980s, it continued to pursue a policy of non-partisanship. The long-standing ideal of being political but non-partisan was evident in how the Institute advised members to engage in the 1980 election. While noting the legal restrictions on partisan political activity among members of the public service, the Institute's leaders certainly wanted members to be highly engaged in politics, urging them to consider:

> Voting for the candidate of your choice;
>
> Belonging to the political party of your choice and contributing funds to that party or its candidates;
>
> Permitting signs supporting the candidate of your choice to be erected on your property;
>
> Expressing your views on political issues in articles or letters to editors;
>
> Wearing buttons that express support for any party or candidate;
>
> Attending political meetings and asking questions or expressing your views.

In that year, PIPSC also hosted forums featuring political candidates from the three major parties, including a luncheon held at the Chateau Laurier.[22]

The repatriation of the Constitution in 1982 did not immediately affect PIPSC, but (as a later chapter will show) the introduction of the Charter of Rights and Freedoms eventually had an impact on all public sector unions. The defeat of the Liberal government in the 1984 election was a watershed moment in Canadian political history. The Liberals had governed the country for most of the 1960s and 1970s. Indeed, the post–World War II era was one of Liberal governments, with Conservatives periodically elected almost as a form of protest and the NDP occasionally supporting minority governments. The Liberals had created the modern public service, and their vision of government and cooperative approach to relations with the public service had remained consistent over time, with the exception of policies like wage and price controls in the 1970s and legislated wage increases between 1982 and 1984. The party managed to dominate the broad centre of Canadian politics by adroitly tacking from left to right (and back) and by appropriating policies of the other two main parties when it was useful to do so. As a result, some Canadians, usually on the political right, raged that the Liberal Party of Canada stood for nothing. In fact, it stood for winning elections.

The early 1980s were also still a period when a national consensus existed that government was a positive force in the lives of Canadians. Things began to change in 1984. As Bob McIntosh recalled, the new Conservative government led by Prime Minister Brian Mulroney initially promised "pink slips and running shoes" for public servants.[23] Mulroney's victory was part of a neoliberal political wave sweeping across industrialized countries. He was friendly with American president Ronald Reagan and British prime minister Margaret Thatcher, yet he did not hew closely to their brand of austerity politics. Mulroney had worked as a labour lawyer in the 1970s and did not actively disdain the public service as his American and British counterparts did. He did begin a process of privatizing crown corporations, such as Petro Canada and Air Canada, while keeping others like Canada Post under federal control.

The Mulroney government had a fraught relationship with organized labour, though relations were better than might have been expected. It sometimes resorted to passing back-to-work legislation, as in the case of a CN (Canadian National Railway) strike in 1987. Liberal governments had already shown a similar willingness to stop strikes through legislative action.[24] The Conservative government also tried to reduce the size of the public service. PIPSC warned its members of the potential impact of the Nielson task force appointed by Mulroney, which recommended a reduction of 15,000 "person-years" in the public service ranks. As the Institute noted, this unusual measure of workforce size reduction didn't consider the fact that the public service lost approximately 18,000 person-years every year through "separation," or normal organizational attrition. The government assured PIPSC members that the Treasury Board was aiming for "zero layoffs." Reducing jobs through attrition reassured public employees but also meant eventual reductions in overall employment numbers. Despite all this, McIntosh recalled that PIPSC was able to negotiate decent contracts with the Mulroney government.[25]

While PIPSC avoided major layoffs and secured decent contracts, it also openly disagreed with the Mulroney government at times. A 1988 letter from Institute president Iris Craig to the prime minister, for example, outlined several concerns with the way the government was treating public servants. Bargaining was stalled. Seventeen professional and scientific groups had been waiting a year for the employer to present a salary proposal. She noted that PIPSC had been able to receive responses to its queries to the government from Robert René de Cotret, when he had been president of the Treasury Board, but Mulroney's latest two picks for that post had been less responsive. Craig also raised the ongoing thorny classification issue, which (although she did not mention this to Mulroney) had vexed the public service for decades. She emphasized that PIPSC's "negotiations are conducted in good faith," which clearly implied that the government was not bargaining in that manner. Craig concluded by reiterating that PIPSC was non-partisan and endeavored to serve the government and people of Canada.[26]

How sympathetic the prime minister's office was to Craig's concerns is difficult to gauge. At the time Craig's letter was composed, the government was preparing for the fall 1988 election, and Mulroney was focused on a single major public-policy issue: free trade with the United States. The government won that election, and the Canada–United States Free Trade Agreement (later replaced by the expanded North American Free Trade Agreement) became law. Mulroney was also trying to navigate the perilous straits of constitutional politics by securing a deal with the provinces that would allow Quebec to sign the Constitution. (In 1982, the province's sovereignist government had been the only one not to agree to the repatriation.) The Meech Lake and Charlottetown Accords that he attempted to pass failed to change Canada's constitutional balance, however, and instead created a national unity crisis. These quixotic policy efforts affected PIPSC members as much as anyone else in the country. The problem for the Institute was that Mulroney's efforts would eventually lead to the fracturing of the Progressive Conservative Party of Canada and the rise of neoliberal politics. By 1990, voices that cast aspersions on the public sector and on the role of government in citizens' lives increasingly dominated Canadian political discourse.

PIPSC in the Media

The Institute continued to promote its policy agenda through popular media, highlighting issues relating to government policy and employment. A 1985 *Toronto Star* article, for example, discussed the Institute's concerns over job security. The Institute had filed a brief with Parliament arguing that because public servants could not sue the federal government for wrongful dismissal, they should have their employment terminated only due to a lack of work, irreparable incompetence, or willful misconduct. Citing PIPSC, the article suggested that the idea of public sector job security was "a myth" that no longer applied to contemporary employment conditions. That last point was also a commentary on public perceptions of what public sector workers did on the job, as much as it was a statement to Parliament. The idea that public sector workers did little work had become a potent line of attack for right-wing politicians in the United States and the United Kingdom. According to Ronald Reagan, the most terrifying words a citizen with a problem could hear were: "I'm here from the government, and I'm here to help."[27] Although Canadian politicians in the mid-1980s were not yet making comments like that, the nature of popular media in Canada was such that the views expressed by someone like Reagan resonated across the forty-ninth parallel. PIPSC was rightly concerned.

Although the Institute courted national media coverage of its concerns in the 1980s, it had less success than other, larger labour organizations. By the end of the 1980s, Canadian Auto Workers president Bob White had essentially eclipsed Canadian Labour Congress president Shirley Carr as the public face of Canada's labour movement. The CAW waged high-profile campaigns and struggles against companies and governments that could be easily packaged into digestible media stories. PIPSC also engaged in important work relevant to the lives of everyday Canadians, but submitting policy papers to parliamentary committees and the like seemed a bit prosaic compared to stories of hundreds of workers on picket lines. Under such circumstances, it was not surprising that PIPSC had a more subdued national media profile than other unions.

PIPSC Members   The voices of individual members more fully illustrate what the changes PIPSC experienced in the 1980s meant to the Institute's members. Debra Dunville worked as an indexer at the House of Commons and also served as a national capital region director on the PIPSC Board of Directors. When asked about whether the union improved her working conditions, she replied:

> Oh absolutely! There was a paternalistic attitude from the employer towards the employees, and when we were in the first round of bargaining to get the very first contract the employer had had a policy of deciding on their own that if a procedural clerk had been out doing a lot of work they would get a few extra days off, maybe up to a week in the summer, an extra bit of time. We were very fortunate because one of our members did [work for] a traveling committee while we were in the process of bargaining, and he kept track of his hours of work and what he was expected to do. And it was very clear that the employer was not properly compensating the employees for the amount of time and that they … were putting in. And it brought an understanding to the table that the employer had to start paying overtime to that particular group of employees.

Dunville also commented on how the union handled issues that were brought forward by women members:

> Absolutely, they were dealt with—not so much at the bargaining table but before they became issues—something as simple as, how do we calculate if someone's on maternity leave? Does that time on maternity leave count towards something else? And we were able to stop something before it became a problem, and the Institute had a lot to do with that.[28]

Other members active in the 1980s shared similar sentiments. Nita Saville, who started working at Industry Canada in 1979 and also served as an NCR director and PIPSC vice president, commented:

> I'm a university graduate, general BA. Industry Canada was a very interesting department because there were a lot of opportunities in many fields, and I would say in the thirty years I had probably eight different positions, … from financial support for industry for R&D export development

[and] business development all the way to being a sector officer. I had some very interesting years as an officer overseeing the Canadian textile industry. It was a great learning opportunity for me, and when I retired, I left a lot of good friends from the private sector, and I got to know all about the textile industry. I ended up writing a profile of the industry, and it was so well received that I think they remembered my name.

Being involved with PIPSC became a major part of Saville's overall career satisfaction:

I became involved with PIPSC through the Commerce Group, which existed at the time, and this would have been in the early eighties. I was asked by— even within the union there was recognition that maybe women needed more opportunity to prove themselves. I was asked by a colleague at work who was actually the president of the Commerce Group at the time if I would like to join the executive, and it was eight or ten members, and I would have been the only woman. It took some convincing. My children were old enough that I wasn't needed at home constantly. I really had to think about it because it's a commitment. I finally said, "Okay, I'll try it. I'll give it a try." And I haven't looked back, actually, so I ended up over twenty-five years as a PIPSC volunteer.[29]

Some former members spoke about the experience of working for the government during periods of restructuring. Bill Giggie, who was a member of the PIPSC Board of Directors for twenty-five years, was employed in the CS Group. He learned about computers on the job:

The first thing is you've got to qualify. So, five or six of us from Toronto came to Ottawa, and they sent us to IBM for five weeks' training. And IBM said to the Post Office, "Oh yes, he can do it." So, the Post Office hired me first as a programmer, a computer programmer, and then I worked my way up to programmer, designer, program analyst, and analyst, and then retired as an analyst. So that's how I got into the Post Office.

That method of hiring and training information technology workers would not endure past the early 1980s as education programs in that field proliferated across Canada.

Giggie talked about working in Ottawa and changes that came when Canada Post became a crown corporation separate from the public service and also about his early involvement with PIPSC:

After five years or so I got transferred here to Ottawa—you know, working with those computer systems people, and some of them were members of the union—of PIPSC. And they were talking about it, and I said, "I think I'll go to a union meeting." And it wasn't very long before they accepted me into the union as a shop steward, and I worked my way up from there. I ran for the Board of Directors of PIPSC. After seven or eight years I ran for vice president of PIPSC [and held that position] for eight years. Then I felt that I needed a rest. So the next election I just ran for director, and I got elected. And I stayed for about eight years.

And during that process, in 1981, Canada Post—or [rather] the government—decided that Canada Post would become a crown corporation. So they passed a law that made Canada Post a crown corporation. And then, of course, they split up—they had unions and wondered what to do with the unions—well, PSAC with their clerks or CRs and so on. The government—or the Post Office—said, "Okay, PSAC, you can keep your members." The letter carriers—well they didn't want to interfere with a powerful union like the letter carriers—so they said to the letter carriers, "You can stay as your own union." Then, of course, there were the inside workers—CUPW [Canadian Union of Postal Workers], I guess—again, another powerful union, 50,000 members or something. When you are a new crown corporation, you don't want to interfere with a union of 50,000 members—exactly the same as the letter carriers—so, "CUPW, you can keep your members."

That only left a few of us—CS people [and] the engineers, and the Post Office had a few nurses working at headquarters. "Oh well, you folks can join PIPSC." And then I stayed there until I retired ... just before the crown corporation was fully operational. And we know there were about 150 CSs recognized as members of PIPSC.[30]

Don Burns, another former PIPSC vice president, worked for Environment Canada, Public Works and Government Services Canada, and Indian Affairs at different points in his career. He was a professional engineer who came to the public service and PIPSC in the early 1980s:

With Environment, I was doing survey work, design work, [and] construction supervision. With Public Works, it was project reviews [and] project management. And with Indian Affairs, it was the same: project review and project management. You're working with consultants. They develop designs. You work with them to make sure we get good value and in an appropriate design. At that point [when I started], I was working for a consulting firm. This would be in the early eighties. I was starting a family. I'd just bought a house. My wife and I decided we were going to have children. The consulting business is a very demanding profession. The public service seemed more of a nine-to-five life. You're able to have a better family life, so my plan was to join the public service. I'd be there for a few years while we started a family and got stabilized, and then I'd go back to the consulting business after. But I loved the job so much. I just didn't see leaving. It was certainly one of the best jobs I had in my life, and it met all my desires for a job.

It [joining PIPSC] was through friends. They were active in the union. They suggested that I might enjoy doing that. I went to a couple of our regional councils. I enjoyed the political side. It was totally separate from what I did for work and fun. There were a lot more social elements to that than there was with work. So yeah—it sort of clicked with me. I enjoyed that.

When asked if being involved in PIPSC had helped his career, he said:

Absolutely! Once I got involved in the union we started getting training. That training helped us do our union job, but it also helped in the workplace—how to better communicate with people, how to express yourself better, how to negotiate better. So, the things that we did within a union and the training that we did certainly helped me in my career. I became more relaxed in a public forum, when you're up speaking in front of people. [That was] not something that I would normally do in my job and [was] something that I'm not comfortable with, or wasn't comfortable with. So it gave me that confidence to get up and speak in front of a crowd, [to] do those things. So that helped me in my job, for sure—you know, meeting with consultants and First Nations. Yeah, definitely it was an advantage for me.[31]

Dunville, Saville, Giggie, and Burns shared comments with similar themes. Both women (Dunville and Saville) felt empowered by their involvement with the Institute and believed that their rewarding careers were made better through union membership. Both rose to important leadership roles

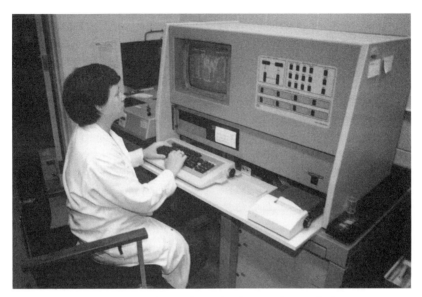

Figure 3-3: A PIPSC member working at the National Research Council, circa 1986. *PIPSC Storage Room, Photo Album 1986.*

in the union and felt that women's issues were being heard, although not all women active in PIPSC in the 1980s would have necessarily agreed with that view. Giggie and Burns also felt that their jobs were rewarding and made better through involvement with the Institute. The fact that all four of them rose to senior leadership roles reveals a key aspect of activism within the Institute: a person could join the board and be elected vice president regardless of his or her paid position in the public service. Dunville, Saville, Giggie, and Burns were members who wanted to be activists, and, like similar people in other unions, they represented a minority of the overall PIPSC membership. They did not get involved in the Institute because they did not like their regular jobs; their elected roles were not an escape from office drudgery. As figure 3-3 suggests, the jobs done by PIPSC members involved considerable training and often required technical skills. People got involved in PIPSC to make things better within the union and the workplace.

A Decade of Change PIPSC emerged from the 1980s changed as much as it had changed during the 1970s. The organization was much larger, and its finances were stronger. The internal divisions experienced in the early 1970s over how PIPSC should deal with bargaining as a union were largely gone. The Institute continued to pay close attention to governance matters and faced a range of new issues, like pay equity. Although collective bargaining became more complex, the Institute had the expertise to successfully reach strong agreements for its members. There were clear challenges for a union that had half of its members and its national office in Ottawa and the other half of its members scattered across a transcontinental country, often in discrete concentrations of regional groupings with diverse local workplace cultures.

A new generation of leaders began to move into leadership roles in the 1980s, including growing numbers of women. The union bargained collective agreements that adhered to the broad parameters of pattern bargaining but also often included unusual clauses that met the needs of specific groups. Those agreements provided decent middle-class incomes and a modicum of job security, both of which were going to be under siege in the next decade. PIPSC remained avowedly non-partisan, an aspect of its internal culture and public persona that drew in people like Phil Jolie. On the other hand, it remained intensely interested in electoral politics and did not hesitate to let the government know what was on members' minds.

While Mulroney's Progressive Conservative government did not, in the end, hand out a lot of pink slips and running shoes during the 1980s, new political ideas and leaders were emerging that would, in the 1990s, challenge the long-standing role of the public sector in Canadian life and have a major impact on the Institute. PIPSC's leaders were aware that change was coming. In 1989, Iris Craig delivered an annual general meeting speech in which she advised members:

> It is clear that our country and, for that matter, the world have entered an era of change—an era that demands new, innovative approaches for Canadians, not only to protect their interests but also to make a positive new contribution to the future development of our country and the protection of our environment. If working Canadians are to be represented effectively, it is clear that many traditional approaches need revision and improvement.[32]

Craig's assessment was timely. She may not have known what to do when she first walked a picket line in 1991, but PIPSC members were well led as they entered into a new decade in which public sector unions faced a far more fractured and hostile public discourse on their role and legitimacy.

Chapter 4

Nothing Can Be Taken for Granted, 1990–99

The 1990s were a challenging decade for all unions, including PIPSC. The country experienced a serious recession in 1991 and a second sovereignty referendum in Quebec in 1995. Neoliberal economic policies had loomed over Canada throughout the 1980s, and those policies began to bite by the early 1990s. The rightward shift in political discourse and practice was evidenced by the fracturing of the federal Progressive Conservative Party and the rise of the Reform Party in the West. The elections of Ralph Klein in Alberta and Mike Harris in Ontario marked the start of increased conflict with organized labour, especially in the latter province. The federal Liberal government led by Jean Chrétien implemented significant cuts to government programs and spending in an effort to deal with the country's systemic budget deficit. Further privatization of crown corporations and agencies disrupted collective bargaining and group affiliations, and Canadians experienced their largest federal public sector strike.

In these circumstances, PIPSC continued on a trajectory that had been set in the late 1960s. It grew through the 1990s, and the nature of its membership continued to evolve as some occupational groups expanded in size and influence. The behaviour of the federal government, as the employer, remained the same in the sense that it routinely made policy and legislative decisions without prior consultation that profoundly affected public service unions. Public sector labour relations grew more complex by the end of the 1990s, and PIPSC made regular use of formal dispute-resolution procedures and practices. After recovering from the legislative interventions of the first half of the previous decade, collective bargaining was again disrupted by government edict and legislation. Wage restraints and massive, unprecedented job reductions required major efforts to support members through an extended period of workforce adjustment.

The Institute's increasing size and organizational sophistication created some internal challenges. For example, conflicts arose between members that required the use of dispute-resolution provisions in the organization's by-laws. PIPSC had to deal not only with the complexity and challenges of bargaining *with* employers but also bargaining *as* an employer. The Institute's staff, which grew substantially, launched a short but contentious strike in 1998. Over the course of the decade, membership demographics and issues continued to evolve, requiring the Institute to develop expertise in new policy areas. Universal classification and pay equity were the two leading policy issues that PIPSC addressed.

The Institute became a more adroit user of the media to present its policy positions, but it more often appeared in news coverage of the National Capital Region than in national news. Provincial and national union leaders regularly cultivated public personas, seeking to attract media attention, and PIPSC leaders were no different in this regard. It was unusual, however, for rank-and-file members to achieve a significant public profile, yet at least one rank-and-file PIPSC member gained such a profile and used it to try to publicly influence government policy in the 1990s (and beyond).

The 1990s solidified the identity change that PIPSC had been experiencing since the 1970s. The internal tension over whether or not the Institute was an organization of professionals or a union persisted. But by the end of the decade the Institute was acting much more like a union than a professional advocacy organization, and the government clearly viewed it in those terms. This chapter follows the basic structure of the preceding three chapters but places more emphasis on leadership and staff, collective bargaining structures and practices, and the PIPSC membership experience. The 1990s was a transformative decade that would lead to even greater change for the Institute as the country approached the new millennium.

Leadership and Staff

Iris Craig led PIPSC into the 1990s, and it did not take long for the Institute to have to deal with serious challenges from the employer. Brian Mulroney's Progressive Conservative government had increased deficit spending in the late 1980s, and the 1991 recession and resulting decline in government revenues led to the imposition of austerity measures in 1992, including public sector wage freezes. Craig outlined challenges such as those in a message to the membership in a *Communications* magazine article, repurposing the famous line Pierre Trudeau had used in 1974 to mock his Progressive Conservative opponent's wage and price control proposal—"Zap. ... You're Frozen"—to shame the government's wage policy. Only four of the Institute's bargaining groups were exempted (due to other, existing legislation) from the 1992 freeze: Architecture and Town Planning, Scientific Regulation, Chemistry, and Meteorologists. The wage freeze and proposed job cuts won public sector workers some sympathetic media coverage, with the *Ottawa Citizen* arguing that "cutting public service jobs should not be a political exercise," which the cuts clearly were. The wage freeze also illustrated the ongoing power of the federal government to unilaterally alter the employment relationship in a way that no private sector employer could.[1]

The challenges facing the Institute in the early 1990s led to increasing competition for elected positions with the organization, with more members aspiring to leadership roles. PIPSC's 1992 elections drew a larger-than-usual range of candidates for vice president and director positions, especially in the National Capital Region. Four candidates ran for the two vice president positions, with Steve Hindle and Blair Stannard winning them. The four national capital director positions attracted five candidates, although there was much less interest in regional director roles. For instance, the candidates from British Columbia/Yukon and Atlantic were acclaimed. The overwhelming majority of candidates that year were also men, which was somewhat unusual considering that the Institute's membership included growing numbers of women and the outgoing president was a woman, Iris Craig.[2]

The 1992 election results revealed not only which groups were most influential within PIPSC but also that many members harboured some ambivalence about actually voting. Members from dozens of different groups participated in that year's election. Yet although the Institute mailed out 25,467 ballots, only 5,473 were returned. That was a 21.5 percent participation rate, which suggests that the organization's activist core was voting while the overwhelming majority of members were not participating. Although the overall voting rate was low, the election results also showed that PIPSC had a very active, engaged, and influential core of activists who did vote.[3]

The election results further showed which groups were influential within the organization. The 25,467 ballots were mailed to members spread across fifty-four different occupational groups. Some, such as Actuarial Science with only three members, were quite small. Others, like Computer Systems Administration (CS) with over four thousand members, were quite large. The CS Group was the largest one in the Institute by 1992, followed by Auditing. Those two groups represented 8,846 members, or 35 percent of the ballots sent out. This meant that anyone coming from one of those two groups had much stronger odds of winning an election than someone coming from a smaller bargaining group like Actuarial Science.[4]

Despite the more contested elections in the 1990s, PIPSC's leadership remained relatively stable, as it had been for some time. Iris Craig's eight-year-long tenure as president concluded in 1993. Her predecessor, Jack Donegani, had been in the role from 1980 through 1985. Craig was replaced by Bert Crossman, who was in office for one two-year term. Steve Hindle became president in 1996, the third baby boomer to assume that role, and his election further solidified the generational shift in the Institute that had begun in the 1970s. Hindle continued to win elections until standing down in 2004.[5]

The types of issues that the Institute's leaders faced in the 1990s continued to involve everyday administrative matters, collective bargaining, media relations, links to the labour movement, and overall interaction with the government as employer. The PIPSC president also had to deal with issues arising from internal organizational conflict, both between members and with the staff. Unlike corporations, unions are democratic organizations, which means they provide the space for rank-and-file members and activists not only to argue with each other but also to openly challenge their leaders, though such challenges are not always welcomed by leadership. Marion MacEachern, who is a life member of PIPSC, a former national board member, and a retiree from the New Brunswick provincial public service, recalled questioning PIPSC president Iris Craig about a union policy matter and Craig's surprising reaction:

> We were at a meeting, and there was a social event afterwards. The provincial groups—we tackled Iris. I can't remember now what the issue was. Iris had been president for quite some time at that point, and she had been a director on the board for years. And I'll never forget what she said to us. She said, "Well, you can just leave the Institute." That was her response. And I looked at her, and I said, "Iris, we will be around a lot longer than you'll be around." And it was true. I didn't call her out [to the membership for her remark], but I can remember thinking, "How dare you say that to us." We were trying to get something fixed.

While it's impossible to know what prompted Craig's clearly inappropriate out-burst—perhaps she was frustrated by the day's proceedings and not in the mood for a challenge to her authority—MacEachern's prompt retort was indicative of the willingness among seasoned activists to challenge their leaders.[6]

As well as dealing with disputes with members, Institute presidents had to mediate disputes *between* members. No organization wants its members fighting among themselves, but conflict is sometimes unavoidable. To its credit, the Institute had a well-defined method for dealing with this problem, one that highlights the Institute's professional ethos. A 1997 complaint filed by a member named Mark S. against two other PIPSC members in the Toronto-area Revenue Canada office where he worked illustrates how PIPSC dealt with such internal conflicts. Marc S. initially filled his complaint in a detailed memorandum to then-president Steve Hindle. To deal with the issue, approved PIPSC dispute-resolution mechanisms were used, including retaining the services of a professional mediator, likely at considerable cost, which was not something routinely done in all unions. Turning to other professionals—namely, mediators—in cases of internal disputes seemed a natural solution to an organization that prided itself on its professionalism.[7]

When considering the range of challenges that union leaders can face, internal issues that lead to open and public conflict between the organization and its members and staff are the most difficult. Many employers gloat when they see union members complaining about their leadership, and the sight of picket lines in front of union offices is an irresistible curiosity for the media. By the 1990s, PIPSC's staff were organized into two unions: the Professional Institute Staff Association (PISA) and the Professional Institute Regional Employees' Association (PIREA). PISA represented staff members in the National Capital Region, and PIREA represented those elsewhere across Canada; the two groups were covered by different collective agreements. While it's common for unions to organize each other's staffs, PISA and PIREA were both unaffiliated unions. As previously noted, PIPSC had experienced a very brief PISA staff strike in 1979. Two decades later, PISA went on strike for three weeks.

The 1998 PISA strike had two key causes, though opinions differ about its impact. The strike was led by PISA president Danielle Auclair, who was a negotiator at the Institute at that time. She came to PIPSC after briefly working at Atomic Energy Canada Limited (AECL), a crown corporation:

> Believe it or not, I answered an ad in the paper. Claude Leclerc was the head of the labour relations officers. I had done a BComm [bachelor of

commerce degree] and most of my courses were in labour relations. I started in labour relations at AECL, and then I did something else. And in 1985, I saw an ad in the paper, and in those days, that's how you found jobs. I started as a labour relations officer, and went through the full gamut of jobs in labour relations at PIPSC—negotiator, section head of collective bargaining, and then manager. So, I spent twenty-five years at PIPSC.

When she ran for her PISA local's presidency, Auclair did not expect to have to contend with difficult organizational politics. Winning the election was not hard because she was essentially drafted into the role by her coworkers:

> The way that happened was Denis [Cardinal] and Bob [Luce] approached me, and we used to kind of rotate who was going to run—Bob Luce and Denis Cardinal. They basically approached me and said, "It's your turn. There's nothing going on. Here, just sign the forms." So I signed the forms and became PISA president. The strike would have been near the tail end of that two-year stint.

The close day-to-day working relationships between PISA members and PIPSC's leadership made for some awkwardness in the office when PISA was bargaining or had to deal as a union with issues like grievances:

> It was interesting. I think being part of the union in a small organization like this [PISA] was awkward, sometimes because you're discussing matters at the table with your immediate supervisor, who happens to be an excluded manager. And sometimes it got really awkward. It's not like Institute negotiators going to meet [the] director of labour relations at DND [Department of National Defence] to talk about a grievance—and then you leave and go back to your office and everything's cool. What made it really quite awkward was this business of negotiating with your immediate supervisors, if you were senior enough in the organization, like I was. I mean—Bob McIntosh and Wayne Rogers and Lorraine Neville [staff managers excluded from union membership]—I was dealing with them on a constant basis at work, and then I was across the bargaining table, or I was presenting a grievance with them. Sometimes it was uncomfortable.

Auclair felt that there were two reasons for the strike:

In my mind, there were basically two key issues. There was a pension issue, and then there was also the issue that at the end (if I recall correctly) they were basically saying, "Sign on this agreement, and then we'll let you know what the economic adjustment [pay raise] is." We would never do that, as PIPSC, as a union, to our membership and say "Yes, we'll sign, and then tell us what the percentage is."

And I don't know how forthright I can be, [but] I think the negotiator on the other side was on a bit of a power trip. It was very acrimonious. I got the sense that he was testing us—he was kind of laughing at us, saying, "Oh, they'll never do anything. They're just a local, hick union." And we got to the point that we thought, "There's no way. This is ridiculous." And this is what I was telling Steve Hindle, who was president at the time: "Steve, you can't put us in that position." And he was saying, "Well, I'm not at the bargaining table." At one point, I got him to try to intervene. And it was basically those two issues: the pension issue and that.

The pension issue that Auclair mentioned pertained to a surplus in the staff association pension plan:

There was a pension surplus, and instead of taking the money and reinvesting it into the pension plan, management took that surplus and distributed it among the excluded staff. Instead of giving everyone a pension contribution holiday, they just gave everyone [in senior roles] huge amounts of cash as a return of contributions—six figures. We hired lawyers in Toronto to give us advice on this, and the bottom line was that it wasn't illegal, but it was immoral. And we took the higher ground. We said, "This is ridiculous. This is our pension." Somebody had, in fact, left on the photocopier a sheet of paper listing the names and amounts. ...

And the irony, too, was that, at that time, PIPSC was suing the government because the federal government had taken the pension surplus out of the Public Service Pension Plan. And there was a huge outcry from PIPSC members and an Institute campaign to bring awareness of this to the public and the media. I remember we distributed thousands of postcards to then treasury board president Marcel Massé.[8]

Steve Hindle, president at the time, agrees that the pension issue was a key one. The Institute, as the employer, was dealing with how to address the surplus associated with each of its three employee groups (PISA, PIREA, and excluded) within the staff pension plan. Hindle noted that the optics of having unionized staff strike against PIPSC were terrible.[9]

The strike, three weeks in duration, proved much more contentious that the shorter staff strike of 1979. PISA sought the support of PIPSC members, which included encouraging people to question Steve Hindle at regional meetings about what was happening in Ottawa. One PISA member named Bill Corcoran, who wrote a strike newsletter called "The Picket Ticket," described what happened at a prairie regional meeting:

> When the participants arrived, there was a PISA information kit at each of the places. No one was able to explain how they got there. Shortly after the meeting began, a hotel staff member arrived with an urgent fax for Barrie Wickware [an auditing group member]. The fax consisted of our list of eight questions to ask Steve Hindle. Barrie got to ask each and every one of them, plus a few more. When he was asked why the fax was sent to him, Barrie replied that he had absolutely no idea.[10]

The strike was relatively brief, but it had lasting effects, particularly on working relations between the Institute's staff and leaders. Steve Hindle described the lasting tensions:

> Certainly, ... some relationships have been damaged or irreparably changed, if not damaged, because of [the] strike action. During the strike in '98 we had a situation with one spouse who had to come to work as an excluded employee and the other spouse was out on the picket line.[11]

Although she defended the strike as principled and necessary, Danielle Auclair also felt it destroyed some personal relationships:

> We just thought, "We can't let them walk over us like this. We have to take a stand." This is what Lorraine Neville and I discussed after the strike—the first day after we came back to work—that same day. It was so difficult on everyone. Sometimes our supervisors were our friends. We would meet with them socially as well. And while we were on strike, we tried to slow them down. We had our picket line, and we didn't want to let them through the picket line. And there we were. It was Bob and Lorraine, ... all of our

friends whom we'd known for a really long time. And the strike broke some friendships and some relationships.[12]

While it may seem ironic to the casual observer that the 1998 PISA strike involved a union as the employer, this was not an unusual situation in labour relations. Such strikes did happen. Canadian Auto Workers staff, for example, went on strike in 2000 over pensions. Even the Canadian Labour Congress' staff representatives went on strike in 2004 after being without a contract for eight months.[13] It's difficult to compare what happened in the 1998 PISA strike with strikes by staff employed by other unions, as there are so few personal accounts of such events. Yet the reasons for the strike in 1998 were common to those of many labour-management relationships, even if the management in this case was a union. The staff felt that they were not being taken seriously during bargaining, and, while they knew the treatment of their pension surplus was legal, they felt it was inappropriate for the surplus to be dispersed in the manner that it was, without consultation.

A strike is an implicit failure of the collective bargaining process, but it is important to emphasize that PIPSC, as an employer, was generally successful in managing its relations with staff. In its five decades as an employer of unionized staff, the 1998 strike was only its second, and none have occurred since. The PISA strike illustrates what can happen regardless of who is on which side of the bargaining table. A workforce can quickly become militant and mobilized over key issues. Managers can make poor tactical decisions, even with institutional oversight in place. Personalities can make a difference, and the effects of a strike can be felt long after it ends. The general feeling with the PISA strike is that it was a learning experience for everyone involved. It certainly reverberated across the organization, particularly since the work that the staff did for the membership was highly valued. Marion MacEachern, a former board member and member of the New Brunswick Agriculture Group, surely echoed the sentiment of many members when she extolled the contributions of the organization's staff:

I can honestly say that we were very, very blessed to have the calibre of staff [that we had] supporting us within PIPSC. I can't speak highly enough of the staff. They are extremely knowledgeable, extremely compassionate, extremely interesting people. They helped us move things forward that we might not necessarily have figured out on our own. With their encouragement, we were able to change PIPSC and make PIPSC more of an organization that did represent small groups as well as large groups, equally.[14]

Governance   The scope of the Institute's internal governance and operations expanded during the 1990s. The fact that PIPSC included dozens of bargaining groups meant that there were by-laws for each group, in addition to regional and national by-laws. The topics discussed at the national level were mostly routine. For instance, a December 1995 board of directors meeting covered matters such as the budget for the coming year, a president's report, and task force reports on human rights in the workplace, women's issues, and member services.[15] Those were the types of routine agenda items that would have been discussed by national boards of many unions in the 1990s.

Some issues dealt with by PIPSC's Board of Directors were more contentious or reflected new concerns that required departures from the norms established between 1967 and 1989. The board's 1998 compensation review for the president's position was one such issue. The Institute hired a compensation consulting firm called Watson Wyatt to conduct the analysis, and the firm used four criteria: the size of the membership the president served and compensation in comparable union organizations, in comparable private sector organizations and associations, and in the senior management of the public sector. The consultant presented some interesting findings, including the fact that the average salary earned by PIPSC members was now $53,013 and that the presidents of other comparable unions were making base salaries ranging from $70,000 to $90,000 per year. Watson Wyatt also found that PIPSC's commissioning of a compensation study was unique, as other unions were not basing their presidents' compensation on comprehensive research. It is unclear if the compensation study was shared beyond the national board, but no one could accuse it of not considering carefully how the president's salary was determined.[16]

Government reorganization of the public service had a profound impact on PIPSC's membership structure. The Public Service Reform Act of 1992 mandated that the Treasury Board merge existing bargaining units. The Treasury Board consulted with unions about the mergers. The upshot was that the entire group structure of PIPSC was radically simplified in 1997, reducing the number of employee groups from twenty-nine to six. This initiative imposed a new order of internal tensions—and opportunities—within the overall

Figure 4-1: The PIPSC office at 53 Auriga Drive, Ottawa, the Institute's headquarters between 1990 and 2006. *PIPSC Photo Database.*

governance of the Institute. The organization's daily operations were complex. For example, 40,000 changes to member files, such as noting changes to job classification, were processed in 1999. The Institute also moved into new offices on Auriga Drive in Ottawa. All of this meant that serving in a governance role required a lot of work.[17]

Financial oversight was another important governance topic since PIPSC had to remain financially sound in order to meet the costs of collective bargaining. By 1999, PIPSC had over $13 million in assets, brought in $14 million in revenue, and represented 36,584 workers. This last figure included nine hundred people who were paying dues but were not actual PIPSC members because they had not applied for membership. (People in job classifications represented by PIPSC automatically paid dues under the Rand Formula, but they did not automatically become members of the union. In fact, PIPSC adopted the term "Rand Member" to describe such workers.) The Board of Directors, which was responsible for the organization's financial health and approving the budget, had to be conversant with basic aspects of financial management and ensure that funds were spent appropriately.[18]

Employers and Collective Bargaining

The collective bargaining environment in which PIPSC operated in the 1990s was far more complex than it had been in the 1970s and 1980s. The size and scope of the issues involved were greater, and the level of expertise required to deal with the employer and complex issues like pay equity became more advanced. The Institute continued to operate in a labour relations environment that was unlike any found in the private sector. PIPSC continued to make regular use of the Public Service Staff Relations Board (PSSRB) and was also an active participant in the National Joint Council (NJC), along with other federal public sector unions. Indeed, the Institute contributed to the NJC's expertise, and former staff members Ken Strike, Muriel Wexler, Dan Butler, Georges Nadeau, and Michel Paquette served on the PSSRB. PIPSC also proved quite capable of meeting the bargaining challenges encountered under the provincial labour laws that governed its members who were provincial civil servants. The 1990s also saw PIPSC engage in its most significant strike activity to date.[19]

The Mulroney government's attempts to reign in its spending at the expense of federal workers provoked a confrontation with the unions. In the 1991 budget, the government declared that for one year no pay increases would be granted unless the federal public sector unions agreed to job cuts, and it capped salary increases to no more than 3 percent for the next three years. Circumstances soon brought matters to a head, as an excerpt from the final report of the Fryer Committee (formally known as the Advisory Committee on Labour Management Relations in the Federal Public Service) describes:

> After the budget, a conciliation board recommended wage increases of 6 percent for the PSAC's administrative workers for the first year and a somewhat smaller amount for the second. The Treasury Board rejected the recommendations and the PSAC called a nation-wide strike. Meanwhile, the PSSRB ruled that the government had bargained in bad faith by insisting that the PSAC accept, as a precondition to bargaining, the restraint policy announced in the budget.[20]

The government responded with legislation extending all unsettled collective agreements by two years, but with no pay increase for the first year and 3 percent for the second year and heavy fines for any strike action.

Before its October 1993 defeat at the polls, the Progressive Conservative government further provoked Iris Craig and other union leaders with passage of the 1992 Public Service Reform Act. This act amended the PSSRA and the Public Service Employment Act (PSEA), among others, to enlarge the grounds for determining managerial exclusions and create a new staffing category called "deployment," which fell outside the merit principle and the appeals process of the PSEA. Those changes diminished employee rights and protections in favour of greater managerial discretion. PIPSC president Iris Craig and other labour leaders characterized this troubling state of labour relations as a naked effort by senior managers, endorsed by key ministers, to write the rules, administer the rules, and rule on the rules. The Fryer Report noted that, by 1993, the unions' disenchantment with the government was total. The presidents of PSAC and PIPSC denounced the Conservative government as the worst employer they had ever had.[21]

Any satisfaction with the demise of the Conservative government was short lived. With its first budget in 1994 the new Liberal government froze wages for another two years, subsequently deepening the freeze by suspending all pay increases based on merit, seniority, and other criteria spelled out in existing collective agreements. The ongoing recession and the depleted state of public finances during this period led to deep cuts to departmental operating funds. The 1995 budget announced cuts of 45,000 public service jobs over the following three years.[22] This staggering number was widely believed to represent the largest workforce reduction ever in either the public or private sectors. To facilitate the departure of so-called surplus employees, the government offered two types of buyout packages: the Early Departure Incentive and the Early Retirement Incentive. The government also suspended the National Joint Council's Workforce Adjustment Directive, which declared that a surplus employee had to be offered and decline a "reasonable job offer" before a layoff could occur, in the most affected departments.

As highlighted later in this chapter, the Institute leadership heavily lobbied government ministers and officials, as well as the media, to ease the angst faced by members during program review and the ensuing turmoil of organizational change. These efforts helped to convince government to permit job swaps between qualified surplus employees who wished to retain employment and employees not declared surplus but willing to avail themselves of one of the buyout programs.

Additional cuts were announced in the 1996 budget. The government expanded its definition of a "reasonable job offer" to "include offers of employment with private sector firms at 85 percent or more of the employee's original salary," a move consistent with the prevailing support for privatization of public services among some senior government officials. The wage freeze was again extended another two years, for a total of six. The Chrétien government finally restored collective bargaining rights in 1997 but passed additional legislation to suspend the unions' rights to binding arbitration for three years and limit compensation increases to about 2 percent per year to "prevent employees from making up for wage increases lost in the preceding six years."[23]

Government cuts to and restructuring of the federal public service made the 1990s a period of turmoil and uncertainty for many Institute members. Morale suffered as the government cut program funding and eliminated jobs. Without collective bargaining, interactions with the employer took on a different focus. The president and other elected representatives engaged parliamentarians, senior officials in government, the media, and various interest groups to mitigate the worst effects of this period.

Collective Agreements   The Institute organized new groups of workers while also negotiating agreements for existing groups, and the overall pattern of pursuing gains at the bargaining table continued. For example, this was evident in the collective agreements that were negotiated for the Engineering and Land Survey Group and Deer Lodge Centre (located in Winnipeg). The former group comprised federal public service workers, while the latter were provincial employees transferred from Veterans Affairs Canada in 1983. PIPSC's 1990s membership was still overwhelmingly made up of federal public sector workers, but the Institute had also organized an increasing number of provincial employees. Common to all PIPSC agreements of this era was a highly unusual clause on the selection of stewards. The usual practice in both public and private sector unions was (and is) for rank-and-file members to elect their local stewards. The practice within PIPSC, codified in these collective agreements, was that the national president appointed stewards, with the agreements giving the employer the right to determine "the geographical area of jurisdiction of each Steward."[24]

In addition to the stewards' clause, the engineering and land survey group agreements included the same type of clauses found in PIPSC agreements negotiated in the 1980s. The 1990 agreement listed six pay ranges corresponding to each classification level of the Engineering Sub-Group and five for the Land Survey Sub-Group. Engineering rates in 1990 ranged from $27,613 for someone starting in EN-ENG-1 to $80,521 for a top-rated employee in EN-ENG-6. Wages were scheduled to increase by just under 8 percent between 1 September 1990 and 22 September 1991. The pay scales for the Land Survey Sub-Group were nearly identical to the corresponding levels of the Engineering Sub-Group. PIPSC did not bargain cost-of-living allowance clauses but clearly did not need to at that point. The rate of inflation from 1990 to 1992 averaged 3.9 percent, which meant that the 1990 wage gains exceeded official increases in the cost of living. The 1990 Engineering and Land Survey agreement also included detailed provisions for travelling, which was part of the job requirement.[25]

The 1992 Deer Lodge agreement shared some clauses with the engineering contract, such as a clause on joint consultation, but the Deer Lodge agreement was only half the length of the other, just over fifty pages compared to over one hundred. The Deer Lodge agreement covered multiple health care occupations including nurses, pharmacists, and clinical psychologists, with a total of eight different job classifications at the health care facility, and included an important provision for pay equity adjustments for nurses. Wages in the first year of the agreement ranged from $30,508 for a person starting in the Nurse II classification to $43,489 for a Clinical Psychologist. The key wording in the agreement that pertained to wages stipulated that increases would equal rises in the consumer price index minus one percent. This meant that the gains made by PIPSC members at Deer Lodge did not match those bargained at the federal level.[26]

There are obvious challenges with trying to compare public sector agreements negotiated at the federal and provincial levels. Deer Lodge was a medical institution funded principally through provincial revenues, and management negotiators could easily fall back on the argument that the province's financial resources did not equal those of the federal government. Yet PIPSC was able to include some aspects of its federal bargaining pattern in the Deer Lodge agreement, even if wage parity could not be achieved. In this sense, the Institute was operating like other national and international unions in Canada that negotiated with employers of different sizes and varying resources. In terms of what provincial bargaining brought to the organization, it provided PIPSC with a chance to broaden its negotiating expertise while adding new members.

Another notable fact evident in the 1990s PIPSC agreements was that most of the organization's members earned wages that exceeded the national average. For instance, the compensation consultant's report on the president's salary commissioned by the Institute in 1998 found that the average wage for PIPSC members was $58,013 per year. The 1996 Census of Canada showed that the average 1995 income in the country was $25,196.[27] Statistics Canada further noted that, due to inflation, the average wage had not really increased since 1985. PIPSC members might not have been enjoying wage increases that exceeded inflation by the late 1990s, but, as qualified professionals with substantial qualifications, they were better off than most wage-earning Canadians, unionized or not.

PIPSC Strike Action   While federal public service strike action is often associated with the Public Service Alliance of Canada, PIPSC was also involved in strikes. As Table 4-1 indicates, PIPSC participated in a series of strikes from the 1970s to the 2000s. As noted previously, PSAC called for a general public sector strike in September 1991, precipitating back-to-work legislation in October 1991. PIPSC auditors did strike between 10 and 16 September 1991. Even before that, members of the CS (Computer Systems) Group had taken job action by targeting vulnerable operations within their area of the public service. In March 1991, for example, they stopped the electronic

Table 4-1: Bargaining Unit Strikes, 1976–2001

Dates	Bargaining Unit
1976 *March–April,* *25 June–29 July*	Aircraft Operations Group
1977 *2–10 May*	Translation Group
1977 *10 December*	Meteorology Group
1978 *4–28 July*	Nursing Group
1979 *December*	Meteorology Group. (This group was the first to have its own strike fund, and it used it during this strike.)
1985 *October*	Veterinary Medicine (NB–VM) Group conducts five rotating one-day regional strikes and a one-day general strike on 17 October.
1988 *August*	New Brunswick Engineering, Land Surveying and Architecture (NB–EN) Group and New Brunswick Agriculture (NB–AG) Group
1988 *September*	NB–EN Group follows through with rotating strikes, leading to general strike on 21 September.
1991 *February–July*	Computer Systems (CS) Group carries out and escalates rotating strike action.
1991 *10–16 September*	AU (Auditing) Group general strike called.
2001 *12 June–6 July*	Organization of Professional Engineers Employed by the Province of Manitoba (OPEEPM)
2001 *17 December*	Canadian Food Inspection Agency-Veterinarians (CFIA–VM) Group in Quebec. (This strike was not sanctioned by PIPSC.)

PIPSC strikes 1976 to 2001. *PIPSC.*

processing of individual tax returns for almost a week when ten members of the group withdrew their services. When excluded managers were eventually put to work processing the returns, the Institute sent the ten members back to work, using the employer's inability to lock employees out to its best advantage. While this tactic did not pay off in improved collective agreements due to the legislative restrictions imposed on bargaining that began that year, it demonstrated that the Institute was capable of tailoring its approach to the needs and capacities of the members of specific bargaining units.

Strikes were periods of great stress for PIPSC members, as they were for members of any union. Stephen Douglas, who was a member of the CS Group, recounted his experience in that group's 1991 strike:

> I was nervous—I'll say that I was apprehensive. I came from a family—both on my side and my wife's side—that identified with workers' right to strike. I didn't have anything on my bucket list that said I want to walk a picket line, but I wasn't in a situation where I wanted to avoid that. I also was aware that I was from Toronto. I was a regional person. Most of the work would be done—and most of the heavy lifting would be done—in the NCR [National Capital Region]. But there were tensions within the group for sure. We always had sizable majorities voting for the conciliation-strike path. I'm not sure ... that people really understood the possibility that [this path meant] they might be asked to go on strike. I think the fact that the Public Service of Canada was an environment where you could strike for an hour and then walk back in and not be locked out was a very weird concept; and we used that to our advantage.

There were no guarantees when PIPSC went on strike, but sometimes the need to stand up for collective bargaining rights overrode members' anxieties.[28]

Pay Equity   The complexity of collective bargaining in the atmosphere of government-imposed austerity in the 1990s was further accentuated by a landmark issue: pay equity. This demand for equal pay for work of equal value was driven by women who rightly felt that they were undervalued and poorly compensated in comparison to men in comparable jobs. Equal pay for equal work had long been a public-policy issue, with the International Labour Organization having adopted it as the Equal Remuneration Convention in 1951. The Canadian Human Rights Act (1977) made it illegal for federal employers to "establish or maintain" different wages for men and women who were performing work of equal value, and the first provincial pay equity legislation was passed in Manitoba in 1986, followed by Ontario in 1987.[29]

The concept behind pay equity is simple. Fundamentally, it means fairly valuing, in social and economic terms, the contributions that *all* workers make. In practice, it is an enormously complex issue as it requires identifying and measuring comparable jobs based on four criteria: skill, effort, responsibility, and working conditions. Public sector workers were at the forefront of the protracted struggle for pay equity in Canada. In fact, pay equity may have taken far longer to introduce across Canada if it had not been for public sector workers because they compelled governments to implement adjustments to realize the policy and legislative goal. After implementing it in the public service, governments subsequently passed legislation requiring private corporations to adhere to pay equity regulations, many of which would otherwise have done everything possible to resist it.

PIPSC members have made contributions to other public-policy developments, including maintaining professional occupational standards and, as following chapters will show, protecting scientific freedom. Yet the contribution that PIPSC members made to the pay equity struggle is equal to anything that they have done on any major policy issue. And from the perspective of women in PIPSC, those contributions had the most lasting impact of any policy effort. The Institute's involvement in the pay equity battle was different from other long-standing campaigns, such as superannuation (pensions), which had been ongoing since PIPSC's founding in 1920, and the scope of collective bargaining, a consistent issue since the late 1960s. Without question, the Institute's leadership viewed pay equity as a fundamental principle that required their support.

Nevertheless, as a male-dominated union, there was an undercurrent of concern, shared by some members, about the implications of implementing pay equity. A prohibition in the law against decreasing wages of a higher paid male comparator group did not remove concern about de facto long-term "red circling" of men's wages—that is, freezing them while women's caught up. Establishing a single evaluation plan capable of measuring work across diverse occupations and professions also held the potential to undermine wage comparisons to outside sector peers and indeed to undermine professional identities and bargaining unit autonomy in favour of one public service–wide bargaining unit.

The organization's leaders and staff have generally been central to pub-lic-policy discussions such as these, and pay equity was certainly no excep-tion. Kathryn Brookfield joined the Institute in 1982 as a research officer and developed considerable expertise on pay equity:

There's a long history. The [Canadian Human Rights] Act was passed in 1977. But I know in 1981 the Alliance [PSAC] laid a complaint—the other union—between the librarians and the historical researchers who worked at the National Library and the then Public Archives of Canada. Soon after that—I think it was in 1982—the dietitians and occupational and physical therapists laid a complaint against five male-dominated groups. The act defined female-dominated as being 70 percent within a group, and the male-dominated groups were all Institute groups. They were the Agricul-ture Group, Chemistry Group, the Biology Group, the Scientific Regulation Group, and there was a fifth group.

In any case we made that complaint. Eventually there was an interim settlement because on the horizon was the joint initiative, which was the large initiative [to institute pay equity] system-wide. There'd been all these little complaints piling up and they [government] realized they had to do something on a systemic basis, so that's what happened there. It had sev-eral challenges. In the first instance, the joint union–management repre-sentatives from the unions and Treasury Board chose a gender-neutral evaluation plan that was with an American firm.

Some of the smaller male-dominated unions, and also the govern-ment of the day, had strong objections to this. ... Some of them [the job evaluations] weren't acceptable because they had no working condi-tions, and the act required [taking account of] skill and knowledge, effort (physical and mental), responsibilities, and working conditions. And they refused to put those in. I don't know how many millions they [the employer] knew they [the consultants] were turning away just because they refused to do that. There were a couple that I wouldn't say who were rejected outright because of this, but I'm not kidding. You walked in the room and they [the consultants] talked to the treasury board people and ignored the union people sitting on the other side—absolutely amazing. So that was a very interesting experience.

Another challenge would be the evaluators. The Institute went through a process of inviting applications—putting out a job description first of all, so in essence they knew what they'd be doing and what they were in for. Then they submitted applications and we did interviews. We wanted a cross-section of members. We had to have some from all the female-dominated groups. So, we did this screening process.

Treasury Board tried to do that [too], but unfortunately the departments weren't very cooperative, and they would give you people that were about to retire or that they had sidelined. I'm not saying all of them were [uncooperative], but a portion of them were, and that proved to be a problem because, let's say, their focus wasn't always entirely there. And that created problems.

There were seventy-two standards alone, and within them there would be a series of what we called levels—they would be called classes in most other unions—numeric [classifications]: one, two, three, four, five, [and so on]. Sometimes within a classification—they called them groups—there would be subgroups. So, for example, in the Home Economics Group, there were the dietitians, the advisors, and [the] home economists, who worked in agriculture doing various things. So that was the system, and it was very unwieldy, especially trying to refresh that number of standards to come up with the changes in technology, changes in policy direction, and so on.[30]

Brookfield also mentioned the contributions that fellow PIPSC member Lyne Morin made to the pay equity struggle, and Morin herself described how she built support within PIPSC to continue the fight:

I was an occupational therapist working at Saint Anne's, the last veterans affairs hospital. I got involved in 1985 in the pay equity file for the OP [Occupational and Physical Therapy], NU [Nursing], and ND [Nutrition and Dietetics] Groups. We created a committee to look after this issue. The complaint was lodged, if my memory is correct, in 1982, but there started to be more activity around 1985. It got resolved by an agreement in 1995. Then I became the president of my bargaining group. Then I became a board member. I was the group advisory council director for about five years.

Then I went to work with Treasury Board [on a secondment in 1997] on the new classification plan that was supposed to solve all the pay equity problems in the public service. That led me to become a consultant, to get the PIPSC stewards trained for classification grievances. But when UCS [the government's Universal Classification System] failed, I [accepted a job offer and] became a classification officer at the Institute, then a negotiator, then the head of negotiations, and then I took early retirement.

Morin had been involved with the Institute since 1985, and it was the pay equity issue and the length of the implementation process that drew her deeper into the union's lengthy struggle to make it happen:

> By the late 1980s and early 1990s, we had huge legal bills. For example, the Institute would spend $600,000 or $700,000 in legal fees in the last few years of the pay equity case because of the complexities of the case. The hearings at the Human Rights Tribunal lasted three years, and then after we got a settlement we withdrew from those. Those costs were because we had a full-time lawyer and a team working on the case—Catherine Mac-Lean, the lawyer who was killed [in a traffic accident in 2001]. So those high legal bills were on display at the AGM by the early 1990s.
>
> At the AGM, there were not a lot of women or younger delegates, and the mostly male delegates found the legal bills very high, and they didn't want to raise the dues. So, Iris Craig said to me, "You're going to have to go and do some lobbying. You'll have to lobby members in other groups, other committees, and the elected officials and get them on your side."
>
> Before the Human Rights Committee, we had the Women's Forum. They were women members of PIPSC who met to discuss women's issues. So, I asked for a meeting to try to get their support because for me equal pay for work of equal value was a women's issue. At that meeting, I was told that neither sexual harassment nor equal pay were women's issues. So that's where I started.

Over time, Morin was able to drum up more support for pay equity, and the greater involvement of women activists in the 1990s helped:

> If I just think back to the first AGM I attended to give a speech to try to get a motion passed to get more money for the equal pay issue, you could see that only 10 percent of the delegates were women—in comparison to the last AGM I attended where you could see more and more women delegates.

Morin stated, "I think for me pay equity was the highlight of my career as a unionist because that's how I became more active and more involved."[31]

Pay equity was thus an issue about which women in PIPSC felt very passionate, and over which they were willing to wage a long campaign to receive redress. They had to develop expertise to successfully navigate the exigencies of the pay equity process, understand emerging laws and regulations, and

convince other members of the Institute to support them. PIPSC AGM delegates may have had to be initially convinced of the necessity of approving the
cost of winning the pay equity struggle, but the organization fortunately had
the resources to persevere to the end. Ruth Walden, who was a nurse and later
a medical adjudicator and who initially came into the pay equity struggle as
a member of the Public Service Alliance of Canada before becoming a PIPSC
member, described Pay Equity in these terms:

> One thing I tell everyone I talk to about this. It was not a pay equity issue.
> It was actually discrimination on the basis of sex. That's a distinction that
> was certainly important to us because, while pay is important and it was
> an issue, it wasn't the only issue, and it wasn't even the main issue. It [the
> gender pay gap] was one of the effects of the discriminatory practice. ...
> Keeping in mind that traditionally—and in our workplace, certainly—most
> doctors were men and most nurses were, and still are, women, it was a
> case of treating the men and the women differently.

When commenting on the eventual settlement with the government, which
was over $100 million, Walden noted:

> There's a lot more to the story than a sizeable pay equity settlement. ... I
> think there were eventually eight hundred individual victims who benefited
> from the settlement, and it covered back all the way to 1978. So that's how
> that sum of money was distributed. And you need to keep in mind as well,
> that [the settlement] only compensated us for some of our losses. It didn't
> compensate for everything we lost over the years.[32]

Despite the shortcomings of the settlement, success in the long pay equity
battle, which began in the public service, was made possible because women
activists like those in PIPSC kept faith that they would prevail.

Universal Classification

Pay Equity was also related closely to yet another
enormously complicated policy issue that came
to a head in the 1990s: job classification. As previously noted, how to compare
and classify public service jobs was an issue PIPSC had contended with since
its founding. Like all major policy issues, job classification sometimes made it
to the forefront of the Institute's policy agenda, while at other times it sim-
mered on the back burner, awaiting re-examination. The United States had

implemented a universal classification system for the federal public service in 1949 with the passage of the Classification Act. This was well before President John Kennedy extended collective bargaining rights to federal workers in 1962 through Executive Order 10988, which meant that public sector workers and their union representatives had not been involved in the creation of the system.[33] The deliberations over pay equity requirements led the Mulroney government to revisit work classification in the early 1990s, and the Liberal government of Jean Chrétien went further by trying to unravel the Gordian knot of comparing jobs through a universal classification system. Unlike in the United States, the proposed Canadian system was one that unions actively sought to shape on an equal basis with the employer.

Brian Beaven, who trained as an academic historian and joined the Historical Research Group in 1989, described universal classification this way:

Now this is the unofficial view because this is my experience. I learned a lot about things in the early period [1987-92] later. It was in the mid- to late nineties that most of us were intimately involved with the universal classification system. The universal classification system started as an initiative under the Mulroney government and it was the effort—and it was an honest effort—to get this monkey off their back. The courts were, systematically through judicial decisions, creating defeat after defeat after defeat for governments because the classification system by definition was never built to deal with equal pay for work of equal value, and that's what they were moving towards.

When I came into the Public Service in 1989, the women archivists were paid on exactly the same scale as the men—and this was true of women across the board. Of course, there were [women's] "ghettos," and there were areas where there was very poor representation of women in a given group. But in terms of equal pay for the same classification, that had been long accomplished.

The problem was the debate had now gone the next step—equal pay for work of equal value, and the Mulroney government responded with a joint union-management investigation of it with the unfortunate acronym of JUMI, which was the Joint Union-Management Initiative. It was an inquiry into pay equity. So that process was started under Mulroney in the sincere hope that they could get the equal pay for work of equal value out of the courts and into something that was more manageable. That morphed, and they changed the name to the Universal Classification System.

In effect, there are two stages to this process—or three counting the JUMI early stage. In the second stage, there was a sincere effort to try and build—using an incremental approach—a mechanism by which you can objectively evaluate all jobs. The problem was that the people who were doing it were in the human resource management area. They didn't have the expertise to do that, and they were making a mess of it.

The unions—who by virtue of their commitment were absolutely dedicated to making sure this worked for the benefit of their members—were much more disciplined. They recruited the people who had the expertise and took over the process. This goes through the early 1990s into the early years of the Liberal regime that takes over under Chrétien.

The unions balked at the formulas that were being developed because there was too many biases—too many assumptions—being built in to the classification model—the criteria of how you would determine the value of a job, because you ultimately had to have an absolutely objective set of criteria by which you could compare apples and oranges [across] the entire federal public service, from people with grade ten education doing entry-level jobs that didn't even require a high school education and people who had PhDs in physics and were doing original research.

Beaven explained that a universal classification system was created but not implemented:

Now to anticipate the result—it was never implemented. The result was, in effect, a huge research project that had created a perfect classification system that, by definition, not only eliminated all bias against women, it eliminated all bias against anybody for anything. It, in effect, created a purely objective frame of reference.

In that purely objective frame of reference, one-third of the entire federal public service was overpaid. Another third was underpaid. It doesn't matter the exact proportions. At an earlier date when I was doing the research for the appraisal of the records involved in all this, I made sure they were preserved. The story is there. It's in the archival record. So that's problem number one. You've created a situation in which, if you actually implemented it, one-third of the public service would be red circled, [have their] salary frozen.

The second step is, of course, in implementing it, by definition, you couldn't reduce the wages of the one-third that were overpaid. I'm using one-third in a figurative sense. But the whole process was to make sure that the people who deserved it—and women in particular—got paid better. You had the base people who were paid about what they should be paid, and the lower overpaid group. ... And you were going to have to red circle them. But then there was the other third. In order to get everything equitable, that third was going to cost one billion dollars per year thereafter. One billion dollars to implement and create the universal classification system. Well as you can anticipate, Chrétien was too good a politician not to realize that this was a non-starter.[34]

Beaven's view of the reason for the failure of the universal classification system were echoed by Lyne Morin:

At the end of the day, UCS didn't work. When we got the last results before they pulled the plug, many PIPSC members would have been under salary protection [red circled] for the rest of their careers. So, for all the pushing and lobbying, UCS was put aside for another attempt at classification reform. The next attempt at classification reform would try to find another way to measure the work with more tailored classification plans. After the plug was pulled on UCS, the Auditor General's report stated it was a waste of money.[35]

Karen Parr, who joined PIPSC in 1992 and worked in Public Works and Government Services, referred to the role of PIPSC in the universal classification effort:

The Professional Institute of the Public Service of Canada were the first ones that went into the universal classification and [were] able to prove it wasn't going to work. The Alliance stood back off that one. I'm not sure why. But basically, we ended up doing most of the work, and of course it cost us a lot of money to do that. And in the long run, they turfed it.[36]

Because of the implications of the UCS for collective bargaining and wage determination, Steve Hindle recalled, many in the public sector greeted its demise with relief.[37]

Hindle, Beaven and Morin undoubtedly captured the underlying issues involved with the failed effort to implement universal classification. Jean Chrétien was too savvy a politician to become ensnared in the fallout that the cost of implementing the USC would have created, and red circling a large portion of the Institute's membership would have been unacceptable to workers.

The universal classification effort was not a complete waste of time for the Institute, though, as it further developed the union's expertise on a long-standing policy priority, and it was closely linked to the successful pay equity effort.

The PSSRB and the NJC   The Institute continued to bring disputes to the Public Service Staff Relations Board in the 1990s and also actively participated in the National Joint Council. These two bodies were (and are) central to federal public sector collective bargaining in Canada but were not well known beyond that particular labour relations sphere. Dan Butler, a PIPSC staff member who eventually became involved with the PSSRB, described how the NJC functioned:

> The National Joint Council was a Whitley Council inspiration. It had to morph into different things over the years, but it was the only game in town for official interaction between the bargaining agents and the government for a number of years—an "old boys" system perhaps. But it did get into the business—by the late 1970s—of actually being more forthrightly involved ... [in] consultation over terms and conditions of employment. ... It was some time probably in the early 1980s that the mechanism was devised that the directives of the National Joint Council ... [concerning] terms and conditions of employment, [such as] travel, isolated posts, [and] all of those sorts of things[, gained the status of collective agreement provisions]. While they were "co-developed"—[that] was the term—in the National Joint Council, in that multilateral framework, they took legal effect by virtue of being deemed as forming part of individual collective agreements.
>
> It [the NJC] has a constitution and by-laws that set out the formal processes for the cyclical review—like a bargaining cycle—a cyclical review of the directives by committees that are composed of union reps, on one side, from different unions, and government [especially the Treasury Board], on the other. They engage in—I was always reticent to call it a bargaining process, but essentially that's what it was. The union side representatives were mandated [given instructions] by the wider staff side of Council [and] ... met every month. All of the union presidents would get together [quarterly] ...and they mandated these people.
>
> There were opting-out procedures, a whole set of mechanisms for some unions. For some unions, there were some NJC matters where they decided not to participate in the NJC. For example, the Public Service Alliance of Canada (PSAC) wanted to deal with the government directly on the

Workforce Adjustment Directive, whereas most other unions co-developed and bargained the Workforce Adjustment Directive that covered procedures for cutbacks and swapping under the aegis of the National Joint Council.

It also established the procedures for the treatment of grievances against NJC directives. ... [There were] different, defined levels in the grievance procedure, which ended up with a grievance being presented before a committee of the NJC. The Travel Committee would hear a travel grievance—both sides. And then both sides would make a recommendation to the Executive Committee of the NJC, which is composed of three union presidents and three senior government people. They would either uphold [the grievance] or sometimes [declare an] impasse. Then there was the right to refer it to a third party—to the board [the PSSRB]. So, two highly developed procedures with rules.

Butler compared the functions of the PSSRB with the Canada Industrial Relations Board (CIRB), which regulated private sector labour relations that fell under federal authority, and with provincial boards, such as the Ontario Labour Relations Board (OLRB):

We're in our fourth incarnation of the board [the PSSRB]. I've been involved in all of them in one way or another, and its mandate has changed significantly over the years. Compared to the CIRB and the OLRB, for example, [the PSSRB's] a different beast. It has all of the classic functions of a labour board—for example, certification, unfair labour practices, the supervision of the bargaining process, the specification of notice procedures, pre-bargaining freeze periods, the dispute-resolution mechanisms, the mediation that goes with collective bargaining. But beyond that, instead of there being a grievance-arbitration function, largely conducted by private arbitrators within the law, it ... has been since the outset the site for grievance adjudication. I've been called different things over time, but they've never used the term arbitrator. ... It's always been adjudicator. ...

So that [settling grievances] has been a huge part of the workload of the board. Probably at least 80 percent to 85 percent of the time of the board is associated with dispute resolution.[38]

The PSSRB may not have been well known outside of the labour relations and legal communities, but it was an important part of an adjudication apparatus that shaped the working lives of all Canadians, whether they realized it or not. Important labour and employment matters are decided every day before labour boards and in civil courts, with the overwhelming majority of cases receiving little media coverage. Labour boards exist as a forum for alternative dispute resolution and were created to move labour disputes out of civil courts. Boards have thus become repositories of expertise on labour and employment matters, and courts look to them when hearing employment law cases. (Boards also read and draw on each other's rulings.) The fact that the Institute had organized many different bargaining units, some of them quite small, contributed to the frequency with which it went to the PSSRB, and PIPSC continued to take disputes to the PSSRB for adjudication during the wage freeze period of the 1990s.

Politics and Community

The 1991 federal public sector strike in response to the Progressive Conservative government's wage freeze was the largest federal public service job action that Canadians had witnessed. PSAC initiated the strike and was the largest union involved. *Maclean's* magazine—hardly a friend of Canadian labour—wryly noted that Prime Minister Brian Mulroney, whose confrontational wage policy had provoked the strike, had disapprovingly commented on the adversarial nature of collective bargaining in a book he wrote prior to winning office. (Mulroney fancied himself an expert on labour-management relations, largely due to his work as a member of the Cliche Commission in Quebec in 1974. However, that commission looked into corruption in the Quebec construction industry, and bargaining in that industry was much different than in the public service.) *Maclean's* noted PSAC's claim that its members were only earning between $20,000 and $25,000 per year, which meant they were earning close to the national average but far less than the wages of PIPSC members. The strike occurred at the same time that private sector employers were imposing austerity and cuts on their workers. In the airline industry, for example, Air Canada and Canadian Airlines collectively laid off 2,000 workers.[39]

PIPSC maintained its official non-partisan political stance throughout the 1990s, but it did become more engaged in the political process through increasing lobbying efforts and raising awareness of issues concerning the public service. For instance, a 1990s lobbying guide created by the Institute detailed how to promote the organization's policy agenda. It stated that the mission of PIPSC was to "represent members individually and collectively." The Institute pursued this objective in three ways: by providing bargaining, labour-relations, and other member services; by promoting and defending the rights and interests of members; and by safeguarding and promoting professional standards. These were broad policy statements, and the positions that the Institute took on issues in the 1990s revealed what the organization's leaders had in mind.

The lobbying guide was particularly critical of the Liberal government's plan to turn Revenue Canada into an independent government agency, a decision that had initially been made public in 1996. A short editorial written by Steve Hindle for *The Hill Times* (and included in the lobbying guide) condemned the idea of a new, more powerful tax-collection agency. PIPSC opposed the creation of the new revenue agency because it would exist outside of the federal public service, which raised questions about the continued applicability of the PSSRA and the Public Service Employment Act for PIPSC members currently working in Revenue Canada. According to the government, this conversion would enhance efficiency, improve service and reduce costs, and strengthen the effectiveness of the Canadian federation. PIPSC argued that the second and third objectives would not be met. The government proposed that the new agency would collect taxes on behalf of the provinces, which would ostensibly lead to greater overall efficiency by eliminating duplication. In fact, as the lobbying document argued, the system would confer enormous power on the new agency and would disadvantage the provinces.[40]

Creating materials that members and activists could use to spread the Institute's policy positions was part of the political process, though getting Canadians fired up about changes to tax collection posed certain challenges. People tend to cringe when the topic is raised, immediately concerned that their own taxes might rise. The messages that PIPSC conveyed in its 1998 lobbying document were nuanced. They did not focus on potential public sector job losses, although the potential weakening of job security was a primary concern. The messages instead emphasized that there were too many unanswered questions involved with the creation of a new tax collection agency, along with the fact that such an entity would be too powerful and invasive. The way that PIPSC interacted with the political process was further reflected in messages that it sent out through the Canadian media.

PIPSC in the Media   The Institute maintained a steady media presence in the 1990s, issuing press releases on topics of concern to the organization, and media sources quoted PIPSC leaders. *The Hill Times*, a small but influential tabloid-style Ottawa newspaper founded in 1989, regularly featured articles on government, Parliament, and related organizations in the National Capital Region. It might not have been high on the reading lists of most Canadian media consumers, but *The Hill Times* was (and is) assiduously read by policy-makers, elected officials, and policy wonks in government. So it offered PIPSC a useful venue in which to voice its concerns over government policy. For instance, in a 1999 editorial Steve Hindle chastised the government for imposing repeated restrictions on public sector collective bargaining rights, noting that the International Labour Organization had rebuked Canada for doing so thirty-three times between 1980 and 1998. He argued that the era of "public-service bashing" that began during the Mulroney years was still going on under the Liberal government.[41]

On other occasions in the 1990s, PIPSC did not directly confront government policy through the media and instead commented on wider problems across the public service. In 1991, the *Globe and Mail* reported on a PIPSC study that found both English- and French-speaking public servants felt that they faced discrimination on the job and that the government was not committed to official bilingualism. Quoting President Iris Craig, the *Globe* noted that this sentiment was found across Canada. English-speaking workers felt that francophones were being accorded preferential treatment, while francophones believed that management was reclassifying jobs to make them unilingual, to the benefit of anglophone employees.[42]

Canadian media also covered the events leading up to the 1991 auditors' strike. Craig used an interview with the *Toronto Star*, which formed the basis of a short article, to draw attention on Parliament Hill and within Canada's business community to PIPSC's concerns. Noting that the auditors had been without a contract for a year, Craig signalled that the Auditing Group was, as a form of protest and a way to put pressure on the government, more strictly adhering to the rules and deadlines with regards to returns filed by major law and accounting firms. Whereas federal tax auditors had usually shown flexibility when dealing with companies due to the complexity of corporate tax law, Craig indicated that this practice was going to end.[43]

The *Toronto Star* also covered the start of the actual strike by the Auditing Group, quoting PIPSC vice president Blair Stannard as saying that the group was on strike partly out of solidarity with the Public Service Alliance of Canada. The auditors estimated that their strike, scheduled to last five days, would cost the federal government $7 million per day and the provinces $3.5 million per day, with the exception of Ontario, Quebec, and Alberta (which managed their own corporate tax system). Although hardened industrial unionists used to open-ended, long strikes might have wondered about the effectiveness of a one-week walkout, at the very least it proved an effective vehicle for PIPSC to capture national media attention.[44]

Members and the   The 1990s proved to be an interesting, challenging
PIPSC Experience   decade for PIPSC members who experienced a public
                             sector strike in 1991, a strike by their colleagues in
the Computer Systems and Auditing Groups, and a short, sharp strike by the union's staff. The actions of the government during the decade pushed members toward greater militancy. As was the case for unions in general, PIPSC rank-and-file members did not automatically become activists by joining the union. They instead often became involved when something happened that convinced them that becoming an activist was a good idea. Michael Forbes's answer to the question of how he became involved in PIPSC, for example, could have come from any rank-and-file unionist anywhere. Like many members, Forbes, who worked as a chemist at the Canada Centre for Inland Waters in Burlington, Ontario, in the 1990s, got involved in PIPSC when his job was under threat and he needed the union's protection.

> I guess it was around the 1990s when they started the universal classification system, and I was nominated to go and work in Ottawa with Treasury Board [in] developing that—the UCS. At the time my boss back in Burlington—I think he wanted to fill my position with some other person—so he was encouraging me to find a job outside the government, and then he was actually writing me out of a job. So, I worked for about eighteen months in Ottawa and then went back to Burlington, and then I had to enlist the help of PIPSC to keep my job. So, I got in contact with Dan Rafferty [staff regional representative for Ontario] in Toronto, and Dan did a very good job. He came and helped me out, and they relented, and I kept my employment as a chemist.[45]

Like Forbes, most PIPSC members in the 1990s did their jobs, paid their dues, and otherwise contended with the periodic vagaries that came with working in the public service. Like most Canadian workers, they did their jobs in relative anonymity, but there were exceptions. Since PIPSC's members generally had a high level of education, some members achieved some public renown. Nobel Prize winner John Polanyi, for example, had worked as a post-doctoral fellow at the National Research Council from 1952 to 1954 and had

Figure 4-2: Nobel Prize-winning scientist Dr. John Polanyi speaking at PIPSC in 1993, with Iris Craig. *PIPSC Storage Room, PIPSC Photo Albums, 1992–1997.*

been a PIPSC member. As shown in figure 4-2, he later returned to PIPSC in 1993 to promote the union's Science and Society initiative.[46]

The Institute clearly valued having members who achieved a measure of public stature, though winning prestigious awards was not the only way some members achieved recognition or even notoriety. Dr. Shiv Chopra, a microbiologist who worked in the Division of Medicine and Pharmacology in Health Canada, achieved his public profile over two matters of public controversy. Chopra had come to Canada from India in 1960, and after completing postdoctoral work he began his public service career with Health Canada in 1969. Almost immediately, he found that the environment was biased against nonwhite professionals and that better qualified Indians and French Canadians were kept out of positions of authority.[47]

Chopra, who was never reluctant to question Health Canada practices and procedures, openly called out the ministry for racial bias. This was certainly his right, but it also drew the ire of public service management. He filed a grievance in 1993 alleging discrimination against Health Canada managers who, when his grievance was heard (Danielle Auclair was his PIPSC representative), admonished him for his relentless criticism of the government. By the late 1990s, Chopra was known within Health Canada and PIPSC as someone who would speak his mind without hesitation if he believed it necessary. Chopra's outspokenness earned him a local profile in Ottawa as a community advocate on race and equality issues and a reputation in the public service as an activist and thorn in management's side.

He soon also gained national recognition over an issue about which the public then knew very little: the presence of recombinant bovine growth hormone (rBGH) in milk. In the late 1990s, Health Canada was considering the synthetic growth hormone, used to increase milk production in cows, for approval. The United States had already approved its use, though Europe did not allow it.[48] Chopra was justifiably concerned about the potential health effects of rBGH on the country's dairy industry and consumers. Chopra disapproved of rBGH, and his public opposition to the drug ultimately gave him a profile that he readily used. He appeared on the popular morning television program *Canada AM* in June 1997 to talk about the health perils of rBGH and was invited to appear again in December 1997 to discuss how Health Canada was pressuring him over his public statements about the drug.[49] Health Canada management was likely tuned into *Canada AM* to see what Chopra had to say because by that time he was attempting to sue the government for harassment. During his regular confrontations with management, Chopra routinely sought PIPSC's support.

Shiv Chopra recounted his full story, which is beyond the scope of this narrative, in a memoir published in 2009. It makes clear that he viewed himself as a whistleblower and social-justice crusader regarding public policy. He proudly noted that Council of Canadians president Maude Barlow described him as a national hero for his opposition to rBGH, and he referred to the "enormous courage and conviction" he demonstrated in blowing the whistle on Health Canada. His memoir frequently referred to the support he received from PIPSC when he came into conflict with management, and he appears to have anticipated automatic union support of his policy positions. The Institute indeed supported Chopra, accumulating thousands of pages of documents in its defence of and involvement in litigation pertaining to him, and it ensured his rights as a union member were respected.[50]

Yet there were clear limits to how far PIPSC could go in representing Chopra. Although any organization would have gladly associated itself with a Nobel Prize–winning scientist of international stature like Polanyi, Chopra's notoriety represented a conundrum for PIPSC: he raised valid concerns on a range of issues, yet the union did not always know how to respond to his fervent, outspoken advocacy based on the certainty of his own convictions. Polanyi and Chopra achieved their high profiles for distinct reasons—one for receiving global recognition and the other for rightly raising alarms about public health threats. Yet they were both scientists who continued a long tradition, dating back to the Institute's founding, of PIPSC members speaking publicly about issues of social concern.

Toward a New Millennium   In the 1990s, PIPSC experienced structural and organizational change unlike anything since the first decade after unionization. Legislation passed in the late 1960s had transformed PIPSC from a professional association into a union, but the Institute had wrestled throughout the 1970s and 1980s with the idea of being one. As is often the case with groups of workers, both organized and unorganized, employer actions had gradually led to changes in how PIPSC members viewed themselves. The Institute's members had been outraged over wage and price controls in the 1970s, legislated wage increases in the 1980s, and wage freezes in the early 1990s. Outrage fueled the membership's growing militancy on the job. PIPSC's leadership also experienced the results of workers' militancy *against* the Institute in its role as an employer when its own full-time staff went on strike.

The 1990s were a decade of major change for Canada as the economy again suffered in the early years of the decade and austerity became part of public policy. The idea that governments had to cut public spending became ubiquitous in popular discourse. Using Google's Ngram Viewer, a tool that searches for how frequently terms appear in over twenty-five million books published over the last five hundred years and digitized by Google, illustrates this point. Although Ngram is not a perfect measure of social change, it does show how ideas were circulated in society. As figure 4–3 shows, the term "fiscal austerity" rarely appeared in published works in 1970, but by the early 1990s it appeared frequently. Similarly, as figure 4–4 illustrates, "privatization" is also a comparatively new term that became common in English-language books in the 1990s. These were influential ideas, rooted in neo-liberal thought, that changed how policy-makers viewed the public service.

Governments at both the federal and provincial levels in the 1990s freely cut public service jobs and used back-to-work legislation to end strikes. The politicians who oversaw those cuts and violations of the right to strike did not dwell on them, but the workers who endured them did. Jean Chrétien noted in his memoir that his government cut sixty thousand public sector jobs, which included the military, and argued that senior public servants concurred with the decision. Brian Mulroney's eleven-hundred-page memoir spilled far more

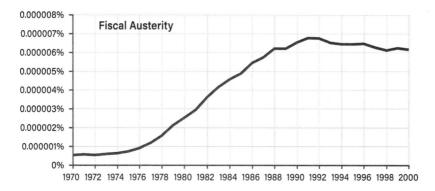

Figure 4-3: Incidence of "Fiscal Austerity" in Publications, 1970-2000. Figures calculated using Google Books Ngram Viewer, Google, accessed 26 April 2019, https://books.google.com/ngrams/.

ink than Chrétien's, yet made not a single references to Canada's public service. (He did note, in a single paragraph, how his government went about privatizing Teleglobe Canada, De Havilland, Air Canada, part of Petro Canada, and other crown corporations.)[51]

In response to government austerity measures, the Institute shifted gears and took its message directly to decision-makers on Parliament Hill and in the executive offices of government and worked to heighten public awareness of the consequences of government actions. PIPSC made significant contributions to the pay equity battle within the federal government, with female staff and activists at the forefront of discussions. Despite considerable work involving PIPSC members, the attempt to create a universal classification system did not succeed due the practical and political difficulties encountered. Yet the group reorganization started by the Treasury Board in anticipation of universal classification transformed the group structure of PIPSC and affected its internal governance. When it was completed, reorganization meant PIPSC had only six groups within the federal public service portion of its membership instead of twenty-nine.

When possible, PIPSC made gains at the bargaining table, as shown with the engineering and land survey collective agreement, although the Deer Lodge contract illustrates that the federal bargaining pattern was not easily duplicated at the provincial level. Internal challenges and conflicts of the 1990s, such as the staff strike, periodic member complaints, and the high expectations of a member like Shiv Chopra, testified to the fact that PIPSC was

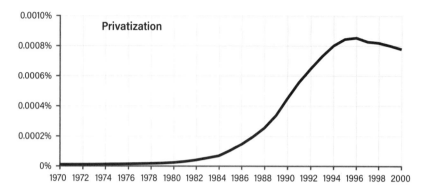

Figure 4-4: Incidence of "Privatization" in Publications, 1970–2000. Figures calculated using Google Books Ngram Viewer, Google, accessed 26 April 2019, https://books.google.com/ngrams/.

an organization that permitted a range of discordant and progressive voices to be heard. Danielle Auclair, who led the 1998 PISA strike against PIPSC, eventually left the Institute for a job in the public service, but she did not bear any animus toward PIPSC over the strike.

On balance, those who had been members in the 1990s described an organization that experienced a lot of change and sought solutions to a range of issues. Governance was the central focus of internal decision-making, and PIPSC continued to expand in membership and assets in the 1990s. PIPSC used local and national media outlets to express positions on different policy matters. As the baby boomers came to dominate senior elected roles, PIPSC election results revealed that the Institute had a core group of people who took a keen interest in organizational politics and that a large majority of members were simply paying dues and were not that engaged. In fairness to the Institute, this pattern of engagement was common in many, if not most, unions. PIPSC grew through the 1990s, and it was in a strong financial position as the twentieth century ended. The difficult trends and increasing complexity of public sector labour relations that emerged in the 1990s would continue into the 2000s, but the organization was also ready to deal with them.

Chapter 5

Into a New Century, 2000-09

The arrival of the year 2000—the start of a new century and a new millennium—was a momentous event in Canada and around the world. Canadian popular culture reflected both the hope and angst that greeted it. Canadians may not have been aware of it, but PIPSC members played a pivotal role in preparing the nation for the over-hyped potential catastrophe of "Y2K"—an initialism for the "year two thousand" that had, by the end of 1999, become universally associated with the prospect of the world's ever more interconnected computers and related electronic control systems suddenly running out of time and crashing due to an inability to cope with a year that started with a number two rather than a number one. This disconcerting prospect arose because, when the earliest computer programs were written, nobody had thought about the consequences of not storing all four digits of the year to allow dates beyond 1999 to be used. (The year 2000 had seemed so far away, and by ignoring the matter, program designers saved valuable space.) As 1 January 2000 approached, fears arose of power outages, planes falling from the sky, and mass chaos across the globe. In fact, all those predictions proved alarmist because most computers and control systems proved to be just as capable, with straight-forward technical adjustments, of operating in the new century as they had in the previous one. The armies of information technology workers hired in the public and private sectors in the 1990s to address system coding problems—which included many PIPSC computer systems' members—ensured (among other things) that the federal government's revenue collection system, pension plans, compensation processes, and other key parts of the public service apparatus were not disrupted. They did much to make Y2K the most over-covered, non-story and biggest anticlimax of the new millennium.

The Y2K issue, which loomed large in the years leading up to 2000 but then quickly (and rightfully) disappeared in the rear-view mirror of popular history, said much about what it meant to be a PIPSC member during the first decade of the twenty-first century. PIPSC members continued to perform tasks that they had been doing for decades, like processing tax returns. Yet they also became increasingly involved in work associated with the challenges of living in an increasingly global economy, such as ensuring the safety of the country's food supply, the integrity of the telecommunications network, and the security of the integrated digital networks that kept everything moving. The twenty-first-century public service was technologically advanced, required well-educated staff, and could be found actively intervening in virtually every area of Canadian life.

The social, economic, and political environments of the 2000s brought further changes to the country and to PIPSC. The issue of Y2K lost its importance in an instant, but the events of 11 September 2001 resonated for years to come. On that day, the United States suffered the worst terrorist attack in its history when airplanes were flown into the twin towers of the World Trade Center in New York City and the Pentagon in Washington, DC. A fourth plane aimed at Congress or the White House crashed in a field in Pennsylvania after passengers on board fought the hijackers who had taken control of it. Although Canada was not the target of these attacks, Canadians did perish in them, including at least one PIPSC member. And the reaction to 9/11 eventually drew the country into an eight-year military operation in Afghanistan, making it Canada's longest war.

Canada entered the 2000s with Jean Chrétien's Liberal government in power, but the election of a reunified Conservative Party led by Stephen Harper in 2006 marked a significant ideological shift to the right for Canada's government. The Chrétien Liberals had enacted severe budget cuts and implemented some tax increases in the 1990s, but the Liberal Party of Canada has historically shown itself to be driven by a pragmatic ideology shaped by a firm conviction that it is the country's natural governing party. The Conservatives had since the era of John Diefenbaker and Leslie Frost in Ontario positioned themselves to the centre-right of the political spectrum. Many former Conservative members of Parliament like Flora MacDonald—a minister in Joe Clark's short-lived minority government in 1979–80—were regarded as political centrists, or "Red Tories," due to their interest in social issues.[1] That big-tent, Progressive Conservative tradition was fundamentally gutted when Stephen Harper became prime minister in 2006. A former insurgent Reform Party MP and past president of the hard-right National Citizens Coalition, Harper came to power at the head of a reconstituted Conservative Party that displayed an ingrained bias against a progressive, activist role for government in the nation's affairs. PIPSC members intensely disliked Pierre Trudeau's 1970s wage controls and Jean Chrétien's 1990s spending cuts. But Harper would be the most difficult prime minister the Institute ever faced.

The 2000s were also important for PIPSC due to changes within the organization. PIPSC continued to fully engage with the labour relations processes first mandated by the passage of the Public Service Staff Relations Act; it achieved tangible gains (including wage increases) through collective bargaining; it recruited new bargaining groups; and it elected to its presidency another woman, Michèle Demers. As its membership continued to expand, so too did its resources. Balancing the interests of members scattered across the country with the half of the Institute's membership that was based in the National Capital Region remained a constant challenge for PIPSC's leaders.

The 2000s brought PIPSC more into the public spotlight than in the past. The Institute moved, slowly, toward affiliation with the Canadian Labour Congress (CLC) and became more involved with public-policy discussions that moved it toward direct interventions in national elections. As it had in the past, the Institute maintained its overtly non-partisan political stance, but it had difficulty not showing its sustained animosity toward initiatives of the new Conservative government.

Leadership and Staff   PIPSC experienced some key leadership changes during the 2000s. The organization entered the decade led by Steve Hindle, whose successful tenure as president ended in 2004. Hindle's nine years in office over three terms made him the longest-serving president in the Institute's history. (After leaving office, Hindle assumed a management position in the federal correctional system, returning to PIPSC to run for president in 2013 and, eventually, serving as vice president for three terms beginning in 2014.) Michèle Demers won the presidency in 2005, the first francophone to hold the post since PIPSC became a union, and she was followed in office by Gary Corbett in 2009. Although each president brought different approaches to leading the Institute, they were all baby boomers who shared an underlying set of goals and assumptions regarding PIPSC.

Figure 5-1: Eddie Gillis and Michèle Demers. *PIPSC photo database.*

Demers may well have led PIPSC for many more years had her life not tragically ended with her sudden death on 10 February 2009. She had been addressing members of the Canadian Food Inspection Agency in Montreal when she collapsed suddenly from a cerebral hemorrhage. Her leadership of the Institute, though tragically brief, was important for some key reasons. PIPSC member Lyne Morin remembered:

> Michèle Demers was my best friend. I used to work in psychiatry. Michèle was a social worker assigned to my team at Sainte-Anne-de-Bellevue veterans' hospital. We started on the Board of Directors the same year [1994]. Michèle was a part-time VP. We didn't have any full-time VPs in those days. And I was the advisory council director. I think she put the word *union* in PIPSC. I think that was the biggest influence she had. Before Michèle, Steve Hindle, and Bert Crossman, we had Iris Craig. She was a great, great woman, but the Institute was more like an advisory body [at that time]. It didn't really have the feeling that we were fighting for rights. And I think that's what Michèle brought with her personality and her conviction, and she tried to change things.[2]

The sentiments expressed by Morin were shared by other current and former PIPSC members and staff. Lorraine Neville also described Demers's importance to the Institute:

> Michèle Demers was from Quebec. I remember the first time she went to the board of directors meeting—I thought she was going to be thrown out. She was determined to bring the Quebec influence to the Board of Directors. [She believed] we should be brothers and sisters, [and] we have to belong to the CLC. And she found the structure abhorrent at the board meetings—that you had to have motions, and you had to pass them, and you had to have support. She was a rebel with a cause.[3]

The comments from Morin and Neville show that Demers was a committed leader who may well have driven herself too hard to change the internal culture and direction of the Institute. She was also a vocal advocate for PIPSC members and did not shy away from criticizing government policy. For example, the problem of ongoing dislike of official bilingualism still existed during the first decade of the twenty-first century, and the advent of the Internet made it much easier for aggrieved parties, however marginal, to vent their frustrations. A self-appointed group called Canadian Oppressed Public Servants (COPS) created a now-defunct website to complain about the administration of bilingual policy in the public service. Demers heard about it and, in the long tradition of PIPSC's support for bilingualism in the federal public service, wrote to the commissioner of official languages urging better French- and English-language training in the public service:

> I am outraged by the COPS Web site. I strongly disapprove of such vicious remarks which border on fanaticism. How could anyone in 2006 cast a doubt over the validity of our "Official Languages"? It is one of the underlying principles that make Canada such a great country, along [with] multiculturalism, democracy and, indeed even freedom of speech. All Canadians must be able to be served by our federal government in the language of their choice. There is no doubt that public service employees face severe shortcomings concerning access to language training, either in English or French. I have repeatedly stated that it is the employer's responsibility to invest the necessary funds and effort in assisting their employees to fulfil their linguistic responsibilities.[4]

Demers also weighed in on highly political public-policy matters. In the mid-2000s, the Liberal government was embroiled in scandal over the misuse of government funds for partisan political advertising in Quebec. Responding to the scandal in the usual Canadian-government way, the Liberals established a commission to investigate the nature and extent of the misuse of funds. PIPSC submitted comments to the Commission of Inquiry into the Sponsorship Program and Advertising Activities, with Demers stating bluntly that Institute members were "appalled by the sordid details that have been uncovered."[5]

Whereas earlier PIPSC presidents had usually confined their public remarks and correspondence to matters pertaining to the federal public service, Demers willingly spoke on a wider range of issues. Her 2005 letter to the British Columbia Teachers' Federation, for example, revealed her interest in broader labour movement challenges. The teachers' union was engaged, at that time, in a difficult struggle with an intransigent, ideologically driven Liberal government led by Gordon Campbell. Although Liberal in name, Campbell's government was closer on the political spectrum to the reconstituted federal Conservative Party under Stephen Harper or its Reform predecessor.[6] Enclosing a $1,000 donation from PIPSC to the teachers' strike fund, Demers wrote:

> We have followed with great interest, through media coverage, the plight of the B.C. teachers on strike. It is extremely frustrating to see how the B.C. government, and most of our governments for that matter, disregard our right to free collective bargaining in favour of hard-handed legislation. This is fundamentally wrong and unacceptable.[7]

The support shown the teachers' union was typical of Demers's willingness to have PIPSC engage politically in labour struggles beyond the federal public sector.

During the first decade of the twenty-first century, occupying the office of PIPSC president continued to require mediating internal disputes between members and addressing membership dissatisfaction with the union. As in earlier decades, Institute members showed little reluctance to convey their concerns directly to the president, and Michèle Demers received her share of complaints. For example, a two-page letter sent by a member of the executive of the Veterinary Medicine Group raised concerns about recent bargaining between the group and the Canadian Food Inspection Agency. The substance of the complaint is less important here than the fact that Demers's response was as lengthy as the member's complaint, a fact that indicated she took member concerns seriously and took time to investigate and respond when issues were raised.

Demers's death left PIPSC momentarily adrift. PIPSC chief operating officer and executive secretary Eddie Gillis described the experience and the key role of the staff in ensuring continuity:

> One of the key moments, I think, that illustrates that role of continuity was when our former president, Michèle Demers, passed away in a very untimely way—of course, with no warning—and the organization was left very much rudderless while we were all in a state of shock for days. And it was the staff, I would argue, that came together and said, "Okay. We have to carry on." And on the senior management side, and throughout the ranks of the staff, we came together. We brought the elected representatives together, and we presented them with plans for moving forward, which they accepted.
>
> At the same time, other members of staff were planning a memorial service for Madame Demers, and that was, for me, one of the most moving events that I've ever been part of as a PIPSC person. And it was extremely well done, and it was extremely well attended. An example that I've used is that staff decided that for the memorial, no vice presidents would be permitted to speak because they would all be potential candidates for president. And we just felt that it was not a time for politics; it was a time to remember Michèle. And they agreed—surprisingly, they agreed. So, it's that kind of leadership and continuity that the staff brings to the organization.

Gillis's last point reflected another reality for PIPSC leaders during the first decade of the twenty-first century. Because they were now leading a medium-sized organization in terms of paid staff, they needed not only the leadership skills to represent their members and the political and negotiating ability to deal with the government but also the management acumen to oversee the internal functions and unionized staff of the Institute.[8]

Despite her short tenure as president, Demers had a lasting influence on the Institute. After her death, others continued to pursue her vision for PIPSC. The idea that PIPSC should be more activist and function like a union rather than an association of professionals became the new centre of gravity for the Institute's leaders and members. The question was no longer whether PIPSC would be activist and act like a union but how it would express this new stance in the future.[9]

Michèle Demers was succeeded by Gary Corbett, who was from Cape Breton. He described how his activism in PIPSC began:

> I got involved in the public service because it was a good job. I was work-ing in the coal industry. I started with a diploma in chemical engineering technology and then a bachelor of science in chemistry. I started working with coal because there was a lot of coal mining going on in Sydney, Nova Scotia. I was formerly a member of the Public Service Alliance of Canada as an EG [member of their Engineering and Scientific Support Group] and then the employer helped me go back to school. In those times there was a lot more benefits for employees, and they helped me with my career. I went back to school, and then I end[ed] up doing a mining engineering degree at McGill University while I was working. Of course, I moved from the technical category into the physical sciences [PC] category, which is a group of the Professional Institute.

Corbett gradually became involved as a PIPSC activist and eventually joined the board in 1999 before assuming a senior elected leadership role.

Not surprisingly given his background, Corbett made science a priority when he was president but melded it with a vigorous defence of the vital role played by professionals in the public service generally:

> So, it comes from the fundamental belief that you should have some [sci-entific] functions in government—even if it's only to the point where you have people to understand what the outside people [in the private sec-tor] are doing. But if you don't have that fundamental understanding in the government—if you don't employ scientists, if you don't have scientists, if you have a manager [without a relevant science background] running a science operation—there's something lost because they don't understand what I call the implication of decisions, the consequences of decisions. When the government makes a decision, there are consequences.
>
> Then the science symposium came from that because I wanted to carry forward the dialogue. "For the Public Good" was a campaign where we put advertisements in bus shelters to help make people aware of the impor-tance of the federal public service, so that when the government decided to cut or ... diminish [the public service] or when the government decided to say "We are going to move everything in the NRC [National Research Coun-cil]," at least people had a basic understanding and could question their

Figure 5-2: Lauren Jain, the 2005 PIPSC Scholarship winner, speaking while Michèle Demers looks on. *PIPSC photo database.*

own government and [could] say, "Why is this happening when professionals are saying this [is not a good idea]?" Let's face it—the professionals are the highly educated ones with the knowledge to actually perform the tasks that the government decides to do—whether it be auditors, or whether it be scientists, or whether it be nurses or doctors or dentists.

Corbett also had broader objectives for the Institute and, like Demers, wanted to see it more active in support of members' interests outside of the workplace. One example was his involvement in establishing a scholarship program:

The scholarship project was a good-news project, and I needed some good news to work on, so it seemed like a no brainer. We should be giving back to the community. After Treasury Board forced our bargaining groups to merge, one of the groups had a big budget left over and had $75,000 that they were wondering what to do with. Steve Hindle was president at the time, and there were some great people, so I started working with them, and then I just did what I do. … I worked to form a committee, and I wrote the report. And it got passed at the AGM. I wrote the criteria for the evaluation of scholarship applications and I think we're still using the criteria today. Then later on, with the Professional Institute Legacy Foundation, the organization got involved, and it is what it is today.[10]

The Institute was thus led during the first decade of the twenty-first century by three presidents from three different occupational backgrounds— computer systems, social work, and engineering—who each brought their own perspectives and strengths to the position. The role of the staff also grew in importance during the decade.

Governance   PIPSC had complex governance by the first decade of the twenty-first century. Each bargaining group had customized by-laws and so did every region (in part because of the group amalgamations around 1997 and in part because PIPSC increasingly operated in multiple provincial jurisdictions and under multiple federal labour statutes). The Board of Directors (its executive committee composed of the president, four vice presidents, and ten directors as of 1998) ultimately presided over all governance matters. PIPSC's president was answerable to the board, and staff leaders were answerable to the president.

Governance continued to be central to the Institute's internal dynamic. Yet despite their importance to the effective functioning of the organization, governance issues can lead to frustrations for those involved in them and can elicit a wide range of views on the utility of focusing on them. Former president Gary Corbett expressed some skepticism about the focus on governance in PIPSC:

Anyone looking at the organization from the inside can only look left or right. You can't be looking in both directions at the same time, so while you're looking this way, there's a lot happening over there that you probably should be looking at. You have fifteen people around the board table who have an opinion, and so they think they're doing something important. The members are saying, "What the hell are you talking about that for? What's happening on my collective agreement? While my boss is screwing me over, you're talking about governance." In a way it [the focus on governance] detracts from the relevance of the organization being a union.[11]

Corbett's view of unionism was rooted in his origins in coal mining and craft unionism, in which there is much less emphasis on internal governance and more on traditional bread-and-butter unionism. As Steve Hindle recounted, members have often shown little interest in running for governance roles:

> Yes—members of group executives, members of branch executives—they hold elected office. [Yet] in a lot of cases, there is not a lot of competition for those positions, so we have a lot of members who are acclaimed into those positions. But occasionally you will find that there is an election. And certainly, over time, the positions on the Board of Directors of the Institute have become more sought-after—they're more likely to see an election, but in some cases, the tradition is that that position is filled by acclamation because only one person puts their name forward.[12]

Governance is also linked to collective bargaining, and the fact that PIPSC appointed stewards rather than electing them was a unique aspect of its internal governance structure, especially since all the senior leaders, along with members of the various group, subgroup, branch, and regional executives, were directly elected. Demers's opinions on this practice are not known, but Hindle and Corbett offered some comments on it. Corbett observed:

> Many of them [stewards] are involved with the right kind of motivations; others may be looking around or may be not be quite sure what it involves or they're on a learning curve. Sure, there are some whose motives may not be entirely altruistic. We try to have an open door to encourage members to become involved as stewards. And I've seen many members develop into excellent stewards.[13]

Hindle commented on stewards by saying:

> They are not elected. They step up, and they say, "I'd like to help out. Can you train me as a steward?" And then we also don't have a strong requirement on what it is stewards have to do or how they have to report or things like that. But we have had a propensity to accept anybody who wishes to be a Steward—there have been some limits, but they've been very few.
>
> I think some of the recognition within the Institute about the potential liability of [appointing] stewards—and just having anybody do it—came about when the veterinary medicine group engaged in "being sick" illegally during a collective bargaining process—and it was the veterinarians in

Quebec who did it—not across the country. As a result, the Institute got embroiled in a lawsuit, which was only recently settled, and that took—from the day they called in sick at the instigation of members of their executive who were [also] stewards to the actual settlement of the suit—about fifteen years. All the vets phoned in sick. Some of them actually were sick, but only a few of them.[14]

The underlying reasons for appointing rather than electing stewards were obviously on the minds of Corbett and Hindle when they expressed their sentiments about stewards and their role in the Institute. Yet if the concern was that elected stewards could pursue their own agenda once elected, the case of the Quebec stewards engaging in illegal strike activity—and thus exposing PIPSC to legal retribution—showed that appointing stewards didn't always mean they towed the line.

Stewards played an important role in the Institute's decision-making during the first decade of the twenty-first century. Some also served in elected roles within the union too. Robert Bowie-Reed, a long-serving steward in the CS group, described his experience in the role and the impact that stewards could have in the organization:

I started working in public service in 1980 as a computer systems developer and I worked there for thirty-three years before they laid me off during the cutbacks [of 2012]. I worked at Statistics Canada. I became a steward in 1984. I attended AGMs for about thirty years. I was NCR director for eighteen years and national vice president for two years. I was the chair of the CS Group for a year—they only had one-year terms—[and] I was on the group executive for several years. I founded a CS Sub-Group at Statistics Canada, an Institute branch at Statistics Canada, and the Statistics Canada Consultation Team. I headed up all three through the years until other people moved up, and then it was time to step back.

At Statistics Canada, my generation wasn't that interested in union activities—they were too scared. So, for a long time, it was me and one other steward holding the fort and keeping things alive in terms of the organization.

That's changed since 2000. [Before then] they were too scared of punishment and retribution. Whether that was realistic or not—I don't think so, but that's what they were worried about. People who say that the generation around 2000 didn't want to get involved do not know my workplace. There were people coming on board around 2000 and getting involved. Prior to that, you couldn't get anybody to do anything. They were glad someone was doing something and glad it wasn't them.

Richard Rice was also a PIPSC member in the Computer Systems Group. Like Bowie-Reed, he not only served as an appointed steward but also as an elected CS official. Rice described his experience:

> I was a steward for about twenty years. I handled a variety of cases, but I was the chair of the Computer Systems Group with Canada Customs and Revenue Agency, and then I stayed on the [group] executive when it progressed through to CBSA [Canada Border Services Agency]. It was quite challenging because the two environments are very, very different. The resources were commingled—both personnel resources and technical resources—when CBSA was formed.[15]

The range of issues the PIPSC members like Rice and Bowie-Reed had to deal with as both stewards and elected officials was at times challenging. Bowie-Reed described the challenge of addressing conflict within the governance process as a member of PIPSC's Board of Directors:

> One of the difficulties we faced on the board is the conflict between the executive committee and the regional directors. Many of the issues dealt with at the executive committee do not come up to the board. We have had formal complaints between members of the executive committee in recent years—people trying to take other members of the executive committee down. There was a vice president who was removed ten years ago.
>
> The board now is more sophisticated. The sorts of mistakes made thirty years ago in terms of staffing and compensation do not happen now. There's a committee called the Executive Compensation Committee, and it's a far more mature process than in the early 1990s. It's still controversial—particularly when it comes to political staff [paid elected officials]—but it's much more sophisticated now.[16]

For some like Rice and Bowie-Reed, being a steward was a path into other leadership roles, but PIPSC stewards were not like those found in most other unions. As noted above, they were not elected, and they also did not directly file grievances on behalf of members.

The employment relations officer on the Institute's staff handled complaints relating to contractual and collective bargaining issues. Former PIPSC staff member Danielle Auclair noted that, as professionals, some Institute members preferred to seek advice and representation from professionals in labour relations rather than from a local steward:

> It depends on the workplace. They're professionals [the members]. They have PhDs and master's degrees. They would say to me, "If you have a problem and you want a divorce, you go to a divorce lawyer. You don't go and see a counsellor if you want to go through with a divorce." So, they wanted to see not only the labour relations officers but the ones who were lawyers, just because of their background and their education.
>
> And the steward may be a CS-2 [a computer systems group job classification], but he's the steward for a workplace that may have members from many different occupational groups. So, a lot of them [members] wanted to work through a labour relations officer. The CSs had a really good strong base of stewards, and members would go to the stewards. But not so for some of the other groups. First of all, there were not a lot of stewards, and they had a hard time attracting stewards. In those days—and I assume it's the same now—it was very difficult to attract stewards. It's not a white-collar type of thing to do.[17]

Governance was obviously complex during the first decade of the twenty-first century as the Institute handled serious issues, from joining the CLC to mediating internal conflict. Gary Corbett's view that too much time was being devoted to governance perhaps has some merit, yet the Institute's size and scope required a robust governance process. For instance, with revenues of slightly over $15 million in 2000, the Institute's finances required effective oversight. PIPSC also needed strong governance to guard against the possibility of incurring legal liability as a result of either actions against the employer (such as the Quebec veterinarians' illegal strike) or as a result of internal issues. Strong governance was particularly important in ensuring that the Institute was prepared to bargain with a hostile employer.[18]

Employers and Collective Bargaining

The 2000s began with the federal government issuing a report on the state of labour-management relations in the public service. The report of the Advisory Committee on Labour Management Relations, known as the

Fryer Report, outlined the current state of labour relations in the federal public service. It listed events that had contributed to a deteriorating collective
bargaining environment, including wage controls in 1975 and 1982; the freeze
on public service salaries in 1991 and 1994, as well as the cuts to operating
budgets in the latter year; the budget cuts in 1995 that led to the loss of 45,000
jobs over three years; the suspension of salary arbitration in 1996; legislation
restricting pay increases in 1997; and delays (to 2000) in implementing pay
equity decisions.[19] And this was not an exhaustive list.

The Fryer Report was an important document because it recorded problems that had persisted in the public service since the advent of collective
bargaining in 1967. The main concern cited by both labour and management
during the Fryer Committee's work was the power the government possessed as both employer and legislator. The report noted that government
had power over labour-management issues beyond what any private sector
employer enjoyed and had used it to do such things as freeze pay and pass
back-to-work legislation.[20]

Yet the problem for public service unions by the mid-2000s was that,
regardless of the structural issues reported by the Fryer Committee, the bargaining environment had deteriorated markedly due to the election of the Conservative government of Stephen Harper. The Harper government was elected
in 2006 with only a minority of seats in the House of Commons, meaning
that it needed support from other parties to govern. That situation changed
when the Conservatives won a majority in 2011 and the New Democratic
Party became the official opposition for the first time in history. The Liberals
endured their worst electoral showing since Confederation and then the ago-
nizing new experience of being the third-place party in Parliament.

PIPSC was not alone in dealing with labour relations challenges under
the Harper government, which demonstrated a particular affection for back-
to-work legislation. Yet the nature of the new government's labour relations
agenda and its attempt to strictly control the messages emanating from government agencies affected occupational groups in PIPSC especially. The most
difficult employment issue for PIPSC members during the Harper years was
not money, pensions, benefits, or even pay equity. Instead, it was the government's sustained assault on the legitimacy and intellectual autonomy of public
servants, in particular those engaged in original research, scientific or otherwise. Yet the Conservatives found themselves vexed on labour and employment issues by the Supreme Court of Canada, which issued a succession of
rulings that positively affected PIPSC and many of its professional groups.

The Conservative government began to impose limits on the free speech of public servants, particularly scientists, shortly after its election. The work the Conservative government wanted to suppress was not subversive or partisan, nor did it represent policy activism on the part of civil servants. Scientific research should be above partisan, political interference, especially from the sitting government, unless it is being deliberately misused and misrepresented by practitioners. As earlier noted (see chapter 1), PIPSC members had a long history, dating back to the introduction of radio in Canada in the 1920s, of speaking publicly on matters of national interest. Yet Stephen Harper, the most controlling prime minister in post-1945 Canadian history, did not want public servants in any capacity expressing opinions that ran contrary to the official policy of the government. PIPSC called it "The Big Chill" and shared information with Canadians about the harmful impact of muzzling scientists and other researchers. An Institute survey found that 90 percent of scientists in the public service felt they were not free to express opinions in the media, 71 percent said that the government's science policy was impeding the development of programs based on scientific evidence, and 24 percent of respondents had been told to alter research findings because the results were not in line with the ideological perspective of the government. The Harper government's egregious effort to muzzle scientists and other professional researchers would continue until it was defeated in the election of 2015.[21]

The first court confrontation with the Conservative government came in 2008 when PIPSC and the Canadian Association of Professional Employees filed a constitutional challenge in Ontario superior court over the government's ongoing refusal to bargain over certain terms of employment, including pensions. As a joint union press release stated, workers had the right to bargain all terms of employment, and employers should not be permitted to circumscribe it. The legal challenge was based on a 2007 Supreme Court of Canada case called *Health Services and Support-Facilities Subsector Bargaining Assn. v. British Columbia (BC Health Services)*. As Larry Savage and Charles Smith note, a set of Supreme Court decisions in 1987 known as the "labour trilogy" had concluded that there was no constitutional right to strike. The Supreme Court had subsequently upheld limits on collective bargaining rights, as it did in upholding the constitutionality of a Northwest Territories law that gave the government the right to decide which employee unions it would bargain with (see chapter 3). Such decisions, especially the labour trilogy, led the labour movement to doubt the efficacy of resorting to the courts to expand collective bargaining rights. That view changed with the *BC Health*

Services decision, in which the court held that collective bargaining within certain limits was a constitutional right. It was, as Savage and Smith note, a landmark decision.[22]

The labour movement's excited response to *BC Health Services* was cooled somewhat by a subsequent ruling—*Ontario v. Fraser*—in which the constitutionality of the Ontario Agricultural Employees Protection Act (AEPA) was upheld. The AEPA extended some bargaining rights to agricultural workers, but not to the extent afforded workers under the Ontario Labour Relations Act. The right to collective bargaining was thus found to be more limited than unions initially thought under *BC Health Services.* Still, the Supreme Court's ruling in *BC Health Services* emboldened PIPSC to challenge the government in the 2008 case. Unions in general, including those in the public sector like PIPSC, were then forging ahead with court challenges. They felt compelled to try to use the courts to expand labour rights since legislative efforts had not led to the desired results.[23]

Court challenges required resources, and PIPSC was well equipped in that regard. Yet litigation was not the organization's central activity, and negotiating agreements and dealing directly with the government always remained the focus of collective bargaining. During the first decade of the twenty-first century, pay equity issues once again asserted themselves at the bargaining table and in PIPSC negotiating strategies, but there was little progress in the face of the blunt refusal of treasury board negotiators to recognize pay inequity. At a more mundane level, however, as the next section shows, the collective agreements that PIPSC negotiated in this era kept up with inflation and achieved incremental improvements across the range of bargaining issues.

Collective Agreements   PIPSC engaged in almost continual negotiations with the government throughout the 2000s and made improvements to collective agreements despite the hostility of the Conservative government. By the 2000s, the Institute's bargaining groups included such diverse occupational groups as clerks in the House of Commons and health care workers at Sunnybrook and Women's College Hospital in Toronto. The Institute continued its established practice of vigorously representing all members, whether they worked in small occupational groups like those in the House of Commons or in large ones like the Computer Systems Group, which was still by far the largest.

The 2006 House of Commons clerks' agreement, like those for other groups, included dispute-resolution language unique to federal public sector labour relations. For instance, the role of the employer in determining the jurisdiction of stewards remained, and several clauses pertained to how members would participate in public service staff relations board hearings, if required to do so. The language on layoffs arising from contracting out was somewhat weak, as it merely stated, "the Employer shall continue the past practice in giving all reasonable consideration to continued employment in the House of Commons of employees who would otherwise become redundant." That kind of language was better than nothing, but PIPSC would have preferred a prohibition on layoffs.[24]

In terms of wages and job classifications, the clerks' contract had three classification levels for Procedural Clerks and two for Analysis and Reference, with a corresponding salary range for each. The salary increments over the different steps were pronounced. For example, someone in Step 1 of the PRL-1 clerk grade in 2003 earned $63,728 while someone in Step 5 made $77,714. Over the life of the agreement, the annual wage increase was 2.5 percent in 2002 and 3 percent in each of the subsequent three years. The average annual inflation rate between 2002 and 2005 was 2.3 percent, so the clerks group gained increases exceeding rises in the official cost of living.[25] At slightly over one hundred pages, the House of Commons agreement was about the same length as those of other groups in the public service represented by PIPSC.

The Sunnybrook and Women's College Hospital agreement differed from the House of Commons agreement in some key respects. Less than half as long, at forty-one pages, it contained standard collective agreement clauses, such as those pertaining to management rights and union security. PIPSC was able to get specific language on health-care benefits and pensions into the agreement, whereas less detailed collective agreements would have merely stipulated that the employer would agree to provide the benefits outlined in the employer's benefit guide. The agreement's salary provisions for its three job classifications—Clinical Coordinator for RT Students, Radiation Therapist and Dosimetrist, and Mold Room Technician—each had several steps, seven for the first two classifications and eight for the third. The salary rates were substantially lower than those found in federal public sector PIPSC agreements concluded in the mid-2000s. For instance, after six years of employment a radiation therapist earned $35,438 in 2004, increasing by 5.3 percent to $37,323 by 2006, an increase slightly above Canada's national rate of inflation (4.9 percent) over that period.[26] Yet the Sunnybrook and Women's College Hospital workers faced a higher-than-average cost of living because they lived in Toronto, which was then tied with Vancouver for highest overall cost of living in Canada.

These two agreements—House of Commons and Sunnybrook and Women's College Hospital—continued a trend that became evident when PIPSC began representing workers outside of the federal public service. These non-federal agreements with public or quasi-public employers, like provincial governments and hospitals, were not as lucrative as those for PIPSC members in the federal public service. Yet it would be unrealistic to assume PIPSC could achieve parity across every agreement. For a start, provincial agreements were governed by applicable provincial labour and employment legislation, which meant that it was difficult to achieve the same level of uniformity as in federally regulated agreements that applied across the country. Employers like Sunnybrook and Women's College Hospital were also smaller than the federal government and were provincially funded. Additionally, most PIPSC bargaining units involved in negotiating agreements with provincially funded employers were smaller and thus had less leverage than most of their counterparts operating at the federal level, though these factors didn't affect the Sunnybrook negotiations and agreements. And some provinces had far fewer financial resources than others, like Ontario, let alone the federal government. Yet the agreements reached with provincially funded employers ultimately included good clauses that benefited the members covered by them.

Dispute Resolution   While PIPSC continued to fulfil its central mandate in negotiating collective agreements, it also continued to administer them, which invariable led to disputes with employers. The Institute made extensive use of federal dispute-resolution processes for individual members and was involved, for instance, in seven cases brought before the Public Service Staff Relation Board in 2000 and ten in 2009. The type of cases brought before the federal board and involving PIPSC were similar to those that concerned other federal public sector unions. Issues of agreement interpretation and statutory responsibility tended to be the focus of the PSSRB's work. For example, the board did not rule on many PIPSC cases involving terminations during the 2000s, but it did decide eight that involved abuses of managerial authority. Most PIPSC cases involved union grievances against government departments and agencies, but individual members and employers also filed cases against PIPSC. In 2009, for example, the board dismissed one such complaint lodged against PIPSC by House of Commons management over PIPSC's refusal to submit to management's attempt to force seven bargaining units into one.[27]

Members' individual complaints against PIPSC focused on issues such as the union's duty to provide fair representation to every member. In another 2009 case, *Veillette v. Professional Institute of the Public Service of Canada and Rogers*, a member filed a grievance against the Institute and one of its vice presidents charging that he had been improperly suspended from his duties as a bargaining agent representative. He alleged a dispute he had had with two other members of PIPSC eventually led to his first year-long suspension. Immediately after the first suspension ended and acting on a PIPSC policy implemented specifically to deal with the suspension of bargaining representatives, PIPSC suspended the griever for a second two-year period. The PSSRB ruled for the complainant, in part, by directing PIPSC to amend the policy, but it otherwise did not provide him further redress.[28]

The complainant in *Veillette* had some limited success before the board, but that case was an exception because labour boards usually rule against member complaints against unions. Duty-of-fair-representation complaints are notoriously difficult to prove in Canadian labour relations because they require members to show that their union devoted absolutely no attention to their issues (not even considering filing a grievance on their behalf, for example). In the 2009 case of *Dubuc v. Professional Institute of the Public Service of Canada and Sioui*, a recently retired member filed a grievance against PIPSC after a three-year-long dispute with the Institute over salary and leave repayments, arguing that the union had not made enough effort to secure her repayments from her employer. The board dismissed the complaint, ruling that Dubuc should have filed the complaint earlier.[29] PIPSC's leadership surely would have preferred to resolve cases like *Veillette* internally using its own dispute-resolution procedures, but all unions faced the prospect of having such disputes brought before the board.

PIPSC's experiences before the PSSRB and the courts proved its willingness to devote considerable attention and financial resources to the fair and reasonable representation of its members. The Institute employed full-time labour relations staff to handle grievances and labour board complaints and hired attorneys to take cases to court. Going before labour boards requires professional expertise and is thus not something done by most union stewards. The cases brought before labour boards and courts were not only part of collective bargaining but were also linked to PIPSC's political and media agenda.

Politics and the Media   The Institute's political and media messaging expanded and became more sophisticated during the 2000s. The Conservative government's attacks on public sector workers made maintaining PIPSC's traditional political-but-non-partisan stance increasingly difficult. By the turn of the new century, PIPSC activists had become adroit lobbyists who knew how to work the halls of Parliament Hill and to meet individual members of Parliament in their ridings. PIPSC gained a higher public profile during the first decade of the twenty-first century because of the Harper government's austerity policies, which forced the confrontation with public sector unions into the media spotlight, and internal efforts to raise the Institute's visibility and rebrand it as, in the words of President Steve Hindle, "the smart guys with the good ideas." The 2002 *Ottawa Citizen* article in which Hindle's words appeared noted that PIPSC, whose members made an average of $64,000, had grown to 44,000 members after dropping to 32,000 during the worst of the Chrétien-era spending cuts. The article also drew some contrasts with the Public Service Alliance of Canada (PSAC) that clearly suggested PIPSC was a better representation option for anyone in a professional occupation.[30]

PIPSC's political and media agenda during the 2008 federal election clearly strained the Institute's non-partisanship. Michèle Demers reminded PIPSC activists that Harper's Conservative government had subjected the public service to "insidious and often unpredictable cuts," and the Institute launched a campaign on food safety, in conjunction with PSAC's Agriculture Union, to raise awareness of the impact of cuts across Canada. PIPSC, Demers's noted, was buying print and radio advertisements in "specific ridings" to explain concerns about food safety. Although Demers issued PIPSC's standard disclaimer—"the Institute is a non-partisan union"—and asserted that she was not telling anyone who to vote for, she made it pretty clear who she thought members should vote *against*.[31]

Demers's 2008 election message was officially non-partisan, and talking about food safety issues supported that approach, but the overall message was that PIPSC members should vote for someone other than the Conservative Party currently in power. It highlighted the increasing difficulty of trying to maintain a non-partisan posture in the face of partisan hostility. Although Demers did not endorse any single opposition party, by commenting so negatively on the policies of the party in power, she provided a tacit endorsement of anybody but the Conservatives. Overall, PIPSC's political messaging during the first decade of the twenty-first century reflected its long tradition

of protecting the interests of its members but not endorsing parties in federal elections.

The Member Experience   By the 2000s, PIPSC members were increasingly diverse in terms of their backgrounds, the
jobs they performed, and the range of occupational groups they represented.
Those who became activists continued to do so for a variety of reasons, and
they championed various causes. Many of PIPSC's newer activists, such as
Waheed Khan, were new Canadians. Khan described how he came to PIPSC:

> I joined the public service in 1999. And before that I came to Canada—five
> years before that. So, I was working for an international consulting com-
> pany for five years. I came from Pakistan. I landed in Toronto and came to
> Ottawa and found a job here. I was living in Ottawa as part of my consult-
> ing career. I got opportunities to consult for the federal government and
> that included Environment Canada. So, I was consulting for Environment
> Canada, and the work kept growing for my skills and expertise. Then they
> gave me an offer and said, "Would you like to work full time?" I have a broad
> background. I studied science—basic science, chemistry, and geology, but
> then later on I also did my MBA [master of business administration degree].
> So, I broadened my background. So even though we were working on tech-
> nologies, there's an element of marketing because you want the market
> to bear the cost of the technologies and be able to sustain them. So that
> was a good combination for me, and I was working on technology transfer
> projects. I was working with technology companies. They were exporting
> technologies. I didn't need to know all the details of every technology, but
> I needed enough to understand how to adapt those technologies into the
> environment in developing countries.
>
> I got involved with the Institute much later actually. I must say that
> for several years I didn't even know that I was supposed to be a member
> of PIPSC. And then somebody did tell me. I think I received some infor-
> mation or papers that I was paying dues to PIPSC and that I could be a
> member if I wanted to. Then I filled in an application form and sent it out,
> and then again I forgot about it. I was not really involved until later. At
> some point I received an invitation to attend an AGM. I filled out a form
> and I was selected as a delegate. That was my first direct contact with the
> union. Steve Hindle was the president of the Institute at that time. I was very

impressed with his speech and the whole AGM, but I never felt the need for a union. I never had issues or problems.

PIPSC approached Khan about serving on a consultation team on employment equity, an employment practice that was initially implemented in the Canadian federal public service in 1986 by the Mulroney government, which was acting on the recommendation of the royal commission headed by Justice Rosalie Abella. The federal public service, since it is supposed to be a potential workplace for any Canadian with the required qualifications, was seen as an appropriate place to start implementing employment equity, thereby leading by example. Aware of the controversies over "affirmative action" policies in the United States, Abella had consciously devised the term "employment equity" to describe the approach through which she addressed the issue. The use of crude quotas in many of the earliest affirmative-action programs in the United States had provoked a strong backlash against implementing policies to hire and promote individuals from designated groups that were underrepresented in a workplace in comparison to the demographics of the community in which the workplace was located. And though the United States Supreme Court had declared quotas unconstitutional several years before Abella's commission, the term affirmative action still carried with it the stigma of so-called reverse discrimination. The fact that Abella's conception of employment equity—and its embodiment in Canadian laws—rejected the use of quotas and instead set targets and objectives for equity hiring and promotion did not prevent employment equity from becoming a political issue. For instance, the Ontario Progressive Conservative Party under Mike Harris ran in 1995 on a platform that included a promise to revoke the "quota law" brought in by the New Democratic government.[32]

Waheed Khan did not see tension in the federal public service when it came to his work on the employment equity group:

There were not a lot of contentious issues. It was more collaborative. At first, we were going through a bit of difficulty in the public sector because of budget cuts. I first started during the days of the budget cuts, but things slowly got better. So, I was just so pleased when I was seeing all those good announcements where the government was making announcements to provide more budget [resources], making things easier with more funding for various programs. That's how employment equity was getting funding as well. There were programs that were happening so everything was good. When I was involved everything was good, with happy public servants.[33]

Khan's involvement with PIPSC and the issues in which he took an interest followed a path taken by many contemporary members. No single specific issue motivated him to become involved, but he became keenly interested in one issue—employment equity—once he had become a member and activist.

Others, like Glen Schjerning, became active in PIPSC because of perceived injustices in their workplaces. Schjerning described how he became involved:

> I was a naval officer for about a little over a decade. I have a background in engineering—mechanical, aeronautical, and nuclear. I worked at Chalk River nuclear labs as a reactor supervisor. I spent a couple of years up there, and I was a PIPSC member there, but I was never active in PIPSC.
>
> I then transferred to the Canadian Nuclear Safety Commission, which was an agency of the government, and it was not unionized. It was one of the very few slices of the federal government that was not unionized. The reason was that back in the late 1960s when the organization [of public sector unions] became legal—it was called the Atomic Energy Control Board at the time—the leaders were ex-military officers much like myself, and they had a pretty good notion of how to take care of their people. So, the staff did not follow the trend [of unionizing] that the federal government followed.
>
> But things change. I'll be a little bit blunt here. So, I showed up quite some time later in 2001. The engineers used to get what was called a terminable allowance—it was essentially retention pay. Depending on your rank, it was worth about $12,000 to $16,000 a year, which is pretty significant—even by today's standards. I was a single parent and I raised a child by myself. At the time, my son and I were living in a one-bedroom apartment, and he was eight. We had four days' notice when they took it [the allowance] away from us. It was harsh. I was the elected representative of the professionals at the Canadian Nuclear Safety Commission. We didn't have a union—so no contract, no dues, no budget, nothing like that. I was their spokesman, but we had no authority whatsoever. A couple hundred of us had just got a massive pay cut with four days' notice.
>
> That's when I got together with PIPSC and we started a certification drive. I believe it had been attempted twice before in the past and failed both times. And both times after it failed management waited a little while

and then fired the people who were the troublemakers who organized the certification drive. Believe it or not, even with a massive pay cut to us with four days' notice, management gave themselves bonuses after they took away our pay. I kid you not. It took us quite a while, but eventually we got certified. I filed the certification drive and put in my letter of resignation on the same day. I gave them two months' notice. What are you going to do? Fire me? We sold union cards for sixty days. I was driving around with my eight-year-old son going to people's houses at night signing union cards.

Because of the fear from the previous failures, we weren't really sure if we would succeed. We weren't sure about the numbers we needed. Fifty percent of what? Because it wasn't defined, and it didn't get defined until later, so we had to shoot for higher than that. Well, we got there—not by a lot, and it was a lot harder than I would have guessed. But all of those 196 people who lost that pay—it took us five years, but we got it, plus back pay. I'm pretty happy with that. I didn't see it coming. Up until that time in my life—I was about forty back then and I'm pushing sixty now—I never saw the reason for a union. I didn't need one. I'd been a military officer. Then all of a sudden, I was thinking that sometimes you need a counterbalance.[34]

Schjerning's impetus for joining PIPSC, and indeed for leading an organizing drive, was his sense the he and his colleagues were being mistreated at work and needed to push back against callous management practices.

PIPSC provided members with ways to become activists if they chose to. The fact that the Institute's leadership appointed stewards did not solve the problem of recruiting enough of them, which is a problem across all unions in both the public and private sectors. The steward role can be thankless, and many rank-and-file members understandably find it unattractive. The experience of being a steward continued to vary depending on members' departments and occupations. The CS group stewards, for example, were an active bunch. Because they were also part of the largest group in the Institute, they would have been working in one of the union's busiest areas and dealing with a greater variety of issues. PIPSC had a vibrant activist core by the end of the 2000s, many of them with expertise on specific issues, such as employment equity or the standards that applied to an occupational group, like engineers. The organization also had considerable expertise within its paid staff. As figure 5-3 shows, PIPSC activism also provided a space for social activities beyond the workplace. This all served to strengthen the organization as it closed out the first decade of the twenty-first century.

Figure 5-3: The 2001 PIPSC Staff Baseball Team, including Danielle Auclair (*front row, second from left*) and Steve Hindle (*front row, second from right*). PIPSC *photo database.*

Beyond 2009   PIPSC ended 2009 stronger in some respects than it had been in 2000, while also dealing with more complex challenges. The Conservative government was still in power and showed ongoing hostility toward the public service and toward evidenced-based policy-making and the independence of government researchers who contributed to it. The union's membership had recovered since the cuts of the 1990s, and as a larger union PIPSC was financially stronger and better able to confront external threats. PIPSC continued to use labour boards and the courts to advance workers' interests.

All three presidents during the first decade of the twenty-first century continued the evolution of the Institute from its origins as an association to an effective union. The hard lessons of the 1990s were not lost on Steve Hindle as he led efforts to stabilize internal operations. Most importantly, Hindle pushed the Institute toward thinking and acting more like a union. This approach was explicitly and militantly adopted by his successor, Michèle Demers, and then continued under the very different personality of Gary Corbett. Demers injected a passion and commitment into the organization to recognize union principles and the value of the Institute to its members. Gary

Corbett reinforced union thinking and the need to explain the value of public services to the public. The fact that PIPSC had elected, in Demers, its first francophone president (not to mention another woman) marked an important milestone in the organization's history. Demers was an inspired and effective leader who commanded respect and a unionist with a clear vision.

The range of bargaining units that PIPSC represented became more varied during the 2000s and included many small occupational groups, even though this meant more work for PIPSC staff and additional costs for the organization. Despite the hostility of the Conservative government in the second half of the decade, the Institute negotiated collective agreements that met or exceeded the cost of living. The baby boom generation occupied most elected leadership positions and, across the union, dominated the steward cadre, developing expertise on a range of issues. Overall, the 2000s were a period of success for PIPSC, but it would face many more struggles in the early years of the coming decade before Canadians elected something approaching a more collaborative government. And, of course, in 2009 nobody had heard of a computer pay system called Phoenix.

Chapter 6

Stepping Up to a Larger Union Stage, 2010-19

T he year 2010 began less auspiciously than 2000. Although there were no dire warnings of computers failing and the global economic crisis that began in 2008 was finally abating, emerging trends in Canada's (and the global) economy did not bode well for working people, including those employed in the public sector. The problem of rising job "precarity," described by authors like Guy Standing, would grow worse even as the economy and financial markets recovered. Precarious work exacerbated the problem of growing income and wealth inequality across Canada. An important study completed by the United Way of Greater Toronto and McMaster University illustrated the enormity of this problem in the Hamilton and the Toronto regions.[1] Although PIPSC members lived and worked across Canada, the second-largest concentration resided in Toronto, which now had the highest cost of living in the country.

These broad trends affected PIPSC members in several ways. The so-called Great Recession led to specious but predictable cries that public sector workers and their pensions were to blame for the economic crisis. PIPSC members were overwhelmingly employed in full-time jobs in the 2010s—and indeed had been since the Institute's founding—and may have seemed insulated from the growing move toward precarious work. But the federal government showed growing interest in outsourcing work, including in the development and implementation of crucial administrative computer systems.

All Canadians faced the problems of wealth and income inequality and work precarity, but PIPSC members confronted two related issues specific to federal public sector workers. The Conservative government continued its policy of muzzling scientists in the public service and enthusiastically out-sourced government work. These policies produced another related problem: the Phoenix payroll system. Phoenix was a grievous disaster that could have been entirely avoided had the Harper government heeded warnings about its potential shortcomings. A Supreme Court of Canada ruling in 2015, which would profoundly affect potential unionization patterns across the country, provided some welcome relief for organized labour in light of the hostile pol-itical climate fostered by the Harper government. And PIPSC and other fed-eral public sector unions received some respite when Canadians voted the Conservatives out of office in 2015. Yet broader issues like lasting structural changes to the national job market persisted.

Although PIPSC grew somewhat larger during the 2010s, further growth was limited for two reasons. First, union density in the public sector generally was already high, 75 percent, meaning that public sector unions now had little room for further growth without venturing into the private sector. Second, the continued influence of neoliberalism on government budgets and priorities meant that population growth was not leading to proportional increases in the size of the public service. In 2019, 287,978 people worked in the federal public service, an increase of 1.7 percent since 2010. Yet Canada's popula-tion—37,314,442 in 2019—grew by 9 percent during the same period.[2]

As the Institute approached its hundredth anniversary, it continued to reflect changes in the composition of Canadian society and its increasingly diverse workforce, especially the growing participation of women, Indigenous peoples, visible minorities, and persons with disabilities. Members of the baby boom generation who had assumed leadership roles in the 1990s and 2000s were now moving into retirement, and PIPSC elected its fourth woman presi-dent. PIPSC made tangible gains through collective bargaining and otherwise promoted the interests of its members through new initiatives and sustained media and lobbying efforts. This chapter describes the Institute's progress from 2010 through 2019 and the challenges and opportunities it faced. Orga-nized much like the preceding chapters, its narrative places the voices of cur-rent and former PIPSC members at the forefront.

Leadership and Staff   PIPSC entered the decade led by Gary Corbett, who was succeeded by Debi Daviau in 2014. Like Steve Hindle, Daviau came from the Computer Systems (CS) Group. Her route to involvement in PIPSC shares similarities with those of other activists in this book. It's impossible to know how similar her story is to those of PIPSC's three former women presidents (Frances Goodspeed, Iris Craig, and Michèle Demers), however, since when the research for this book was conducted she was the only one still alive to be interviewed. As Daviau recalled:

> I was a young mother who was experiencing some of my own workplace issues and certainly riled up about some of my colleagues' issues. I had from time to time tried to advocate on behalf of my colleagues and been told that it was really none of my business. And I suppose it really wasn't. So, I became a steward so as to make it my business. I was in the CS Group. I had gone to Algonquin College to get a computer programming degree, and I had done a work term with the government. And that ended up leading eventually to a term job in the government. I started working for the government in a term position in 1996. ...
>
> In my field there were very few women—maybe one in ten—and very few other workers had family obligations. I was a single mother, so I had a lot of family obligations. I remember working so hard but needing to take leave to look after sick kids or to make sure that we were meeting our family appointments. Sometimes it also meant that you needed time off, and that time off was provided through our collective agreement, but it was frowned upon for us to take it. So, there was a lot of pressure not to use up your sick leave and not to use up your family-related leave. I'll never forget I was about four months into my first full-time CS-2 position and my boss called me in to chastise me for having taken four days of leave—one day per month—which was really the minimum amount of time I could take to get through family obligations.
>
> I remember asking him, "In the four months that I've been here, have you received any complimentary comments from clients? Do you have anything positive you want to say to me about the work that I'm doing here, or are you just calling me in because I've taken the leave that I was rightfully entitled to?" And he said, "Well, yes, I receive comments from clients all the time, and, by the way, maybe you're doing too much because you're making your colleagues look bad." And that was our reality. I helped that boss to find his way out of our branch after that, because obviously this was a person who was not ready to uphold the values that I think all public servants [should] have in the interest of serving Canadians. I may have been one in ten women, but I packed a punch, and I was probably noticed for it. Ultimately, it was the union that won my heart, and so that sort of focused my efforts from pretty early on in my career.

Daviau's motivations for getting involved in her union—the desire to ensure management respected her rights and those of her colleagues and the concern for balancing the needs of work and family—also motivated other activists interviewed for previous chapters, including Glen Schjerning (see chapter 5). Daviau also described her journey to the PIPSC presidency: "I became a PIPSC member in 2003. I was elected initially to be director of the National Capital Region. That was a part-time position. And then, in 2010, I was elected as a full-time vice president, so that's when I came to be working at the Institute full-time on behalf of the members."³ After four years as a vice president, Daviau won election to the Institute's top job.

She found the transition to the president's job eye opening and full of challenges. Unlike the leadership of private sector organizations of a size similar to PIPSC or to managers in the public sector, union leaders like Daviau are elected, which adds to the challenges. Union leaders must juggle many duties, including dealing with the important day-to-day management and administration of the organization, addressing member concerns, being the public face of the organization, dealing with employers, and essentially being in continual campaign mode. As C. Wright Mills famously wrote in 1948, a labour leader is a "manager of discontent, ... an army general and a parliamentary debater, a political boss and entrepreneur, a rebel and a disciplinarian."⁴ Daviau's comments on the experience of becoming the president reflected some of what Mills described:

> I think one of my biggest challenges was making the transition from being a workplace steward and a worker to being a union leader and a manager of some 170 staff and 1,500 steward volunteers. For me there was a lot of learning on how to manage people—some fundamental stuff. I think it's interesting that we very often find people in management roles that have no training or experience to back them. They've made their way there because of their aptitudes or their skills in the field that they're in—not because they have any information on how to lead people. An executive coach shared this comparison with me. If you went to the hospital and you needed a nurse to take blood and you got a nurse who had never taken blood before—so she was actually just learning, trying to get a vein—you really wouldn't find that acceptable. But somehow, we find it acceptable to put people into leadership roles and not to train them to be able to take care of things that could become quite problematic if they're not dealt with correctly. So, I think my first [and] biggest challenge was learning

Figure 6-1: PIPSC office at 250 Tremblay Road in Ottawa. *PIPSC Photo Database.*

administratively how to manage people. I was already a leader, but not
necessarily a manager.

To the list of roles that Mills described as being part of a union leader's job,
Daviau's comments suggest that skilled administrator should be added.[5]

The 170 paid staff that Daviau referred to also reported to the Institute's
chief operating officer and executive secretary, Eddie Gillis. Gilles commented
on what he felt were the issues facing PIPSC in the 2010s, including administration of the Institute's new office building, the purchase of which added
landlord to the other duties the union's leadership was responsible for:

> One of the most significant decisions by the Institute—and led by its Board
> of Directors in 2004—was to move from Auriga Drive to a new building.
> We looked, for a great deal of time, for a building that ... had the [loca-
> tion,] size, and space that we were looking for. After a search that lasted a
> couple of years, we came upon the building at 250 Tremblay Road, which
> was very much larger than our needs. And so there was a very significant
> and important set of discussions held at the board of directors level about
> whether or not this was a wise move—to use the resources of the orga-
> nization to buy a building which would make us commercial landlords, in
> that we would be leasing space to others. That decision was made, and we

entered into the largest and most expensive project in the history of PIPSC, I would argue.

So, on Labour Day 2006, we opened officially the Institute's headquarters at 250 Tremblay Road and created, at that same time, a board of governors of a new corporation that we launched called the 250 Tremblay Road National Office Corporation. And that, of course, still exists today, governing the operations related to this major asset of the organization. For the first ten years, the building was fully occupied—100 percent occupied for the entire first ten years, and we've struggled a bit in the last couple of years. There is a very difficult real estate market in the city, and very aggressive actions by the federal government as a tenant. The federal government was our tenant for the first ten years. It was, to me, a rich irony that our mortgage would be paid, in many ways, by the employer. We've managed to make the building a successful venture for us, and our members and our staff are very comfortable.[6]

By the 2010s, the relationship between PIPSC's leaders and the Institute's unionized staff had improved since the days of the 1998 strike. The staff's union representation had also changed somewhat. Both the Professional Institute Staff Association (PISA) and the Professional Institute Regional Employees' Association (PIREA) had been founded as independent unions. But in 2010, PISA members chose to affiliate with a national union, becoming Unifor Local 3011 in 2013. This decision was not unusual for a small, independent local. It is possible for a local union to be directly chartered by the Canadian Labour Congress (CLC), but it cannot expect a lot of support in those circumstances beyond access to resources like basic steward training, advocacy, and advice on bargaining. Affiliating with a national or international union gives a local access to more resources, including comprehensive bargaining expertise, better training, and a strike fund. The potential downsides for a small local include minimal representation at national and international union conferences and having to compete with much larger locals to have the voices of its members heard.[7]

PIREA remained independent, but after 2010 its members were covered by provincial rather than federal labour law. It became the Professional Institute Regional Employee Council, as its members across Canada had to bargain under the labour laws in their respective provinces. This added more complexity to the labour relations process at PIPSC because it meant adhering to different labour laws in each province, even if they were generally similar.

All workplaces invariably have some tensions, but the sentiment after 2009 was that PIPSC provided a good work environment overall. Turnover among the PIPSC staff was low, which suggests that the Institute was (and is) indeed a decent place to work.[8]

Governance   Governance processes continued to be at the core of the Institute's activities after 2010, and the annual general meeting was at the core of governance. Many national and international unions do not meet annually. The International Association of Machinists and Aerospace Workers, a private sector union with 600,000 members, only holds a convention every four years.[9] Unifor, Canada's largest private sector union with 315,000 members, has a constitutional convention every three years. The Canadian Union of Public Employees, the country's largest at 680,000 members, holds a convention every two years.[10] Unlike these larger unions, PIPSC, with a membership of over 60,000 workers, has an annual meeting. The fact that PIPSC brings delegates together from across Canada much more frequently than other major unions reflects how seriously PIPSC takes the issue of democratic governance.

PIPSC's interest in governance is also reflected in the comprehensiveness of the Institute's by-laws. PIPSC's by-laws are longer than Unifor's, and the latter's membership is over five times larger. This is not to suggest that other unions like Unifor do not take governance issues seriously; instead, it shows that PIPSC has developed a comparatively intensive governance process. Other national and international unions such as Unifor also do not elect their top leaders through direct, individual membership ballots like PIPSC does. The way PIPSC is governed, from its annual general meetings to the democratic election of its leadership, provides much opportunity for direct member involvement in governance and elections.

The annual general meeting (AGM) required significant advance planning and work by the Institute's staff. Eddie Gillis described the work involved:

> Some members think that the AGM is only about the business—the business of resolutions and by-law changes and policy changes. Other members think that the networking opportunities and the ability to come together with fellow activists is the most important part. We, on the staff side, understand we have to accommodate both of these points of view, and so we have to create enough space to get the business done without entirely cutting out great opportunities for networking, for breaking bread

together, for seeing old friends and colleagues whom you wouldn't see except at the AGM."

The AGMs after 2009 still dealt with routine business matters like the approval of budgets, but they also addressed more pressing issues like those relating to internal democracy, collective bargaining, and the terms of federal public service employment. To improve internal democracy, for example, PIPSC adopted a ranked-ballot system—the British Columbia Single Transferable Vote, or BC-STV—at the 2012 AGM and used it first in the 2015 elections. The AGM minutes described "how BC-STV works":

> In single-winner elections, the votes from the person with the fewest votes are transferred to the voter's subsequent choice until a winner is obtained. For multiple-winner elections, a minimum threshold is needed to be elected. Surplus votes above the threshold are transferred to other candidates as per the voters' ranking preference. All voters have a say in the election of all winners.[12]

The Institute's 2016 AGM passed a number of resolutions that signalled the Institute's then-current priorities, if not its political direction. Convention resolutions do not automatically lead to concrete change, but they do reveal approved changes in the union's priorities and reflect the concerns of convention delegates and rank-and-file members. In the case of the resolutions below, all were endorsed later by the PIPSC Board of Directors, "imbedded in [the union's] strategic directives," and given budgetary support. One resolution launched a campaign for tax fairness:

> Whereas the legitimacy of an advanced democracy's tax system is predicated on its integrity and fairness; and
>> Whereas the Government of Canada's Budget 2016 announced new spending expected to yield more than $12 in revenue for every $10 invested in the Canada Revenue Agency (CRA); and
>> Whereas restoring public faith in the integrity of tax system demands investing in the staff and structure needed at the CRA to catch international tax cheats and provide much-needed revenue for federal government programs;
>> Therefore be it resolved that PIPSC calls on the federal government to:
>> Establish a world-class tax fairness initiative with a $600 million investment to recoup $6 billion in revenue;

> Investigate complex cases and prosecute offenders; [and]
> Target corporate tax cheats.[13]

The resolution on tax fairness is an example of social unionism, as it did not reflect concerns specific to PIPSC members but rather a concern for tax equity for all Canadians.

The 2016 AGM also addressed the pressing issue of scientific integrity, an issue that combined the specific concerns of PIPSC members with a wider concern for the public good. This issue remained a major concern despite the change of government in 2015:

> Whereas public science requires rebuilding after nearly 10 years of muzzling and cuts by the previous federal government;
>
> Whereas there exists a significant shortage in the number of scientists, engineers and researchers to meet the ongoing research and regulatory needs of the Government of Canada;
>
> Therefore be it resolved that PIPSC engages the current government to support public science by investing in innovation and science at the federal level;
>
> Be it further resolved that PIPSC calls on the federal government to hire additional federal scientists to reverse the impact of dangerous cuts over the previous 10 years and increase funding for conference attendance; and
>
> Be it further resolved that PIPSC campaign vigorously to enshrine scientific integrity into collective agreements in order to ensure no future government can muzzle federal scientists again.[14]

AGM delegates also debated and passed a significant resolution on contracting out of work. Since 2009, the Canadian government had continued the extensive use of contract labour, a practice that understandably drew criticism from organized labour:

> Whereas the contract between public employees and the federal government is breaking down as more and more services are outsourced for longer and longer periods of time; and
>
> Whereas outsourcing government services does not ensure Canadians get the best expertise available when it's needed, more efficiently or at a lower cost; and

Whereas the federal government currently spends $10 billion a year on outsourced services, more than the budgets of several large federal departments combined;

Therefore be it resolved that we call on the federal government to reduce reliance on outside IT [information technology] and other professional services and reinvest a portion of the savings into training to enhance the government's internal capacity; and

Be it further resolved that the Institute build a multi-pronged campaign to raise member and public awareness of the harms of contracting out/outsourcing and continue to lobby the federal government to reverse the trend towards an over-reliance on private sector solutions.[15]

AGMs during the decade were typically well attended, with all bargaining groups assigned representation. For example, 458 delegates attended the 2018 AGM, the size of each group's delegation ranging from forty-two for the CS Group (still the largest in the union) to one for very small groups such as the Canadian Museum of History.[16] The resolutions passed were a starting point for setting the union's priorities going into collective bargaining. And bargaining was difficult.

The Phoenix Payroll System   PIPSC enjoyed gains through collective bargaining after 2009 but was confronted with one grievously vexing labour relations issue that took years to resolve. Collective bargaining can involve focusing on a broad or narrow range of issues. Management, whether in the public or private sectors, prefers to narrow the scope of bargaining and to keep as many issues as possible away from the bargaining table. In contrast, unions prefer a wide scope of bargaining and hope to include all possible aspects of the employment contract in their collective agreements. Management prefers shorter and less detailed agreements, while unions prefer them to be lengthier and more exact in their terms.

A fundamental aspect of the employment relationship, one so obvious as to require (usually) no mention, is that employers pay employees for their work. To put it another way, employers hire people at specified compensation rates, and the employees sell their labour with the expectation that employers will pay as agreed. Employees' refusal to perform the work they are paid for (except in the case of a strike or lockout) or employers who don't compensate people for the work performed violate the employment contract. Although employees in the private sector might face situations in which they don't get paid—when a small business can't make payroll during an economic downturn or a company goes bankrupt—the general expectation is that public sector employees are almost immune from such occurrences. The administration of government programs may re-organize work or change priorities and policy directions, with the consequence that public sector workers face layoffs. Nevertheless, both public employees and the public expect that governments will compensate their employees in accordance with their terms of their employment. Yet that basic employment arrangement broke down in the Canadian federal public service after 2016 due to the introduction of IBM's Phoenix payroll system.

Phoenix, initiated under the Conservative government of Stephen Harper and rolled out under the Liberal government of Justin Trudeau, was intended to simplify and improve the efficiency of the federal payroll system. Organizations of all sizes in both the public and private sectors rely on increasingly sophisticated systems to support their operations. Payroll is absolutely central to maintaining the employment relationship and is part of human resources, which is (unfortunately) not considered a core function of most organizations. Prior to 2016, the federal government used several different payroll systems, which was not an efficient way to ensure that current workers and retirees would receive their pay. Having one system *should* have proven more efficient, but the obvious catch was that the single system had to work.

Canada was not the first major industrialized country to try the Phoenix system created by IBM. The Australian state of Queensland introduced Phoenix in 2010 to compensate 78,000 workers in health-related occupations, and the activation of the system caused chaos. Thousands of workers were not properly paid. While Queensland was grappling with Phoenix's deficiencies the Harper government was considering using it. Despite warnings from Australians about the perils of the system and, more importantly, despite the fact that sufficient information technology expertise existed within the public service to implement a new payroll system without using a third-party contractor, the Canadian government went ahead. It purchased Phoenix in 2011 with the expectation of implementing the system in 2016.[17]

The decision to activate Phoenix in 2016 fell to the recently elected Liberal government, which gave the rollout the go-ahead. Immediately, problems arose, and the system was found to be faulty. Significant numbers of public servants were paid incorrectly or not at all, problems that in many cases stretched on for months, even years. In all, Phoenix negatively affected 146,000 public service employees and retirees. It took a huge toll on public

Figure 6-2: Nix Phoenix. *PIPSC website, https://www.pipsc.ca/.*

sector workers who, without pay, were unable to meet their financial obligations. One person told the CBC that she could not afford to pay for her mother's funeral. This fiasco, heavily covered by the national media, was not only an example of government mismanagement but also meant the largest employer in the country could not properly pay its workers. The minister responsible for fixing Phoenix admitted that it was an embarrassment for the government.[18]

PIPSC responded at once to the Phoenix fiasco through several means. It started a media campaign, as illustrated in figure 6–2, offered financial assistance to members, and lobbied the federal government extensively to fix the system. PIPSC members, wanting an even more robust response, questioned why they could not go on strike or sue the government. The Institute argued that a strike would be illegal while collective agreements were in place. Canadian law also prevented unionized public sector workers from engaging in class action lawsuits against the government. Consequently, PIPSC's leadership concluded that the most viable strategy was to combine with other federal public sector unions to force the government to repair or replace Phoenix as quickly as possible and to demand compensation for their members. The terrible impact that the faulty system had on individual members was further compounded by the fact that the federal government collected dues, via payroll deduction, on behalf of the various public sector unions. The Phoenix system malfunction hampered correct dues deduction for thousands of public sector unionists, depriving the unions of revenues.[19]

In the summer of 2019, PIPSC and fourteen other federal public sector unions reached an agreement with the federal government to compensate affected civil servants for their lost pay, as well as for the hardships they endured. The agreement provided compensation to affected employees for fiscal years 2016 to 2019 inclusive and also awarded up to five paid leave days for all members of the fifteen bargaining agents (or the option of cashing out those days for former employees and the survivors of deceased workers). Debi Daviau commented on the agreement when it was reached:

> Despite not getting paid properly, our members have come to work each
> and every day to give their best in service of the public. We can't erase

the loss and suffering that Phoenix has caused for these dedicated public service professionals. It took a lot of hard work by the unions to obtain a fair settlement. The hard work was worth it, because with the commitments and the compensation enshrined in this settlement, the Treasury Board has taken important steps forward.[20]

The 2019 agreement marked a major step toward ending a difficult period in the Institute's history.

The disastrous Phoenix debacle will, the Institute and others hope, serve as a cautionary tale for future governments that want to rely on third-party entities to supply essential operating or administrative systems. The Harper government had no pressing reason to buy Phoenix, other than its dogmatic faith in contracting out government work. The Trudeau Liberals came to power after the system was on its way to implementation and likely concluded that backing out of an agreement with IBM would have caused headaches at a time when seemingly more important policy issues had to be handled. In time, Phoenix will become a bad memory, and one hopes that the government will never again have difficulty meeting its contractual obligations to its workers.

Scientific Integrity

The Phoenix fiasco affected all federal public sector unions equally, but the compromising of scientific integrity under the Harper government and the disruption it caused to the lives and careers of public servants disproportionately affected PIPSC. As the preceding chapter described, from the time the Harper government came into office it systematically muzzled scientists in the federal public service. PIPSC commented frequently in the media about the danger of governments trying to suppress science and also made it a bargaining issue. The new Liberal government agreed in 2016 to include language in collective agreements that protected the right of scientists to speak publicly about their work and research. Debi Daviau commented that the change in government was positively influencing public policy by acknowledging the intellectual integrity of PIPSC members. The Liberals reintroduced the long-form census, for example, which the Harper government had eliminated, and took steps to repeal anti-union legislation.[21]

PIPSC member Matthew MacLeod, who works as a scientist in the Department of National Defence and is president of the Research Group, discussed the importance of and researchers' focus on scientific integrity:

I've never been directly involved with the Science Advisory Committee who did the studies [*The Big Chill* and *Vanishing Science*, both about the Harper government's attack on scientists' independence], but certainly those issues came to us as a group executive as well. Our members [were] saying there [were] huge issues around muzzling and access to resources and [their] ability to get to conferences. I saw some of that in my own workplace as well. With the government having passed legislation that changed the rules of bargaining—including obligating us to be on the strike path [rather than, as in the past, allowing bargaining agents to choose arbitration], which was not a normal thing for researchers to think about, and painting the public service in a very negative light—we made the conscious decision to focus on issues that were more integrity based.

You certainly see in the media whenever there's news about a potential job action, management always tries to portray it as being all about money. Then when you actually are able to get interviews with the union representative, you find out—no, it's about scheduling, or it's about all these other things. I'd say a good number of researchers, especially those who are further along in their career, are not that worried about their salary.

What they were worried about was their ability to get their work done and to talk about their work. So, we focused on those as our major issues. That led to us bundling those under this scientific-integrity banner.

Even things that had been monetary issues in the past—for example, there used to be a government policy that if you had a patent made of your work, you were eligible to receive a certain percentage of the revenues that the government generated from that. It was capped at a fraction of your salary. But that was pushed down to departments to implement or not. It had mostly gone away. We brought that back as a bargaining proposal. How we proposed it is that it would go back into the research program—not even to the person as a monetary benefit. This was how much the scientists were struggling to get their work done. They would rather have the resources for their job than remuneration.[22]

Recovering from the deliberate and sustained effort to prevent federal scientists and researchers from speaking to Canadians about their work would take some time, and PIPSC made a significant gain at the bargaining table—a contractual guarantee that scientists could speak publicly about their research. This bargaining achievement went beyond just benefiting workers and their workplace, as Canadians benefitted from having public servants who could inform them about important research that could shape their lives. Enshrining the un-muzzling of scientists in collective agreements will help prevent future governments from trying to politicize scientific research to the detriment of public discourse.

RCMP Unionization

As the previous chapter demonstrated, PIPSC has willingly used the courts to defend its members' interests. The 2015 Supreme Court of Canada decision—*Mounted Police Association of Ontario v. Canada*, or MPAO—was a landmark ruling that could potentially transform the country's labour relations, and it had immediate significance for PIPSC. Uniformed and civilian employees in the Royal Canadian Mounted Police (RCMP) had long been prevented from unionizing for reasons of national security.[23] Other police services across Canada were allowed to unionize, though with limitations that included an inability to strike and mandatory binding arbitration to resolve bargaining disputes.

Describing the full background and details of MPAO is beyond the scope of this discussion, but the important point is that the decision had the potential to further extend the right to collective bargaining to other occupational groups currently prevented from unionizing. As Larry Savage and Charles Smith have noted, the court emphasized that its ruling mandated a "meaningful" collective bargaining process rather than a specific labour relations model.[24] This means that future court decisions may potentially limit the scope of what currently excluded groups, such as managers, can expect when they want to engage in collective bargaining.

Unions nonetheless celebrated the MPAO decision. Uniformed RCMP officers were required to bargain separately from their civilian colleagues and in a union that only represents them, which is the practice with other police services in Canada. However, many civilian RCMP employees fell into job classifications, such as computer systems, already represented by PIPSC. So, the Institute began negotiating on behalf of six civilian groups within the RCMP. Relying on courts to protect and expand labour rights comes with uncertainty, and unions would prefer to achieve gains through bargaining and collective action. Yet the Supreme Court of Canada has provided bargaining rights to previously excluded workers and enabled PIPSC to extend membership benefits to them, including codifying rights and obligations in collective agreements.[25]

Collective Agreements   PIPSC continued to win tangible improvements for its members through collective bargaining, despite the hostile environment for public sector workers created by the Harper government until 2015. This was clear in agreements negotiated on behalf of the Research (RE) Group and the Applied Science and Patent Examination (SP) Group in 2014. The names of these bargaining groups, like those discussed in preceding chapters, further illustrate the range of activities covered by PIPSC members. The research agreement covered people working in Historical Research, Mathematics, Scientific Research, and the Defence Scientific Service. The applied science and patent examination contract included workers in Actuarial Science, Agriculture, Biological Science, Chemistry, Forestry, Meteorology, Physical Sciences, Scientific Regulation, and Patents. Both collective agreements included language that was found across various PIPSC agreements, such as a clause that stipulated that provisions agreed to by the National Joint Council were part of the PIPSC agreements, including directives on a range of issues from bilingualism bonuses and the public service health care plan to uniforms and motor vehicle operations. The agreements also had a clause recognizing the need for workers to engage in career development, something not found in most private sector agreements.[26]

The two agreements differed in their job classifications and salary scales. The research agreement outlined grades and salary steps for four different occupations. For instance, the Mathematics occupation was divided into seven grades from MA-1 to MA-7, with from one to seven salary steps in each. The salaries for 2017 ranged from $32,002 for MA-1 step one to $130,638 for MA-7 step five. The SP agreement outlined grades and salary steps for nine different occupations. As an example, the agreement divided the Patent Examination classification into seven grades, each with one to nine salary steps. The 2018 salaries for that occupation began at $35,731 for step one in SG-PAT-01 and rose to $136,098 for step nine in SG-PAT-07. The salary ranges across both agreements were quite similar, with a few thousand dollars' worth of variation at both ends of the salary scale. The agreements awarded wage increases of just under 2 percent per year over three years, which exceeded increases in the cost of living in Canada during that time.[27]

The two agreements also reflect the complexity of federal public service bargaining in the 2010s. By 2019, the Treasury Board was negotiating twenty-nine separate collective agreements for seventeen different bargaining agents. PIPSC bargained six of those agreements, one for each of its bargaining units: Architecture, Engineering, and Land Survey (NR) Group; Applied Science and Patent Examination (SP) Group; Audit, Commerce and Purchasing (AV) Group; Computer Systems (CS) Group; Health Services (SH) Group; and Research (RE) Group. Each of the occupations covered by those agreements was subject to regular job evaluation, and that process required considerable expertise from management and labour. (The federal government and public sector unions consult on job evaluation for the many occupations covered by collective agreements.) For instance, someone working as a mathematician had to meet a minimum standard that included "graduation with a degree from a recognized post-secondary institution with specialization in mathematics, statistics or operational research or with specialization in one of the physical, life or social sciences combined with an acceptable number of courses in mathematics, statistics or operational research at the level of a recognized post-secondary institution."[28]

Because such minimum standards and further required steps for progression in an occupation were (and are) subject to periodic consultation and negotiation, PIPSC collective bargaining continued to grow in complexity during the 2010s. The Canadian government had many job classifications and, since a universal classification system was never implemented, every job needed evaluating and re-evaluating on an ongoing basis. This process shaped who was hired for given jobs, and that in turn led to labour-management disputes if union members felt they had been unfairly denied selection for new jobs or if their compensation was not correctly determined.

Dispute Resolution   Passage of the Federal Public Sector Labour Relations and Employment Board Act in 2013 altered the dispute-resolution process in federal labour relations, turning the Public Service Staff Relations Board into the Federal Public Sector Labour Relations and Employment Board. The resulting acronym—FPSLREB—was less sonorous than the previous PSSRB, yet the board's mandate continued to focus on adjudication and mediation, and its scope grew to include regular and reserve members of the RCMP. PIPSC continued to take issues to the board for adjudication and mediation, and so too did the employer. The practice of employers, in this case federal departments and agencies, seeking redress from labour boards is not replicated at the provincial labour boards; private sector employers are less likely to bring matters before labour boards.

Two cases, one from the beginning of the decade and one from the end, exemplified the highly technical issues that both PIPSC and employers brought before the FPSLREB. The first, a 2010 case titled *Treasury Board v. Professional*

Institute of the Public Service of Canada, revolved around differing interpretations of what constituted an essential services agreement. The second, a 2019 case called *Professional Institute of the Public Service of Canada v. Treasury Board*, involved a dispute over the employer contemplating withholding pay increments for poor performance.[29] In both cases, the labour board ruled in PIPSC's favour. The adjudicator's ruling in the first case does not describe the facts extensively, but in the second case the adjudicator did, revealing enormously complex legal issues. In that case, the labour board ordered the Treasury Board to remove any references in documents to withholding pay increments for poor performance. PIPSC staff counsel handled both cases, and the intricate analysis involved obviously required representation from either an attorney or someone enormously well acquainted with the relevant issues and jurisprudence. Those cases show, along with the job evaluation process discussed above, that resolving disputes between the Treasury Board and other agencies and public sector unions required expertise from everyone involved.

National Joint Council   So too did PIPSC's role in the National Joint Council (NJC). Well known and respected in the public service, the NJC is largely unknown to the wider Canadian public. In the 2010s, it continued to be the central mechanism for addressing labour-management issues that broadly affected the entire public service. In 2019, it comprised all the bargaining agents of federal employees, including PIPSC and PSAC, and five employer groups, including the Treasury Board Secretariat.[30] The Public Service Alliance of Canada was still the largest federal public sector union in Canada, with just under 180,000 members by the mid-2010s, and PIPSC remained the second largest, with slightly less than 60,000. Some of the unions in the NJC, such as the Association of Justice Counsel (AJC) that represents federal crown attorneys, are small enough that they are not counted in government surveys of labour organizations. That association had only 2,600 members in 2019. Interestingly, AJC members had formed an independent union in 2006, which included the former PIPSC Law Group (of approximately one hundred members). Knowing that they would still benefit from participation in the National Joint Council, law group members felt confident being out from under PIPSC's umbrella.[31]

The NJC provided a vehicle for sectoral bargaining and consultation in the federal public service, and, crucially, it enabled small unions to benefit from the gains achieved by their larger counterparts. The NJC also provided an alternative dispute-resolution mechanism that was less formal than the

FPSLREB. Grievances could be brought before the council if an affected party thought that a council directive had been violated. For example, the NJC resolved disputes arising from violations of its bilingualism bonus directive, which mandated additional compensation for workers proficient in both official languages.[32]

Advocacy, Media, Community

Canadian citizens hear about public sector unions like PIPSC through the media and the advocacy campaigns mounted by the labour movement. They also unfortunately hear negative critiques of labour by the business community and political right. PIPSC's public profile was higher in the 2010s than in any preceding decade. This resulted from a deliberate policy move driven by threats to scientific integrity and Phoenix. PIPSC ran public awareness campaigns on both issues that were meant to pressure the government and to inform Canadians about how their public service was being harmed. Mostly because of Phoenix, the media paid attention. For example, CBC News quoted Debi Daviau sixty-one times between 2012 and July 2019.[33]

PIPSC also adopted policy positions on Canada's First Nations communities, which included recognizing treaty rights through a land acknowledgement, in the wake of the Truth and Reconciliation Commission's calls to action. In 2019, the Institute's board adopted the following motion brought forward by Indigenous PIPSC member Greg Scriver:

> Whereas Canada's unions continue to work towards reconciliation, relationship building and trust with First Nations, Métis, and Inuit peoples. In that spirit, by acknowledging traditional lands, the Institute has an opportunity to move forward with Truth and Reconciliation.
>
> [Be it resolved] that the Board of Directors recommends that a permanent land acknowledgement plaque be installed at the Institute Headquarters. The Board also recommends that all PIPSC Regional offices do the same.[34]

Scriver commented on his role in PIPSC and his interest in Indigenous advocacy:

> I became a member of the Institute through what is known as an Order-in-Council which was issued for Shared Services Canada back in 2011. I came from another union called the Research Council Employees' Association,

or RCEA, which is a union for employees of the National Research Council. I'd spent my entire public service career there. I started back in 1999. So now as I look back, it's twenty years of service as a proud public servant as a CS.

I was providing IT services for the National Research Council and then the Order-in-Council came along and I had to resign as a second vice president for the RCEA. I started working with the task force for creating Shared Services Canada. That was really my first look at what the Institute was, how they operated, and the different aspects of the Institute. In 2014, I ran for election as an NCR regional director, as a member of the Board of Directors, and I successfully won a one-year term. The following year, in 2015, I ran again for the position of NCR regional director, and successfully completed a three-year term on the Institute board.

I'm now actually working with the Canadian Labour Congress at least two days a week, organizing the first ever Indigenous Lobby Day, which is very important to me because of my heritage. I was very proud last year that I brought a motion to the Board of Directors to actually start making land acknowledgments at the beginning of each and every board meeting, and we have been doing that since last year. One thing the Institute doesn't do is actually have members self-identify, and that's something that we are starting to look at—to have the Institute actually have individuals self-identify. I know of a handful of individual members who are Indigenous, but really there isn't a lot of committee work or a lot of other work [on Indigenous issues] that's being done right now with the Institute.

I'm trying to work with the Board of Directors right now to recognize Indigenous people in this great country of ours. We need to start looking at different values and different areas within the Institute, and ways that we can have that land acknowledgement. The board has just agreed to sponsor a First Nations' event in the BC/Yukon [region], with Director Rob MacDonald spearheading that for the summer solstice on June 21, 2019, so that will be another sponsorship that the Institute is involved in. They have been involved in a few other sponsorships over the years but not as many as we probably should have been.

I come from Kahnawake, which is on the South Shore of Montreal. My grandmother was actually born and raised there. When she moved away from the reserve, she actually lost her status, and it wasn't until around 2011 when there was a new bill passed that indicated that any grandchildren of a grandmother that lost status during that time period were able to qualify for full status. My three sisters and I all applied, and we now have full status. I've gone back to the reserve quite a few times.[35]

The Institute's efforts on behalf of First Nations people is particularly significant because it represents people who have spent decades working in First Nations communities. Sharon Trasatti, who was a nurse in remote First Nations communities, joined PIPSC in 1978. As well as expressing gratitude that her small occupational group was able to be part of PIPSC, she expressed great satisfaction with the work that she did over the years, and felt that First Nations people had a lot of respect for the service provided by her and other nurses.[36] Ginette Tardif, a nurse and PIPSC activist, also worked in remote Indigenous communities:

I'm an Acadian from New Brunswick originally. I'm a nurse. I went to work in Ontario in a remote nursing station, and most of the nursing stations for the First Nations and Inuit Health Branch, at the time, were remote. Perhaps twenty-six out of thirty are isolated, meaning they are "fly-in" communities—you have to take a small plane to get there. You feel quite isolated when you start working there, ... [and] you don't know much about what's going on in the outside world. And when I started, back twenty-something years ago, communication was not very good in the North. We had no Internet, the phone system didn't work that well—you had CBC North, which was snowy on the TV. We felt very isolated.

You may have heard in the news ... [about] the state of emergency in the Cat Lake nursing station—how bad housing is, the mold, and all that. Actually, Cat Lake is one of the nursing stations where I worked. Working in the North is a different kind of work. The isolation gets to you. The nurses work away from their family. There's no accommodation to accommodate families. ... You are on site 24/7, so that makes it very difficult. So, our challenges are a little different from regular employees. ...

A few AGMs ago, we wanted to mark the issue of the First Nations' murdered and missing women. We had a day where we asked the members who were attending the meeting to wear red. We tried to move the story up front so that members could be more informed about what was going on. So, we tried to bring that issue as a focus for the AGM delegates.[37]

Rob MacDonald, a member of the Board of Directors for British Columbia/ Yukon, described his region's First Nations advocacy:

Figure 6-3: APTN Indigenous Day, 22 June 2019, Whitehorse, Yukon. Shown in the photo-graph are (*from left*) PIPSC BC/Yukon Director Rob MacDonald; Yukon Federation of Labour President Ron Rousseau; PIPSC CLC Indigenous Representative Greg Scriver; PIPSC mem-ber Kathleen Chapman; PIPSC President Debi Daviau; and PIPSC Yukon Branch President Mike Paré. *PIPSC photo database.*

Our BC First Nations' bargaining group is a fascinating group in the sense that they were part of Health Canada. Through a devolution process, that service was devolved to the First Nations Health Authority. The nurses and IT folks there, and some other professionals, decided to stay with PIPSC. So, we created a separate group for them that is just limited to the borders of BC. They are a very small group and very diverse, but they are on the cutting edge of healthcare. I've had a chance to meet some of these nurses and some of these other professionals, and it's incredible what they're deal-ing with. They are going to small communities. They are at the front and centre of healthcare in some of the most vulnerable parts of our community. They're under incredible pressure to provide services with a limited amount of money, and, at the same time, they must bargain a collective agreement and deal with health and safety issues and deal with consultation issues.[38]

The activism of people like Greg Scriver and Ginette Tardif testified to the diversity of PIPSC's membership and its activists. The election of Norma Domey, an African Canadian who grew up in Nova Scotia, to one of two full-time vice president positions in 2018 also highlighted the diversity of PIPSC members. Domey commented on her involvement in PIPSC and her advocacy interests:

> Thirty-one years ago, I entered the Public Service of Canada, and initially I was a drug evaluator with Health Canada. And a position opened at Environment Canada doing the same type of evaluations. Instead of looking at human health endpoints, I was looking at environmental endpoints, essentially keeping the toxins out of our environment. I've got a degree in biochemistry at the undergrad level, and I've got a master of science degree in toxicology from the University of Western Ontario. Any new commercial substance that was about to be commercialized would come through us from chemical companies worldwide. We'd look at all the studies, and we would make a recommendation. Is this going to be toxic to the environment if there is unlimited manufacture or importation into Canada? Or we would recommend banning it if we thought that the substance would be harmful. It was very interesting work—from ingredients in your shampoo to ingredients in the paint to biochemicals, biopolymers, Alberta tar sands, to artificial snow for the Olympics.
>
> An opportunity came up with the union—the Professional Institute of the Public Service of Canada. Initially I was going to volunteer as the national capital region director, but I have a tendency, when I get involved, to really get involved. I jump in with both feet. So, I would have had a full-time job that I got paid for and a full-time job that I didn't get paid for [NCR director]. Another opportunity was available and that was as vice president, which was a full-time paid position. I was lucky enough that my years of service with the union as a volunteer on national executives for the science professionals paid off for me.
>
> I would like the powers that be in the government to help us [get] action and get some traction on proposals that were put forward today, which were the same proposals that were put forward thirty years ago. The committees that I was on as a young black woman—whether it be for the black community or for the women—these are the same proposals. You could take those proposals from thirty years ago and present them today and it would be the same. Nothing has changed. So, we need—for the women—we need the men to come in and be involved. Your career shouldn't be any more important than my career. When the call comes to go pick up your child because they're sick at the daycare, why is it always

Figure 6-4: The 2019 PIPSC National Executive Board. In the front row are (*from left*) vice presidents Steve Hindle (part-time) and Stéphane Aubry (full-time); President Debi Daviau; and Vice-President Norma Domey (full-time). In the back row are mostly NCR and regional directors: (*from left*) Rob MacDonald (BC/Yukon); Waheed Khan (NCR); Nancy McCune (Prairie/NWT); Peter Gilkinson (Ontario); Vice-President Gary Corbett (part-time); Jennifer Carr, Dave Sutherland and Jennie Esnard (NCR); Kim Skanes (Atlantic); and Advisory Council Director Chris Roach. Not pictured is Yvon Brodeur, director from the Quebec Region.

the women going? Our careers are just as important. So, let's spread the work out.[39]

Domey's perspective reflects that of an engaged activist. She was the first African-Canadian woman to be elected to the position of full-time vice president on the PIPSC executive and took a leadership role in the cause of greater visible-minority representation. The boards of directors of all organizations are works in progress but, as shown in figure 6-4, the PIPSC board is certainly representative of the diversity of the organization.

Supporting Indigenous rights and increasing the representation of visible minorities in PIPSC leadership positions were only two of the campaigns that PIPSC actively engaged in after 2009. PIPSC did not advocate a partisan position when it came to federal elections, but it showed an increased interest in being politically active. Debi Daviau commented on the decision to join the Canadian Labour Congress in 2011:

Affiliating with the CLC can be seen as a political statement. I saw it as the next logical step for an organization such as ours that wanted to be part of important social change on behalf of Canadians. That's not just looking inwards at our own jobs but looking at issues like gender equality or pharmacare or fair pensions for all with an external lens because I think we can all agree that we do enjoy decent provisions in the public sector in this regard.

I think what we want to do is bring everybody up to the same bar so that it doesn't become a race to the bottom where nobody has anything, but rather that all Canadian workers have access to prescription drugs. And all Canadian workers have access to a fair pension. And all Canadians can expect reasonable terms and conditions of employment that protect them from harassment and take care of them when they're ill. Those are the kinds of things that we defend through our affiliation with the broader labour movement, not necessarily through our campaigns that we run in house. But for me, the single most important reason for us to affiliate with the CLC was about what we could bring to the CLC as a professional union with a strong and credible voice. What can we do to help improve the Canadian labour movement's chances [of] addressing some of these broader social issues that affect not just our own membership but all Canadians?[40]

Individual public service workers also showed an interest in becoming politically active during PIPSC's tenth decade. A 2015 CBC report, in which Daviau was quoted, described how thirty-five federal workers sought permission to run in that year's election, compared with eleven in 2011.[41] PIPSC also articulated the following position on partisan versus political action in advance of the 2015 election, making clear its anybody-but-Conservatives approach:

Some members believe PIPSC should not participate in the upcoming federal election as it is against the PIPSC constitution [by-laws] to be political. In fact, the Institute has always been political, taking positions on issues that affect its membership. It is not against the PIPSC constitution to be political; it is against the constitution to support or endorse a specific political party or candidate. PIPSC is always political but never partisan. ...

We are sometimes asked by members: Who should I vote for in the upcoming election? The answer is: That is a decision you will have to make yourself. Tell the person to look at the information from other parties (we're all familiar with the Conservative record by now) and to ask themselves: Who best represents my interests? Which party will stop the cuts and restore the balance that's needed for the public sector?

This may lead to the same question in a different form: Who has the best chance in my riding of defeating the Conservatives *based on what is known.* Again, the answer is: You will have to decide that for yourself.

This election is a very tight race and in the final four months public opinion polls may and likely will change significantly. It's impossible to predict who has a better chance of winning, but by following online news campaign coverage and websites such as www.threehundredeight.com you'll be better informed about the race and your options.

One thing's certain: If you and those you speak to want change, you must get informed about the alternatives to the current Conservative government, and be prepared to ask the candidates that come to your door what they intend to do to stop the cuts and restore the public service.[42]

PIPSC was also keen to tell Canadians about the value of public services. A 2017 study by the Institute for Government in the United Kingdom ranked Canada first in the world for public services, and PIPSC quickly shared that information with its members and the general public. PIPSC developed a robust public-policy agenda after 2009, including campaigning through the CLC to advocate for First Nations peoples and trying to improve the diversity of its leadership.[43]

Belonging to PIPSC   Despite the hostility that PIPSC members sometimes felt directed at them by the Harper government and elements of the media, members generally expressed continued satisfaction with the work. Madeleine Blais, who joined the public service in the mid-1970s, felt her work as a PIPSC member at Nav Canada was valued by management. She stated, "I hear so much dissatisfaction of people who often work in the public service not feeling that their work is valued. I would say that's not the case at Nav Canada. I would equate it as a union friendly shop."[44]

As noted earlier, PIPSC continued to experience further generational change during the 2010s as baby boomers retired and members of the so-called millennial generation became activists. Andrew Wigmore described his involvement in PIPSC and the public service:

I've been involved in the public service since I was seventeen. I started in high school as an FSWEP (Federal Student Work Experience Program) student [in 2005] and just doing filing at … the civilian side of DND [Department of National Defence]. Basically, I just did filing and then they kept bringing me back from summer of grade eleven through grade twelve and all the way till I finished at university. Then I was bridged as an indeterminate employee for Department of National Defence this time, but as a civilian doing materiel management work.

Around 2012, Harper first instituted the cuts to the public service, and, lo and behold, my position was cut during that time. When I had the meeting with the colonel who was explaining to me what would happen, I didn't have any union representation there. Once that had happened, I wanted to know more about why this was happening [and] what could the union do for me.

Once I found a new position at Public Works—which is now Public Service and Procurement Canada—I ended up getting more involved because I sat adjacent to Lynn Morris, who is [now] a retired member. Lynn encouraged me to become a steward and helped me figure out the way to learn more.

I think many of the younger members don't know what their union does for them. We had our young workers' conference this past February [2019]. It had a combination of more experienced younger members and newer younger members. There were a lot of people who said that they didn't really know what the union did. It's a great opportunity for PIPSC to put something like that on to try [to] engage younger members and get them to know more about what the union is and why it's important.[45]

Some PIPSC members continued to face issues on the job and in the union that needed further work to resolve them. Gordon Bulmer, who has worked in the public service for almost thirty years and is an activist in the union and in the LGBTQ (lesbian, gay, bisexual, transgender, and queer) community, commented on his involvement in PIPSC:

I joined the federal public service twenty-seven years ago [in 1991]. I actually have a bachelor's degree in fine arts—photography—and that didn't pay the rent, so I started doing temporary work. And after about a year and a half, I got a CR-4 position in DSS [Department of Supply and Services] at the time and was a member of the Public Service Alliance of

Canada. That government department is now PSPC [Public Services and Procurement Canada]. I've seen a number of departmental name changes over the years. I did that for two years, and then applied to a CS-1 competition, and I've been a CS ever since—computer systems. I've worked my entire career for PSPC.

I got involved in the union fifteen years ago. A colleague on my team was involved in the union. She started inviting me to the local events at the branch level, and it turned out that there was a need for CS representation on one of the branch executives, so I put my hand up and said, "Sure. I have no problem helping out." And she indicated to me that there was a need for stewards in the workplace. I had always assumed that they had enough stewards.

When I started in the federal public service twenty-seven years ago, the magic was being able to change the floppy [disc] so that you could spell check in WordPerfect. That was the new thing. They were just getting rid of the giant orange glass ashtrays for smoking in the office. There was an IBM Selectric typewriter at every desk. I know when I reported to work at Parliament Hill to support the senator whose office was on Parliament Hill, I just said hello to the security guard. No badge was required. Nothing. Now you have to go through what's like airport security.

When I started in federal public service twenty-seven years ago, I could have been fired for being gay. Colleagues were still deep and darkly in the closet because, while it was essentially illegal to do it, management was still behaving badly. When I started in the federal public service, I had to put up with an awful lot. I've always been incredibly open about who and what I am. I've had senior management say some very nasty things that today I would be able to file a human rights complaint about. ... So, things have changed considerably, particularly in the LGBT community within the federal public service.

But the history of not being open at work still has an impact, because all management has to do is find a reason to deny you your security clearance and you've lost your job. Everybody has to have a security clearance. Even if it's just the basic enhanced security. With the new security protocols that were introduced by Treasury Board about five years ago, if you fail your security clearance for any reason, they can fire you. And you have no recourse. I don't get as much hate mail anymore from members when I announce that the NCR is participating in the Pride Parade. I only got two this year. Usually I get about fifteen or twenty—seriously.

As PIPSC members, we are all professionals, but we come from very diverse ethnic backgrounds. While you may not see it in terms of our activists or it may not initially be very visible at the board level, you just have to look at our AGMs. A lot of our professional members are immigrants. We have a very large, very diverse ethnic membership, which of course brings all of the regular biases that having a very diverse membership brings.

I have a standard answer for all the members who yell at me for how can I spend union dues on supporting an LGBT event. It's like, as an openly gay activist, "I'm sorry that you feel that way, but you are still invited to the parade. Thank you very much." It's one of those things. I'm not surprised. I wouldn't tell [a young LGBT person] to work in the federal public service, but I wouldn't discourage them because of being LGBT. The chances of senior management being openly homophobic is ... [not very high because] if they are—senior management will slap them hard. I just won a Public Service Award of Excellence for the work I did within my own department, developing a trans-support guide for members in transition. Not every manager manages well. The ones who manage well, we never hear from. The union only hears about the ones who manage badly.[46]

As Bulmer's comments show, there is still some work to be done in PIPSC when it comes to addressing discrimination in the workplace. Yet working for equity and inclusion is a continual effort in all organizations, and progress has been made for LGBTQ people in the public service. PIPSC members continued to do varied work in the 2010s, like Wigmore and Bulmer, and the generational change that is taking place should help bring the Institute into engagement with many new workplace discrimination issues.

Moving Ahead   The decade after 2009 saw PIPSC encounter difficulties and challenges, but overall the decade was an improvement over the ten years that preceded it. Phoenix was an egregious disaster that tested the bounds of management's obligation to fulfil the terms of employment, but PIPSC worked with other public sector unions to get members through it, resolve the problem, and get restitution for affected members. With the defeat of Harper's Conservative government in 2015, PIPSC made major progress on protecting scientific integrity. PIPSC remained a vigorous participant in collective bargaining, dispute-resolution processes, and the National Joint Council. Although it did not expressly endorse any political party in the 2015 election, it welcomed the change in government. The

Institute experienced leadership change that fostered greater diversity. PIPSC members were also part of a national labour market that featured increasingly precarious employment through short-term, contract, and casual work. They lived in a country that suffered from a huge gap between people with assets and good jobs and others who lived on the brink of economic disaster. PIPSC members were fortunate, as they were part of a strong union that would advocate on their behalf and help them engage in advocacy and activism if they chose to. The organization was stronger by 2019 than in 2010, with 60,000 members, and well poised to meet the future.

Conclusion

This analysis of PIPSC's first one hundred years has covered a lot of ground. It was structured chronologically, with each chapter covering specific themes and topics. The thematic approach to each chapter facilitates answering the three main questions posed at the start of this book: What was PIPSC? What did it do over the past century? And how did it shape its members lives, while (at the same time) being altered by them? The answers to these questions are complex. PIPSC evolved over time, with the introduction of formal public sector collective bargaining being an especially important event. Indeed, the history of the Institute is really demarcated by the passage of the Public Service Staff Relations Act in 1967—the year it became a union.

Leadership and Staff   PIPSC's leadership changed markedly during the Institute's first century. Changes in the leadership—and staff—and the scope of their responsibilities, reflected not only changes in the Institute but also wider shifts in Canadian society. Photographs of PIPSC leaders from the 1920s to the 1950s show a succession of stern-faced, male public service professionals, a reflection not only of prevailing social norms regarding portrait photography but also a purposeful attempt to convey an image of professionalism, competence, and respectability. PIPSC members have always been comparatively well-educated and credentialed, and that was especially true in the interwar decades, between PIPSC's founding in 1920 and the Second World War. In those days, the Institute was a non-partisan advocacy group and a small one in terms of organizational complexity. PIPSC ran entirely on volunteer labour. It had no paid staff, and elected executive members served short terms.

In the early 1940s, PIPSC members contributed to Canada's war effort, and, in the 1950s and 1960s, the organization grew as the public service expanded.

Figure C-1: Living Current and Past PIPSC Presidents, 2019: (*from left*) Steve Hindle, Debi Daviau, Bert Crossman, and Gary Corbett.

Canada grew economically and demographically during those decades with a postwar baby boom that touched virtually every facet of society. Women gradually entered leadership roles, and Frances Goodspeed became the first woman elected president. The growing size and complexity of the Institute's work on behalf of members led to the hiring of paid staff, and in the 1960s that staff grew beyond a three-person shop, with people like Executive Director Leslie Barnes playing important roles in policy decisions. Yet the Institute's internal operations were still small and its finances rudimentary, with (as Lorraine Neville described in chapter 1) members able to pay their dues in postage stamps rather than cash.

The 1967 passage of the Public Service Staff Relations Act (PSSRA), which allowed federal public servants to unionize for the first time, was a watershed moment for PIPSC and marked the beginning of its transition from a voluntary professional association to a full-fledged union. PIPSC felt the full impact of the PSSRA in the 1970s. The Institute was now the bargaining agent for multiple employee groups, which added to the complexity and volume of its work. The full-time staff increased, the organization's revenues and membership expanded, and PIPSC's leaders wrestled with how to move forward. Despite its flaws, the 1972 McGill Report commissioned by the union represented a serious effort to chart a future course for the Institute and significantly shaped its organization.

The 1980s ushered in further changes at PIPSC. The Institute's interwar leaders, who had done much to mold PIPSC into a voluntary association of professionals, were now long gone, and the baby boom generation began entering leadership roles, a trend that accelerated through to the first decade of the twenty-first century. Newer activists, such as Jack Donegani, assumed senior leadership positions, and Institute members elected Iris Craig as their second woman president, the first since unionization.

By the 1990s, PIPSC's membership, especially its activist core, were more conversant with collective bargaining and more comfortable with the idea of seeing themselves as union members, not just professionals. New members valued professionalism, but they had no memory of PIPSC as a voluntary association. Members and activists did not hesitate to exercise their right to challenge senior leaders and felt empowered to question the union's current and future direction. Leaders in the last two decades of the twentieth century, like Iris Craig, thus led an organization that differed substantially from the one leaders like Frances Goodspeed had known in the 1950s and 1960s.

By the early 2000s, PIPSC had begun to act even more like other public sector unions, with its leaders both reflecting and driving this change. Michèle Demers, whose term as president was tragically cut short, had a profound impact on the Institute's future direction. She recognized the need for the union to engage politically—though without abandoning the Institute's tradition of non-partisanship—especially with the broader Canadian labour movement. She accelerated PIPSC's move to become a member of the Canadian Labour Congress (CLC). President Steve Hindle, who was an activist from the time that he joined the public service and was elected president several times, could not secure approval of CLC membership while he was in office. His successor, Gary Corbett, brought the Institute into the CLC in 2011, at a time when the government was showing increasing hostility toward public sector workers. As baby boomers gradually retired from the Institute and its leadership, generational change occurred again when Debi Daviau became the first president of PIPSC from "Generation X." As images of the board show, the union's senior leadership was a much more diverse group in 2019 than it had been in 1960.

Between those two dates, PIPSC saw its staff grow considerably. And despite the tensions caused by two staff strikes in 1979 and 1998, turnover among PIPSC's staff was consistently low, and workplace relations were stable and productive. The staff was composed mainly of people who were themselves professionals, with most of them hired from outside of the union's ranks. The paid staff helped provide continuity because they remained in their roles while elected leaders came and went. The union's administration grew into progressively larger office buildings from the 1970s to 2006, when the union purchased its own office building at 250 Tremblay Road, a move that saw it playing the role of landlord to, for a time, the federal government. Both before and after 2006, the Institute's offices tended to be used for administrative and meeting purposes, not as a community space. Unlike many industrial and craft unions, PIPSC does not have a hall that can be used as a recreational space.

Governance   Governance is an imperfect but necessary part of democratic workers' organizations. Although it can be cumbersome and time-consuming, the alternative would be a top-down hierarchy that would make a union look more like a corporation. Throughout its history, PIPSC has taken—and takes—internal governance seriously. Much larger Canadian unions do not hold annual conventions as PIPSC does, nor do their members directly elect their national leaders. So, comparatively speaking, PIPSC affords rank-and-file members considerable democratic rights, with the exception of direct election of stewards. The PIPSC governance process is, though, like those found in other unions, as it tends to engage only the union's activists. Most rank-and-file union members don't spend much time poring over by-laws.

Considering the range of imperatives that it had to address, the Institute's governance process was (and is) ultimately effective. From its earliest days, the PIPSC's Board of Directors and its national executive has presided over governance across the entire union. Yet each bargaining group has had its own by-laws and executive, and so has each region. The union has had to be mindful of concerns raised by members—60,000 of them, at the latest count—who live across all of Canada's provinces and territories, and it has had to be capable of addressing their concerns in both official languages. Not all unions in Canada and few of PIPSC's size have included such geographical and occupational diversity as the Institute, unless they also organized workers in all provinces. A strong governance process was also central to successfully pursuing key policy initiatives. The long fight over pay equity, for example, would not have been nearly so successful without the support of the PIPSC Board of Directors and annual general meeting delegates, nor would the efforts to defend scientific integrity and to reach out to First Nations communities.

Collective Bargaining   The collective bargaining process for unions under federal authority was (and remains) complicated and fraught. From the time they were given the right to engage in collective bargaining, unionized public sector workers have been subjected to considerable vitriol from certain groups, some of which oppose the very idea of unionized public servants. In the 1960s and 1970s, for example, groups like the Canadian Manufacturers' Association routinely complained to governments of all levels about workers, like teachers, having the right to strike.[1] The federal public sector has also faced periods of hostility from government, particularly since the rise of neoliberalism in the 1980s. The neoliberal attack on public sector workers that Stephen Harper's government exemplified had clear intellectual underpinnings. Whereas policy-makers in Canada adopted Keynesian economic practices from the late 1940s to the 1970s, the views of thinkers like Friedrich von Hayek increasingly held sway by the late 1980s and 1990s.[2]

Government hostility has been one challenge faced by PIPSC and other unions in the federal public sector's collective bargaining system. Yet the nature of the public service has blunted some of the worst effects of the neoliberal attack on unionized workers. There were limits to what even hostile public sector employers could do to their unionized employees. A government department cannot easily send public service jobs offshore, particularly because of security and privacy concerns. A government department or agency cannot be closed down on a Friday and reopened the following Monday in another country. So public sector unions did not face anything like the mass wave of deindustrialization, which accelerated in Canada in the middle of the first decade of the twenty-first century, and the accompanying loss of well-paid, unionized jobs to other countries. The fact that PIPSC members are well educated and highly skilled has also meant that a hostile government could not simply lock them out (even if that were permitted under public sector employment laws) and bring in replacements to do their jobs.

The highly skilled nature of PIPSC members' work and their dispersal throughout the country and across government departments has made the collective bargaining process quite complex. PIPSC has organized a wider range of workers than unions of comparable size. From the start, the Institute organized its members by occupational group rather than by department or agency, making it more akin to a traditional craft union (which organized workers by skill) than an industrial union (which organized all workers at a given workplace location, regardless of skill). This distinct organizational structure, derived from the government job classification system, predated the unionization of PIPSC members following passage of the PSSRA in 1967. A direct line exists between PIPSC's origins as a voluntary association of public service professionals and its existence as a de facto coalition of many bargaining groups of professionals in one big union.

PIPSC's structure has insulated members from some of the problems faced by other public service unions. Most importantly, being organized by professional occupation has meant that PIPSC members could usually maintain their affiliation with their employee groups and their union even as government reorganizations swirled around them. Far from being monolithic, the federal government as an employer includes multiple ministries and agencies, meaning multiple workplaces. The number and composition of ministries had changed often during the hundred years since PIPSC's founding in 1920. Donald Savoie, who has studied the growth of federal ministries and agencies, notes that Prime Minister William Lyon Mackenzie King's government had nineteen ministries in the 1940s, Brian Mulroney's oversaw forty in the 1980s, and Jean Chrétien had twenty-seven (plus eight secretaries of state) in the 1990s. (During Justin Trudeau's first term as prime minister, his government was composed of thirty-four ministries.)[3] Particularly when a new government comes into office, governments frequently reorganize and merge existing ministries and create new agencies, and public employees often find themselves shifted around into other workplaces. Unlike members of unions that are organized by work location, such as PSAC, and who might find themselves shifted into new bargaining units by a reorganization, PIPSC members tend to remain in the same bargaining unit.

Over time, the Institute developed considerable bargaining expertise, negotiating collective agreements that generally brought gains over previous rounds. Salary improvements, for example, commonly met or exceeded the cost of living, though provincial agreements were sometimes an exception to that pattern. Unlike in private sector bargaining, in which unions often try to insert a new negotiating objective into a collective agreement through a letter of understanding signed with an employer, PIPSC more commonly negotiated new objectives directly into new clauses of its agreements, which made them more enduring. (Letters of understanding remain in force for an agreement's duration only and must be renewed every time negotiations take place.) The collective bargaining process did not always lead to negotiated settlements, and PIPSC had to resort to dispute-resolution processes, including (rarely) strike action by some groups.

Although throughout much of its history PIPSC has focused more on negotiating economic gains for its members than on engaging in broader "social unionism," it would be wrong to categorize PIPSC as being driven solely by a "business unionism" approach. People who study and work with unions— academics, attorneys, union staff members—have long distinguished between these two strains of unionism. Business unionism involves focusing solely on achieving economic gains through collective bargaining, with membership as a form of insurance against job loss and other risks, like punitive management. In contrast, social unionism looks beyond bread-and-butter bargaining issues, envisioning a larger role for unions in bettering not only their members lives but also society. As Stephanie Ross notes, most union activists prefer not to be associated with the term "business unionism." On one hand, PIPSC has definitely focused intensely on economic gains for its members, which is a core mission for any union, relying on its professional, paid staff to handle collective bargaining matters. On the other hand, it has waged long fights over issues such as pay equity and scientific integrity that are well beyond the scope of basic economics and are instead issues of social justice and public well-being. While pursuing gains through collective bargaining, then, the union has, especially since the 1990s, worked to advance social justice issues as part of the larger union movement in Canada.[4]

Since PIPSC members were first unionized in the late 1960s, two basic facts have dominated collective bargaining with the federal government. First, unlike private sector employers, the government has the power to set and then unilaterally alter the legal framework in which bargaining occurs. PIPSC members felt the reality of the government's unilateral power, for example, when it imposed wage controls in the 1970s. More generally, Canadian laws governing public sector bargaining impose limits on its scope, meaning some terms of employment cannot be included in agreements. For instance, the PSSRA explicitly excluded pensions from the scope of collective bargaining. So, though PIPSC has shown consistent interest in the public service pension plan, its collective agreements don't include pension provisions. Seniority rules, to cite another example of an issue that features prominently in private sector collective agreements, were set by the Public Service Employment Act, which determined the order in which employees would be laid off (by reverse order of merit). Layoff and recall procedures were further addressed by a Workforce Adjustment Directive (WFAD) agreed upon by representatives of the government and other federal public sector unions under the auspices of the National Joint Council.

Such directives highlight the second fact that underlies PIPSC's negotiations with the government. That is, some aspects of bargaining with federal employer groups take place outside of the regular collective bargaining process—namely, through the National Joint Council (NJC). The NJC, created in 1944, was derived from the Whitley Council model of bargaining (discussed in chapter 1), which was first introduced in Britain in the 1920s and then also in Canada. The Whitley model, a form of sectoral bargaining, is understudied in Canada compared to the better-known Wagner model that came to dominate private sector collective bargaining beginning in the 1930s. The original idea behind the Whitley Committee Plan, according to Daphne Taras, was that sectoral bargaining would involve unions in all industries. In Canada, the Whitley model deviated from this ideal. Used initially as a model of union substitution in the public sector, it now only exists within the National Joint Council.[5]

Overall, the bargaining of specific issues on a public-service-wide basis has been beneficial to PIPSC and other unions, with only a limited downside. The main benefit of the Whitley-based system is that it provides sectoral bargaining of an extent only dreamed of by private sector unions, which have often pursued a strategy of pattern bargaining, or trying to get employers in a given industry to adhere to common employment terms. Autoworkers' unions, for example, were able to achieve pattern bargaining with Detroit automakers from the 1950s to the 1990s. Being able to negotiate important terms of employment, such as the layoff provisions covered by the WFAD, in cooperation with the other federal unions through the NJC has provided a major benefit for PIPSC and the other unions that belong to the council.

Even before the PSSRA legalized public sector unionization, the NJC—the Whitley-based model used in Canadian federal public sector labour relations—gave workers access to limited collective bargaining rights and permitted the establishment of sector-wide negotiations on some aspects of the terms of employment that were common to all federal employee groups. The absence of a Whitley-based council like the NJC would have enabled the government to avoid pattern bargaining across the federal public sector and, before the legalization of public sector collective bargaining, to avoid any kind of bargaining with its workers at all. The NJC made possible the successful negotiation—albeit outside of the regular collective bargaining process—of across-the-board wage increases and important agreements on issues such as pay equity and scientific integrity. These would have been more difficult to achieve without the NJC.

A primary criticism of the Whitley model is that it is the domain of experts and rank-and-file union members and activists cannot easily navigate it. The Wagner-based system used across Canada (especially in the private sector) is complex, but the Whitley-based system is a labyrinth in comparison, and the federal public service is more Whitley than Wagner. Some of the member complaints described in this book are attributable to members' frustration with and alienation from collective bargaining and dispute-resolution processes. Once problems that arise in the workplace move into the dispute-resolution system, they are taken out of the hands of the people who were initially involved. In fact, Whitley-style committees like the NJC were created originally to do just that—and thus to blunt worker militancy by taking disagreements out of the hands of rank-and-file members and channeling them into defined dispute-resolution processes. Adding to the distancing of members from these processes in PIPSC is the fact that the Institute's staff is more centrally involved in dispute resolution than is the case in many other unions, especially in the private sector where stewards, for example, play a much greater role. On balance, however, the Whitley council model and the bargaining practices used by PIPSC provided members with more benefits than detriments.

Advocacy, Media, and Politics

The roles that PIPSC adopted as a public advocate, its media presence, and its political activism changed markedly during the Institute's first century. Although the public radio talks of the Institute's early years seem genteel from a twenty-first century vantage point, a common thread runs through the history of the Institute's public advocacy. From its earliest days, PIPSC members viewed themselves as professionals, and they wanted to educate Canadians about weighty issues, especially scientific ones. They grew accustomed to being heard by the government and the public and felt both respected their views. This tradition of engaging with the public on issues of importance and of scientific concern helps explain why the union objected so strenuously to the Harper government's attempt to muzzle public sector researchers. PIPSC members, for whom non-partisanship was a source of professional pride, also reacted vociferously because they believed (rightly) that the suppression of scientific evidence was an effort to distort the truth and otherwise align public policy-making with an ideological agenda.

The Institute's media presence became more sophisticated as decades passed, partly in response to the emergence of new media forms. Television and radio gradually displaced print media before themselves being challenged by Internet-based content and social media. PIPSC's portrayal in different forms of media revealed a basic fact about the union: it was, simultaneously, a national union (with members across Canada) and a local union (with half its members in Ottawa). PIPSC appeared more regularly in *The Hill Times* and *Ottawa Citizen* than the *Globe and Mail* or *Toronto Star*. The relative lack of regular national coverage stemmed from the fact that media outlets, drawn to controversy, found little of interest in a union that successfully represented its members and preferred cooperation over confrontation in its labour relations. Images of striking union members battling replacement workers on a picket line make for more marketable television viewing than news that a public sector union based in Ottawa had successfully bargained a new collective agreement without needing to resort to a strike.

In recent decades, PIPSC has used the media to criticize the flawed Phoenix payroll system and to advocate for important social justice issues, such as pay equity. A leader in the fight for pay equity, PIPSC continues the struggle for equal pay for work of equal value. Officially, PIPSC has long drawn a careful distinction between political engagement and partisan political activity. In the 1970s (as chapter 2 noted), Val Scott drew the ire of activists for attending a New Democratic Party meeting. The union has never formally endorsed any political party. It has always sought good relations with whatever party was in government and encouraged individual members to engage in electoral politics, regardless of the parties that they supported. Adopting a non-partisan stance meant that PIPSC did not, by endorsing a winning party, have a guaranteed friend in Parliament but also did not, when that party fell out of power, face an avowed enemy in its rival. That changed in 2006 when the Conservative Party under Stephen Harper returned to power. That government's unprecedented attacks on the integrity of the public service eventually led PIPSC to adopt an any-party-but-the-Conservatives stance in the 2015 election. PIPSC may still maintain an officially non-partisan stance, but it does so while keeping a close eye on political threats.

Belonging to PIPSC

PIPSC members are like those in any union in the sense that they pay dues, are represented in the workplace through an exclusive bargaining agent, and are able to use collective bargaining and formal dispute-resolution processes to achieve gains in their working conditions. Those improvements, in turn, have a salutary effect on members' lives outside the federal public service. The change that PIPSC experienced in 1967—when it went from being an association to a union—still reverberates five decades later. Some PIPSC members still seem hesitant to call PIPSC a union. Of the dozens of people interviewed for this book, only one—Gordon Bulmer—routinely used the term *union* to describe PIPSC. Members, activists, and leaders still wrestle with the organization's identity. As Larry Savage and Michelle Webber have noted, discussions about professionalism have an impact on unionization patterns and the methods adopted by workers organizations.[6]

What it means to be a PIPSC member has changed notably over the past century. While in 1920 membership was restricted to professional employees with degrees, the 2020 membership requirements are much broader:

> To be eligible for membership, a person is required to occupy a posi-
> tion in a Canadian public service or equivalent Canadian employment,
> where such employment is in a professional capacity or in the direction
> or administration of professional work, and to satisfy one (1) of the follow-
> ing qualifications:
> a) is engaged in the application of specialized knowledge ordinarily
>   acquired by a course of instruction and study resulting in gradua-
>   tion from a university or similar institution;
> b) membership in the corporate body of a profession;
> c) qualifications equivalent to the above; or
> d) occupy any position which falls within a bargaining unit defined
>   by the applicable legislation when the Board [of Directors] is satis-
>   fied that such bargaining unit is professional in character.[7]

Over its history, the number of bargaining groups PIPSC represented grew, with some groups like the Auditors Group defecting from PSAC to PIPSC. In a few notable cases, member groups have left the Institute. Some members, like those in the Law Group, decided they wanted to be part of a union that exclusively represented their profession, even though (as the foregoing analysis shows) the lawyers enjoyed decent salary gains under PIPSC. Other groups left over policy differences. For example, the Economists, Sociology, and Statistics Group (ES) left in 1975 because of a dispute over membership fee increases, among other issues.[8]

In general, the members interviewed for this book expressed positive feelings about their membership in PIPSC and their careers in the civil service. A considerable literature exists on the degradation of work and workers' feelings of alienation; the modern workplace can be mind-numbing, soul-destroying. Yet, while the interviews conducted for this book have certain limitations in the sense that the interviewees were activists and not simply rank-and-file PIPSC members, none of the interviewees seemed to view union activism as an escape from workplace drudgery. None of them cast aspersions on the quality of the services that they provided as public employees or raged against management. Some certainly expressed concerns about issues like the outsourcing of work and attacks on professionalism, but nobody said the Government of Canada was a terrible place to work.[9]

PIPSC and Canada

In fact, the people interviewed for this book expressed a sense of mission about their work, about what they had done and would continue to do for Canadians. They felt that they had helped move the country forward. That sentiment also permeated the Institute's archival materials, held by PIPSC and Library and Archives Canada. All members who sat and talked about their experience in PIPSC felt that the union had made a difference in their working lives and that it had a positive impact on Canadian society. Thomas Landry, a member since 1989 who worked in the Department of Fisheries and Oceans, explained:

> I think being a public servant is more of a vocation than a career. To me, it's something that is beyond just deciding to have a career in science. So, PIPSC definitely gives you the confidence and the ability to stay focused on what you want to do in order to serve Canadians. I think it would be very difficult for us as public servants to keep ourselves reminded of that mission if it wasn't for a union like PIPSC. They definitely make sure that you recognize the value of your work in terms of serving the public.[10]

Glenn Maxwell, a member since 2000 and a civilian employee in the Department of National Defence, commented positively on PIPSC's decision to engage more in the wider labour movement and in shaping public policy:

> So how it's changed—as far as the Institute goes, things move a lot faster. We're now lobbying governments—which we never did before—which I think is fantastic. And I think we're effecting change at the highest levels of governments. We joined the CLC—which gives us the opportunity to actually lever[age] the support of 3.3 million other Canadian labour people—and I think that again is another fantastic opportunity.[11]

Susan O'Donnell, a member since 2004 and a senior research officer at the National Research Council, felt that PIPSC still had more work to do when it came to advancing women's issues, though she also stressed the positive work PIPSC has done in that direction:

> PIPSC—certainly at the national level—will agree that we have a long way to go in terms of advancing women, and I think the [union's] Women in Science initiative is one really bright light that may serve as an example for how other initiatives at PIPSC can happen. There's a lot of women in leadership roles in the organization—which is fantastic—because, you know, they're doing really great things in terms of role modelling and, I think, helping a lot of women see how they can move forward.[12]

Terry Peters had been a PIPSC member since 1971 and worked for the Canadian Food Inspection Agency. He took pride in the work he did as a public servant to ensure the safety and quality of the Canadian food supply. He noted, "the safety and quality of foods is the section that I worked in. We worked hard to minimize the outcome of food-borne illness [and] outbreaks, [to ensure] the quality of foods, and [prevent] the adulteration of foods ... [including] fraud [in] the selling of foods—what its label says is one thing, but it's actually not that." More generally, he spoke of the vital role that public servants play in Canadian society. They act as a vital link between the government and the public, an "intermediary" and a means of two-way communication.[13]

Some members stressed the opportunities available in the public service. Bonnie Pratt, a member since 1996, worked in the Canada Revenue Agency and felt that working in the public service afforded some specific benefits that were not often available in the private sector:

> When I did actually some recruiting—and this was at a time when the oil patch was very strong in Calgary—and we had to be very persuasive to get people to look at us as a future employer. And one of the things I was able to tell people with good faith, and all honesty, is there were numerous areas you could work in, so you weren't confined to your job as accounts payable clerk for the next fifteen years. You may not have gotten paid as well, but there were certain benefits and there were certain protections, and you had a contract, and job security was not as volatile as it was in the oil patch—those were certainly some benefits I could speak to.[14]

Terry Sing, who joined in 1992, worked at Public Service and Procurement Canada and commented on misconceptions about the public service:

> When you look at the majority of the people in the public service—they are hardworking, dedicated, professional people, trying to do a really good job. And not just the professionals [but also] the support people and all the people in the government take pride in their work, generally speaking. They want to be recognized for doing valuable work. Nobody wants to go to work saying, "Oh, this job isn't needed, and I'm not really valuable." A lot of the people in the public service get up, looking forward to going to work and doing a really professional active job—making a contribution, not only to their organization, but feeling that, overall, they're able to contribute to Canada. And you know it sounds trite—but it's actually true. A lot of my colleagues—that I know—and the people that I've worked with over thirty-five, forty years are really dedicated to doing a good job.[15]

Barrie Wickware, a member since 1989 who worked at the CRA, shared similar sentiments:

> Personally, I was very proud to be in the public service. I think we did do a very useful job—finding people who weren't paying their taxes. I understand a lot of people think that we just sit there and do nothing all day long. It's just not true. We certainly contribute to the betterment of Canada.[16]

Steve Hindle, who saw PIPSC from a range of elected positions, concluded:

> I would certainly want the Canadian public to know that our members are proud of the work that they do, and that they consider the work that they do is on behalf of Canadians—much more than on behalf of the Government of Canada. Even though the legal relationship would say they work for the government, our members think they work for Canadians and that they add value, and they want to be able to talk to Canadians about the work that they do.[17]

All of these people expressed a sense of pride in their public service roles and PIPSC membership. The idea that public service workers are not engaged in their jobs is an entirely unfair fiction devised for partisan political purposes by organized labour's foes.

Founded as an association of professional workers who wanted to further their mutual interests, the Professional Institute of the Public Service of Canada has experienced significant change during the hundred years since its founding in 1920. Yet it has also showed considerable continuity in its values and its mission. Whether as the professional association it was for its first five decades or as the union it became with the passage of the Public Service Staff Relations Act, PIPSC has always been concerned with protecting and promoting the interests of its members who, though concentrated in Ottawa, can be found across Canada. (Indeed, in the 1970s, PIPSC even had an office in London, England, to represent members employed as diplomats.) As Canada has changed, PIPSC members have shown their dedication to public service by doing the work that keeps Canada's government and the vital services it provides going. Unknown to and unrecognized by many, if not most, Canadians, PIPSC members have—for the past century—played significant roles in their lives. The food Canadians ate was safe because of the work of PIPSC members. The planes on which they flew travelled without incident due to the contribution of people in PIPSC. Pension cheques and tax returns were processed, the Canadian Armed Forces deployed, museums opened and closed, and First Nations communities received health care because of the work of unionized professional employees. Even Parliament itself functioned with the skillful help of the Institute's members. PIPSC has not always been a perfect union—such an entity only exists in theory or, at least, has yet to be organized—but its members absolutely helped lead Canada's progress between 1920 and 2020, the Institute's first hundred years.

List of PIPSC Presidents

Year	Name	Legacy Group
1920	Dr. C. Gordon Hewitt	Entomological Society
1920	Dr. Merton Yarwood Williams	Geologists
1921	K. M. Cameron	Public Works Engineers
1922	Dr. James Malcolm Swaine	Entomologists
1923	George A. Mountain	Railway and Highway Engineers
1924	Frederic Hatheway Peters	Survey Engineering
1925	Robert M. Motherwell	Astronomers
1926–27	Fred Cook	Editors
1928–29	D. Roy Cameron	Forestry and Forest Products
1930–31	Leonard S. McLaine	Entomologists
1932	Dr. Edgar Spinney Archibald	Agriculturalists
1933	John McLeish	Chemical, Mining and Metallurgical Engineers
1934–35	Dr. Alne Edward Cameron	Veterinarians
1936	Thomas Andrew McElhanney	Forestry and Forest Products Engineering
1937–38	J. Clément Beauchamp	Technical Translators
1939	R. D. Whitmore	Chemists
1940	Sedley Anthony Cudmore	Statisticians, Economists, and Actuaries
1941	W. N. Keenan	Entomologists
1942	James G. Wright	Forestry and Forest Products Engineering
1943–45	N. T. Allan	Designers, Draughtsmen and Cartographers
1945–46	Robert C. Berry	Patent Examiners
1946–47	Dr. Cecil R. Twinn	Entomologists

1947–48	Col. Albert R. Whittier	Canal Engineers
1948–49	William H. van Allen	Editors and Public Relations
1949–50	G. E. Blake Sinclair	General
1951–52	Harold McLeod	Statisticians, Economists, and Actuaries
1952–54	Dr. Harold Archie Senn	Biologists and Anthropologists
1954–55	James H. Lowther	Statisticians, Economists, and Actuaries
1955–56	F. G. Ardouin	Chartered Accountants
1956–58	R. J. Loosmore	Statisticians, Economists, and Actuaries
1958–59	Dr. C. Lloyd Francis	Statisticians, Economists, and Actuaries
1959–60	Z. W. Sametz	Statisticians, Economists, and Actuaries
1960–61	Wilfred M. Marshall	Electrical and Electric Engineering
1961–62	Frances E. Goodspeed	Chemists
1962–63	Leslie W. C. S. Barnes	Defence Inspection Services
1963–64	C. F. Gilhooly	Professional Accountants
1964–65	Dr. Blake B. Coldwell	Chemists
1965–66	Alfred C. Kilbank	Statisticians, Economists, and Actuaries
1966–67	James F. Mazerall	Topographical Engineers
1968–69	Eric F. V. Robinson	National Research Council
1970–73	Ken J. Harwood	Economics, Sociology and Statistics
1973	Donald R. Buchanan	Economics, Sociology and Statistics
1974–75	Ernie S. Eaton	Economics, Sociology and Statistics
1975–79	Chesley L. Lockhart	Scientific Researchers
1980–85	Jack E. Donegani	Meteorologists
1986–93	Iris L. Craig	Biologists
1994–95	Bert Crossman	Biologists
1996–2004	Steve Hindle	Computer Systems
2005–09	Michèle Demers	Social Work

| 2009–13 | Gary Corbett | Engineering |
| 2014– | Debi Daviau | Computer Systems |

Professional Institute Medal Winners

BRONZE	Year
Dr. John Hubert Craigie	1937
Harold Loomis Seamans	1938
Herbert Marshall	1939
Dr. Frederick S. Burke	1941
John Patterson	1942
Monson Fraser Goudge	1942
Dr. Lloyd Montgomery Pidgeon	1943
S/Lt. A. Hardisty Sellers	1943
Dr. Walter A. Bell	1944
William Masson	1944
Ernest C. Desormeaux	1945
Cecil Herman Ney	1945
Professional & Technical Workers, Radio Branch, NRC	1946
Walter A. Rush	1946
Dr. Charles Camsell (Special)	1946

GOLD	
Otto Maass	1947
James H. Lowther	1947
E. W. Griffith	1948
Dr. Edward Wm. Richard Steacie	1949
Dr. Frederick W. Jackson	1950
Harold E. Seely	1951
Andrew Thomson	1952
Dr. C. H. Goulden	1953
Dr. Wilfred Parsons Warner	1954
Dr. Karl A. Clark	1955
Dr. Omond McKillop Solandt	1956

H. R. Balls	1956
Dr. Hugh Lyle Aubrey Tarr	1957
Major C. Austin Bell	1957
Dr. Carlyle Smith Beals	1958
Dr. Nathan Keyfitz	1958
Dr. Leo Marion	1959
Howard Hillen Kerr	1959
Dr. Har Gobind Khorana	1960
Elmer A. Driedger, Q. C.	1960
Dr. Donald Charles Rose	1961
A. H. Richardson	1961
Dr. Thorvaldur Johnson	1962
Dr. Clarence A. Morrell	1962
Dr. David Keith Chalmers MacDonald	1963
Dr. William Elgin Van Steenburgh	1963
Defence Research Board responsible for the Alouette Satellite Project	1964
Dr. Joseph W. Willard	1964
Mr. Alison DeForest Pickett	1965
Mr. L. Dana Wilgress	1965
James Merritt Harrison	1966
Honourable Andrew G. L. McNaughton (Special)	1966
Dr. Frederick Thomas Rosser	1967
Dr. Gerhard Herzberg	1969
Mr. C. W. Martin	1969
Defence Research Board Laser Team, Valcartier	1971
Robert Arthur Douglas Ford	1971
Alfred W. H. Needler	1973
Jack W. Grainge	1975
Albert Wesley Johnson	1975
Dr. Victor E. F. Solman	1977
Clarence Powell	1977
Mr. D. J. McLaren	1979
Ms. J. R. Podoluk	1979
Norbert L. Kusters	1981
Dr. William G. Schneider	1981
Hans Grieger	1981
Winnipeg Bread Wheat Research Team	1983

Polly Hill	1983
Kenneth James Jenkins and Michael Hidiroglou	1985
Ray Thorsteinsson, Robert Christie, and Hans Trettin	1987
Vera Roberts	1987
R. K. Downey, S. H. Pawlowski, A. J. Klassen, G. A. Petrie, D. I. McGregor, B. M. Craig, and C. Youngs	1989
E. Fred Roots	1989
Alan R. Longhurst	1991
Walter Slipchenko	1991
Leroy Stone	1992
Ling Suen	1994
Leo Margolis	1995
Peter V. Cooney	1998
Dr. James F. Whitfield	1998
Dr. Harold J. Jennings	1999
David Allan Vardy	2000
Dr. Ewen C. D. Todd	2001
Aly M. Shady	2002
Dr. J. R. Jocelyn Paré	2003
Dr. Kutty Karthy	2004
Dr. Derek C. G. Muir	2005
Dr. James E. Clark	2006
Dwight Williamson	2007
Dan Beavon	2008
Dr. Keith U. Ingold	2009
Richard C. Bennett	2010
Dr. Ronald DePauw	2011
Dr. Bernard C. K. Choi	2012
Dr. John A. Percival	2017
Dr. Xiaolan L. Wang	2019

Groups Within the Institute, 1970

Actuarial Science
Agriculture
Aircraft Operations
Architecture and Town Planning
Biological Sciences
Chemistry
Commerce
Computer Systems Administration
Defence Research Board—Defence Scientific Service Officers (DSSO)
    —Scientific and Professional Category other than DSSO
Dentistry
Economics, Sociology, and Statistics
Engineering and Land Survey
Forestry
Historical Research
Home Economics
Law
Library Science
Marine
Mathematics
Medicine
Meteorology
National Film Board—Administrative and Foreign Service
National Research Council—Communications Officers
    —Information Services
    —Library Science
    —Translation
    —Research and Research Council Officers
Nursing

Occupational and Physical Therapy
Organization and Methods [never certified]
Pharmacy
Physical Sciences
Psychology
Scientific Regulation
Scientific Research
Social Work
Translation
University Teaching
Veterinary Science

Groups Within the Institute, 2019

FEDERAL PUBLIC SECTOR LABOUR RELATIONS ACT (PSLRA)

Employer: Treasury Board

AV	Audit, Commerce and Purchasing
CS	Computer Systems
NR	Engineering, Architecture and Land Survey
RE	Research
SH	Health Services
SP	Applied Science and Patent Examination

Employer: Canada Revenue Agency (CRA)

AFS	Audit, Financial and Scientific

Employer: Canadian Food Inspection Agency (CFIA)

CFIA-IN	Informatics
CFIA-S&A	Scientific and Analytical
CFIA-VM	Veterinary Medicine

Employer: Canadian Nuclear Safety Commission (CNSC)

NUREG	Nuclear Regulatory Group

Employer: National Energy Board (NEB)

NEB	National Energy Board

Employer: National Film Board (NFB)

NFB	National Film Board Professional Group

Employer: National Research Council (NRC)

NRC-IS	Information Services
NRC-LS	Library Science
NCR-RO/RCO	Research Officers and Research Council Officers
NCR-TR	Translation

Employer: Office of the Superintendent of Financial Institutions (OSFI)

OSFI	Professional Employees

PARLIAMENTARY EMPLOYMENT AND STAFF RELATIONS ACT (PESRA)

Employer: House of Commons
  HOC   Procedural Clerks, Analysis and Reference
Employer: Senate
  SEN   Legislative Clerks

CANADA LABOUR CODE

Employer: Canadian Nuclear Laboratories (CNL)
  CRPEG   Chalk River Professional Employees
  WPEG   Whiteshell Professional Employees
  WTEG   Whiteshell Technical Employees
Employer: Canadian Commercial Corporation (CCC)
  CCC   All Employees
Employer: Canadian Museum of History (CMH)
  CMH   Scientific Researchers
Employer: Canadian Museum of Nature (CMN)
  CMN   Research Scientists, Collections Managers and/or
                 Collections Specialists
Employer: Canadian Tourism Commission
  CTC   All Employees
Employer: National Gallery of Canada (NGC)
  NGC   All Curators
Employer: NAV CANADA
  NAVCAN   Professional Employees
Employer: B.C. First Nations Health Authority (BCFNHA)
  BCFNHA   B.C. First Nations Health Authority
Employer: Yukon Hospital Corporation (YHC)
  YHC   Yukon Hospital Corporation

PUBLIC SERVICE LABOUR RELATIONS ACT OF NEW BRUNSWICK

Employer: New Brunswick Board of Management
  NB-AG   Agriculture
  NB-EN   Engineering, Land Surveying and Architecture
  NB-VS   Veterinary Science

NB-CC   Crown Counsel

NB-CP   Crown Prosecutors

Employer: New Brunswick Legal Aid Services Commission

NB-LA   Legal Aid Lawyers

LABOUR RELATIONS ACT OF MANITOBA

Employer: Civil Service Commission

MAGE   Manitoba Association of Government Engineers

Employer: Deer Lodge Centre (DLC)

DLC-MD   Medicine

DLC-NU   Nursing

ONTARIO LABOUR RELATIONS ACT

Employer: Regional Cancer Centres Employers Association

MP   Medical Physicists

Employer: Hamilton Health Sciences

JCC-RT   Juravinski Cancer Centre—Radiation Therapists

Employer: Sunnybrook Health Sciences Centre

SUN-MET   Sunnybrook—Mechanical and Electronic Technologists

SUN-RT   Sunnybrook—Radiation Therapists

Employer: Thunder Bay Regional Health Sciences Centre

TBH-RT   Thunder Bay—Radiation Therapists

Employer: Windsor Regional Hospital

WRH-RT   Windsor—Radiation Therapists

Employer: University of Ottawa

UOITP   University of Ottawa Information Technology
Professionals

List of Interviews

Danielle Auclair, former PIPSC negotiator and staff union (PISA) president
Lucienne Bahuaud (AFS Group), chair of the 100th Anniversary Committee
Brian Beaven (RE-HR), former RE Group executive member
Madeleine Blais (NAVCAN), former NAVCAN executive member and
    branch president
Robert Bowie-Reed (CS), life member and former vice president
Kathryn Brookfield (staff), former head of PIPSC's Research Section
Gordon Bulmer (CS), life member, former board member, and chair of the
    national capital region (NCR) executive
Don Burns (NR-EN), life member and former vice president
Dan Butler (staff), former head of negotiations, general secretary of the
    National Joint Committee, and Public Service Staff Relations Board
    (PSSRB) member
Gary Corbett (NR-EN), life member, current vice president and former
    president
Debi Daviau (CS), current president (as of 2020)
Randy Dhar (NR-AR), former board member
Norma Domey (SP-PC), current vice president
Stephen Douglas (CS), former president of the CS Group
Debra Dunville (HoC), former board member
Michael Forbes (SP-CH), former president of the
    Hamilton-Burlington Branch
Bill Giggie (CPC-CS), former board member
Eddie Gillis (staff), chief operating officer and executive secretary
Neil Harden (MAGE), former board member and Prairie/NWT region
    staff member
Steve Hindle (CS), current vice president and former president, and Bob
    McIntosh (staff), former head of negotiations and senior policy advisor
    to the president

Waheed Khan (SP-PC), current board member

Pat Kinnear (CS), life member and former board member

Thomas Landry (SP-BI), chair, Professional Recognition and
    Qualifications Committee

Bob Luce (staff), former negotiator, and Phil Jolie (AFS-AU), first chair of
    the Auditing Group

Rob MacDonald (SP-PC), current board member

Marion MacEachern (NB-AG), life member and former board member

Matthew MacLeod (RE-DS), current research group president

Glenn Maxwell (CS), former board member

Lyne Morin (SH-OP), former board member and lead, Task Force on Pay
    Equity, 1990s

Ed Napke (MD), former vice president

Lorraine Neville (staff), former executive secretary

Susan O'Donnell (NCR-RO/RCO), former president of the
    NRC-RO/RCO Group

Karen Parr (AV-PG), former PG group executive and PIPSC Service
    Award laureate

Nicholas Pernal (staff), current negotiator and former president of Unifor
    Local 3011

Terry Peters (CFIA-S&A), life member and former vice president,
    CFIA-S&A Group

Bonnie Pratt (AFS), former board member

Richard Rice (CS), former AFS group executive member

Nita Saville (AV-CO), life member and former vice president

Glen Schjerning (NR-EN), NR group president and former NCR chief steward

Greg Scriver (CS), former board member

Terry Sing (AV-CO), life member and president, Retired Members Guild

Blair Stannard (CS), life member and former vice president

Ginette Tardif (SH-NU), former president of the Health Services (SH) Group

Sharon Trasatti (BCFNHA), president, B.C. First Nations Health Authority

Ruth Walden (SH-NU EMA), lead, PIPSC Gender Equality Case Victory, 2012

Max Way (staff), president, Professional Institute Regional Employee
    Council

Barrie Wickware (AFS), former Prairie/NWT executive and president,
    Edmonton Branch

Andrew Wigmore (AV-CO), PIPSC Young Professionals

Note on Sources

The primary sources in this book are held by the Professional Institute of the Public Service of Canada (PIPSC). The union's records are voluminous and organized by box number, though not always in a consistent manner. There are no finding aids. The records contain organizational files, but they are not arranged using methods employed in formal archives. Terms like PIPSC Storage Room, PIPSC Central Records, PIPSC Storage Cage, and PIPSC Photo Database were devised to describe how the union's records are currently stored. The interviews conducted for this study were scheduled by PIPSC, and the union stores the audiovisual recordings of them. The formal archival materials on PIPSC that are referenced in the book are found at Library and Archives Canada, Professional Institute of the Public Service of Canada Fonds, MG28-I36. The author has also made use of Statistics Canada census data and cited several decisions issued by the Public Service Staff Relations Board and its successor.

Endnotes

Introduction

1. Eugene Forsey, *Trade Unions in Canada, 1812–1902* (Toronto: University of Toronto Press, 1982); Brian Palmer and Greg Kealey, *Dreaming of What Might Be: The Knights of Labour in Ontario, 1880–1900* (Cambridge: Cambridge University Press, 1982); Sam Gindin, *The Canadian Auto Workers: The Birth and Transformation of a Union* (Toronto: James Lorimer, 1995); David Sobel and Susan Meurer, *Working at Inglis: The Life and Death of a Canadian Factory* (Toronto: James Lorimer, 1994); Jamie Swift, *Walking the Union Walk: Stories from the CEP's First Ten Years* (Toronto: Between the Lines, 2003); Wayne Roberts, *Cracking the Canadian Formula: The Making of the Energy and Chemical Workers Union* (Toronto: Between the Lines, 1990); Eileen Sufrin, *The Eaton Drive: The Campaign to Organize Canada's Largest Department Store, 1948–1952* (Toronto: Fitzhenry and Whiteside, 1982); Julia Maureen Smith, "Union Organizing in The Canadian Banking Industry, 1940–1980" (PhD diss., Trent University, 2016).

2. See, for example, Craig Heron, *Lunch-Bucket Lives: Remaking the Workers' City* (Toronto: Between the Lines, 2015).

3. Stephanie Ross, "The Making of CUPE: Structure, Democracy, and Class Formation" (PhD diss., York University, 2005). On the public sector generally, see Stephanie Ross and Larry Savage, eds., *Public Sector Unions in the Age of Austerity* (Halifax: Fernwood, 2013).

4. Jack Nevin, AFGE-*Federal Union: The Story of the American Federation of Government Employees* (Washington: AFGE, 1976); Marjorie Murphy, *Blackboard Unions: The AFT and the NEA, 1900–1980* (Ithaca: Cornell University Press, 1990); Francis Ryan, AFSCME's *Philadelphia Story: Municipal Workers and Urban Power in the Twentieth Century* (Philadelphia: Temple University Press, 2011).

5. John Swettenham and David Kealy, *Serving the State: A History of the Professional Institute of the Public Service of Canada, 1920–1970* (Ottawa: Professional Institute of the Public Service of Canada, 1970).

Chapter 1: Starting as Professionals, 1920-69

1. Robert MacGregor Dawson, *The Civil Service of Canada* (Oxford: Oxford University Press, 1929), 8

2. Dawson, 19, 23.

3. Dawson, 56, 186.

4. J. E Hodgetts, *The Canadian Public Service: A Physiology of Government, 1867–1970* (Toronto: University of Toronto Press, 1973), 33, 109, 160, 242.

5. Craig Heron, ed., *The Workers' Revolt in Canada, 1917–1925* (Toronto: University of Toronto Press, 1998). See Maggie Craig, *When the Clyde Ran Red: A Social History of Red Clydeside* (Edinburgh: Birlinn, 2018) for a full account of the immediate post-World War I years in Glasgow.

6. Michael Bliss, *Northern Enterprise: Five Centuries of Canadian Business* (Toronto: McClelland and Stewart, 1987), 345, 373–74.

7. Eric Tucker and Jude Fudge, *Labour Before the Law: The Regulation of Workers' Collective Action in Canada, 1900–1948* (Oxford: Oxford University Press, 2001), 108–13.

8. Tucker and Fudge, 123.

9. Jonathan Rees, *Representation and Rebellion: The Rockefeller Plan at the Colorado Fuel and Iron Company, 1914–1942* (Boulder: University Press of Colorado, 2010); William Lyon Mackenzie King, *Industry and Humanity: A Study in the Principles Underlying Industrial Reconstruction* (New York: Houghton-Mifflin, 1918).

10. *The Civil Service of Canada, A Special Issue of the Civilian* (Ottawa: Government of Canada, 1914), iii, 191; "Federal Government Employment, By Department, Branch and Service, 1900 to 1977," Statistics Canada, https://www150.statcan.gc.ca/

11. Whyeda Gill-McClure, "Adaptation, Evolution and Survival? The Political Economy of Whitleyism and Public Service Industrial Relations in the U.K., 1917–Present," *Labour History* 59, no. 1 (2018): 16.

12. John Swettenham and David Kealy, *Serving the State: A History of The Professional Institute of The Public Service of Canada, 1920–1970* (Ottawa: Professional Institute of the Public Service of Canada, 1970), 6.

13. Swettenham and Kealy, 7, 23.

14. "The Canadian Medical Association: Proud History, Strong Future," iPolitics, 15 May 2017, https://ipolitics.ca/.

15. Swettenham and Kealy, 8.

16. J. L. Granatstein, *The Ottawa Men: The Civil Service Mandarins, 1935–1957* (Toronto: University of Toronto Press, 1982).

17. "Degrees Awarded by Canadian Universities and Colleges, by Sex, Canada, Selected Years, 1831 to 1973," Statistics Canada, accessed 1 August 2019, https://www150.statcan.gc.ca/.

18. Library and Archives Canada (hereafter LAC), PIPSC Fonds, Box MG28, I36, Vol 1, Annual Meeting, 1920 to 1923, Report of the Committee on Reclassification, 1922.

19. LAC, PIPSC Fonds, Box MG28, I36, Vol 1, Annual Meeting, 1920 to 1923, 1922 Annual General Meeting.

20. LAC, PIPSC Fonds, Box MG 28, I 36, vol 18, Radio Talks 1930–1934, untitled memorandum on radio talks.

21. Untitled memorandum on radio talks.

22. "Civil Service to Fix Tariff: Sir Robert Falconer Suggests This May Come in Future," *Globe and Mail*, 2 November 1921; "Unity Plea of Canadian Dean: McGill Professor Addresses Members of the Dominion Civil Service," *Christian Science Monitor*, 24

November 1925; "Urges Revision of Salary Rate: Wants Higher Compensation for Officers in Technical Services," *Globe and Mail*, 6 April 1922.

23. LAC, PIPSC Fonds, Box MG 28, I 36, vol 2, Annual Meetings 1930 to 1935, Annual Meeting 1935.

24. Jim Coyle, "The Weirdly Effective Reign of Mackenzie King," *Windsor Star*, 20 May 2017, https://www.ourwindsor.ca/. For the Snyder decision, see Privy Council Appeal No. 99 of 1924 (The Toronto Electric Commissioners v. Colin G. Snider and others), 20 January 1925, a copy of which can be found on the British and Irish Legal Information Institute website, https://www.bailii.org/.

25. Craig Heron, *The Canadian Labour Movement: A Short History*, 3rd ed. (Toronto: Lorimer, 2012), 71–72.

26. L. W. C. S. Barnes, *Consult and Advise: A History of the National Joint Council of the Public Service of Canada, 1944-1974* (Kingston: Queen's Industrial Relations Centre, 1974), 39, 49, 88.

27. See, for example, Ian MacMillan, "The Passage of the Public Service Staff Relations Act, 1965-67" (master's thesis, University of Guelph, 1983), 2.

28. Barnes, 105.

29. PIPSC Storage Rooms, *PIPSC Journal*, April 1964, 9.

30. MacMillan, 2.

31. MacMillan, 5–6.

32. A. Gray Gillespie, "The Public Service Staff Relations Board," *Industrial Relations/ Relations Industrielles* 30, no. 4 (1975): 637.

33. MacMillan, 61–65.

34. PIPSC Storage Room, *PIPSC Journal*, April 1967, 9.

35. Patrick Kinnear interview, 17 November 2017.

36. "In Memoriam: Frances Goodspeed (1923-2018), 1st Woman President of PIPSC," PIPSC website, 17 July 2018, https://www.pipsc.ca/. See also "Grace Hartman, CUPE National President, 1975-1983," CUPE website, 30 April 2003, https://www.cupe.ca/.

37. Lorraine Neville interview, 12 July 2018.

38. Ed Napke interview, 12 July 2018.

39. Reg Whittaker and Gary Marcuse, *Cold War Canada: The Making of a National Insecurity State, 1945-1957* (Toronto: University of Toronto Press, 1994), 27.

40. Whittaker and Marcuse, 163.

41. "In Memoriam: Frances Goodspeed."

42. "Federal Government Employment, by Department, Branch and Service, 1900 to 1977," Statistics Canada, accessed 8 December 2018, https://www150.statcan.gc.ca/

Chapter 2: We Are a Union, What Do We Do Now? 1970-79

1. For example see Craig Heron, *The Canadian Labour Movement: A Short History*, 3rd ed. (Toronto: Lorimer, 2012); Bryan Palmer, *Labouring the Canadian Millennium: Writings on Work and Workers, History and Historiography* (St. John's: Canadian Committee on Labour History, 2000); Joan Sangster, *Transforming Labour: Women and Work in Postwar Canada* (Toronto: University of Toronto Press, 2010).

2.   PIPSC Records Room, *Professional Public Service*, January 1970, 2–3. (All subsequent citations to issues of this publication are also from the PIPSC Records Room.) PIPSC publications indicate that Edweena Mair was married. At a time when women often found themselves excluded from workers' organizations, Mair's work as an activist in PIPSC represented an enormous commitment since she, like other married professional women at that time, also carried the additional burden of maintaining a domestic sphere at home.

3.   *Professional Public Service*, January 1970, 3–5.

4.   *Professional Public Service*, January 1970, 6, 11; *Professional Public Service*, February 1975, 5–12.

5.   *Professional Public Service*, May 1979, 3.

6.   Lorraine Neville interview, 12 July 2018.

7.   *Professional Public Service*, April 1979, 12–13.

8.   *Professional Public Service*, January 1970, 16.

9.   *Professional Public Service*, October 1970, 22.

10. *Professional Public Service*, October 1970, 22.

11. *Professional Public Service*, April 1970, 22.

12. Ellen Terrell, "When a Quote is Not (Exactly) a Quote: General Motors," United States Library of Congress, 22 April 2016, https://blogs.loc.gov/.

13. *Professional Public Service*, April 1970, 18.

14. *Professional Public Service*, October 1970, 19. This was equal to $4.8 million in 2017 dollars (calculated using the online Bank of Canada Inflation Calculator, Bank of Canada, accessed 11 September 2017, http://www.bankofcanada.ca/).

15. *Professional Public Service*, October 1970, 18.

16. PIPSC Storage Room, Ed Napke Collection, Box 3, Envelope Ernie Eaton, PIPSC President to Board of Directors, 26 April 1974; PIPSC Storage Room, Ed Napke Collection, Box 2, H.S. Weiler letter to PIPSC President E. Eaton, 3 March 1974.

17. PIPSC Storage Room, *Journal of the Professional Institute*, March 1973, 5; "Trusted Arbitrator Frances Bairstow Dies at 93," *Tampa Bay Times*, 27 September 2013, http://www.tampabay.com/; Archie Kleingartner profile, UCLA Meyer and Renee Luskin School of Public Affairs, accessed 12 September 2017, http://luskin.ucla.edu/; "Latest on Dispute Resolution: An excerpt from the State of the Art and Practice in Dispute Resolution Symposium to honour the late Dr. Bryan M. Downie," Queen's University IRC website, November 2002, http://irc.queensu.ca/.

18. PIPSC Storage Room, *Rebuilding the Professional Institute, Part I*, October 1973.

19. Ed Napke Collection, Box 2, "Organization Committee Report on Institute Restructuring," 5.

20. See Jean-Claude Parrot, *My Union, My Life: Jean-Claude Parrot and the Canadian Union of Postal Workers* (Halifax: Fernwood, 2005) for more on postal worker militancy.

21. Heron, *Canadian Labour Movement*, 96–98.

22. Heron, 110.

23. "The Professional Institute of the Public Service By-Laws, March 1967," Delegates Package, First Biennial Convention and 48th Annual Meeting of the Professional Institute of the Public Service of Canada November 1–3, 1967, Chateau Laurier

Hotel, Ottawa, Section C; "By-Laws and Regulations," Special Isssue, *Journal of the Professional Institute* 58, no. 2 (1979).

24. "By-Laws and Regulations," 2.

25. "By-Laws and Regulations," 2–5.

26. "By-Laws and Regulations," 5.

27. D. R. Buchanan (Chair, Finance Committee), Notes on the proposed fee increase, Minutes of the 53rd AGM, November 17, 1972; PIPSC *Journal* 51, no. 10.

28. "By-Laws and Regulations," 2, 8–9.

29. "By-Laws and Regulations," 2, 9.

30. "The Professional Institute of the Public Service By-Laws, March 1967." See By-Law 8.6—Regional Representation.

31. "By-Laws and Regulations," 6, 10. See, especially, By-Law 12—Regions and Regional Structures.

32. "By-Laws and Regulations," 6, 10.

33. "By-Laws and Regulations," 10.

34. J. G. Hollins, letter to the editor, PIPSC *Journal* 83, no. 5 (1974): 9.

35. *Public Service Staff Relations Board, Third Report: 1969–1970* (Ottawa: Information Canada, 1971), 8, 18.

36. "Federal Legislation Ordering Postal Workers Back to Work in 2011 Unconstitutional," National Union of Pubic and General Employees, accessed 11 September 2017, https://www.nupge.ca/.

37. Pattern bargaining is another strategic objective that unions often pursue. This practice sets common employment terms across an industry with many employers. For instance, autoworkers' unions have long sought to establish common work standards for every company with which they negotiate. In the 1960s and 1970s, pattern bargaining was often successful with larger companies and in wealthier industries, but it would become more challenging in the 1980s and 1990s.

38. PIPSC Central Records, File 217MD, Medicine, 1969–1982, Medicine Agreement 1969–1970, 2–3.

39. Medicine Agreement 1969–1970, 12–14.

40. Medicine Agreement 1969–1970, 10–12.

41. Medicine Agreement 1969–1970, 46, 50.

42. Medicine Agreement 1969–1970, 54.

43. Medicine Agreement 1969–1970, 78–80.

44. PIPSC Central Records, File 226SW, Social Work, 1969–1983, Social Work Agreement 1969–1970, 2–4.

45. Social Work Agreement 1969–1970, 54–56, 66, 78.

46. Social Work Agreement 1969–1970, 90.

47. Ed Napke Collection, Box 2, File Medical Bargaining, Department of National Health and Welfare, 11–12, 16.

48. Ed Napke Collection, Box 1, File 1972 Medical, Dr. A. C. Roy, memorandum, 16 May 1974, and Medicine Group letter to Ed Napke, 16 October 1974.

49. "Can Two Solitudes Be Avoided in the Civil Service?," *Globe and Mail*, 1 October 1970.

50. "Institute Proposes Changes in Bargaining Rules," *Globe and Mail*, 28 April 1971; "1,600 Nurses Reject Public Service Offer," *Globe and Mail*, 5 February 1975.

51. Patrick Kinnear interview, 17 November 2017.

52. Lucienne Bahuaud interview, 17 November 2017.

53. Statistics Canada, *1971 Census of Canada*, Volume V, Part I, 32.

54. Randy Dhar interview, 17 November 2018.

55. Bob McIntosh interview, 18 December 2017.

Chapter 3: Achieving Better Results for Members, 1980-89

1. PIPSC Storage Room, *Communications*, 1 February 1980, 1. (Subsequent citations of other issues of *Communications* are also from the PIPSC Storage Room.)

2. Dan Butler interview, 13 March 2019.

3. Lorraine Neville interview, 12 July 2018.

4. *Communications*, 15 July 1988.

5. "Understanding Your Language Rights," Office of the Commissioner of Official Languages website, accessed 1 January 2020, https://www.clo-ocol.gc.ca/.

6. PIPSC Storage Cage, Box 85, Policy and Planning 1973 to 1989, Minutes 1986, Policy and Planning Committee Meeting, 1 December 1986.

7. Don Burns interview, 17 November 2017.

8. Blair Stannard interview, 11 July 2018.

9. PIPSC Storage Room, PIPSC Financial Statements, 1989, 3–4.

10. Andrew Jackson and Sylvain Schetagne, "Solidarity Forever: An Analysis of Changes in Union Density," *Just Labour* 4 (Summer 2004): 63.

11. Neil Harden interview, 13 March 2019.

12. Steve Hindle and Bob McIntosh interview, 18 December 2017.

13. Larry Savage and Charles W. Smith, *Unions in Court: Organized Labour and the Charter of Rights and Freedoms* (Vancouver: University of British Columbia Press, 2017), 97–98.

14. Phil Jolie and Bob Luce interview, 12 July 2018.

15. Steve Hindle and Bob McIntosh interview.

16. Hindle and McIntosh.

17. PIPSC Central Records, File 303CS, Computer Systems, 1969–1979, Computer Systems Agreement, 1981–1983, 55–56.

18. PIPSC Central Records, File 214LA Legal 1970–1983, Law Group agreement, 1981–1982, 18.

19. Computer Systems Agreement, 1981–1983, A-1–A-2; Law Group agreement, 1981–1982, 18; Statistics Canada, *1981 Census of Canada*, Volume 1, Table 1.

20. *Communications*, 23 October 2019.

21. Public Service Staff Relations Board, *Fourteenth Annual Report, 1980–1981* (Ottawa: Minister of Supply and Services Canada, 1981).

22. *Communications*, 1 February 1980, 1.

23. Hindle and McIntosh interview.

24. Marcus Gee, "A Short and Angry Strike," *Maclean's*, 7 September 1987.

25. Hindle and McIntosh.

26. Iris Craig to Brian Mulroney, 6 July 1988, cited in *Communications*, 15 July 1988. See also *Communications*, 21 June 1985, 3.

27. "Public Servants Want Security Against Layoffs," *Toronto Star*, 5 November 1985; Mitchell Baird, "Reagan Was Wrong: The Nine Most Terrifying Words Are, 'I'm a Libertarian and the Market Will Save You,'" Huffington Post, 25 May 2011, https://www.huffingtonpost.com/.

28. Debra Dunville interview, 17 November 2017.

29. Nita Saville interview, 17 November 2017.

30. Bill Giggie interview, 17 November 2017.

31. Don Burns interview, 17 November 2017.

32. PIPSC Storage Cage, Box AGM 1981 to 1983, "On the Move: Preparing for the 1990s," Speech by President Iris Craig, 70th Annual General Meeting, 2.

Chapter 4: Nothing Can Be Taken for Granted, 1980-89

1. PIPSC Storage Room, *Communications*, December 1992, 1. (Subsequent citations of other issues of *Communications* are also from the PIPSC Storage Room.)

2. *Communications*, December 1992, 7.

3. *Communications*, December 1992, 7.

4. *Communications*, December 1992, 7.

5. See "List of PIPSC Presidents" in this book's appendices.

6. Marion MacEachern interview, 14 March 2019.

7. PIPSC Storage Cage, Box Complaints, 1996–2000, Judith H. Clarkson, Mediated Solutions Incorporated, "Fact-Finding Report for the Professional Institute of the Public Service of Canada," 28 February 1997.

8. Danielle Auclair interview, 13 March 2019.

9. Steve Hindle, email message to the author, 7 May 2019.

10. "The Picket Ticket," private collection of Laureen Allan.

11. Steve Hindle and Bob McIntosh interview, 18 December 2017.

12. Danielle Auclair interview.

13. "CAW Staff on Strike for Better Pensions," *Globe and Mail*, 22 May 2000, https://www.theglobeandmail.com/; "CLC Staff on Strike," Members for Democracy Archive, 12 February 2004, http://www.m-f-d.org/.

14. Marion MacEachern interview.

15. PIPSC Storage Cage, Box Board of Directors: August 1995 to December 1995, Duotang: Board of Directors Meeting Number 11, 5 December 1995.

16. PIPSC Storage Cage, Box Board of Directors: August 1995 to December 1995, "The Professional Institute of the Public Service of Canada (PIPSC): External Compensation Review for the Position of President," 26 June 1998.

17. PIPSC Storage Room, Annual Reports, 1999 Annual Report.

18. 1999 Annual Report.

19. Hindle and McIntosh interview.

20. Advisory Committee on Labour Management Relations in the Federal Public Service, *Identifying the Issues: Final Report, May 2000* (Ottawa: Government of Canada, 2000), 28, https://www.tbs-sct.gc.ca/.

21. *Identifying the Issues*, 29.

22. *Identifying the Issues*, 30.

23. *Identifying the Issues*, 31.

24. PIPSC Central Filing, File 210EN Engineering and Land Survey 1990–1993, Engineering and Land Survey Agreement, 1990–93, Article 14.

25. Engineering and Land Survey Agreement, 1990–93, Article 18, Appendix A. The cost of living calculation is from the online Bank of Canada Inflation Calculator, Bank of Canada, accessed 19 April 2019, https://www.bankofcanada.ca/.

26. PIPSC Central Filing, File 927DLNU Deer Lodge Nursing 1984–2005, Deer Lodge Agreement 1992–94, Appendix A.

27. "External Compensation Review for the Position of President"; The Daily, Statistics Canada, 12 May 1998, https://www150.statcan.gc.ca/.

28. Stephen Douglas interview, 17 July 2018.

29. "Fact Sheet: Evolution of Pay Equity," Government of Canada, accessed 20 April 2019, https://www.canada.ca/.

30. Kathryn Brookfield interview, 29 August 2018.

31. Lyne Morin interview, 14 March 2019.

32. Ruth Walden interview, 13 March 2019.

33. The American system is outline in United States Office of Personnel Management, *Introduction to the Position Classification Standards* (OPM, 1991; rev. 2009), https://www.opm.gov/.

34. Brian Beaven interview, 29 August 2018.

35. Lyne Morin interview.

36. Karen Parr interview, 17 November 2017.

37. Hindle email to the author.

38. Dan Butler interview, 13 March 2019.

39. Anthony Wilson-Smith, "Mulroney Versus the Unions," *Maclean's*, 23 September 1991, http://archive.macleans.ca/; "Brian Mulroney Takes On Organized Crime," radio audio clip from *Five Nights*, aired 9 December 1974, CBC Digital Archives, Canadian Broadcasting Corporation, accessed 19 April 2019, https://www.cbc.ca/archives/.

40. PIPSC Storage Room, Box PIPSC Miscellaneous Documents 1990s, Revenue Canada position paper, 1998.

41. Steve Hindle, "Public Servants Waiting For a Sign of Good Faith," *The Hill Times*, 30 August 1999.

42. "French, English Complain of Bias: Civil Servants Question Commitment to Bilingualism," *Globe and Mail*, 6 March 1991.

43. "Tax Auditors Take Hard Line on Companies," *Toronto Star*, 12 June 1991.

44. "4,000 Auditors Join Strike," *Toronto Star*, 11 September 1991.

45. Michael Forbes interview, 17 November 2017.

46. PIPSC, "PIPSC President Iris Craig and Guest Professor John Polyani Launch 'Science and Society' to Mark National Public Service Week," press release, 15 June 1993.

47. Shiv Chopra, *Corrupt to the Core: Memoirs of a Health Canada Whistleblower* (Caledon, ON: KOS Publishing, 2009), 4, 13, 15.

48. Chopra, 48; "Recombitant Bovine Growth Hormone," American Cancer Society website, accessed 22 April 2019, https://www.cancer.org/.

49. Chopra, 122.

50. Chopra, 206.

51. Jean Chrétien, *My Years As Prime Minister* (Toronto: Alfred A. Knopf, 2007), 62; Brian Mulroney, *Memoirs, 1939–1993* (Toronto: McClelland and Stewart, 2007), 387.

Chapter 5: Into a New Century, 2000–09

1. "Flora MacDonald, Veteran Canadian Politician, Dies at Age 89," *Toronto Star*, 26 July 2015, https://www.thestar.com/.

2. Lyne Morin interview, 14 March 2019.

3. Lorraine Neville interview, 12 July 2018.

4. PIPSC Storage Cage, Box Office of the President Correspondence Michèle Demers, Michèle Demers to Dyane Adam, 22 December 2005.

5. PIPSC Storage Cage, Box Office of the President Correspondence Michèle Demers, Michèle Demers to Sheila Marie Cook, 28 October 2005.

6. PIPSC Storage Cage, Box Office of the President Correspondence Michèle Demers, Michèle Demers to Ginny Simms, 31 October 2005.

7. PIPSC Storage Cage, Box Board of Directors, January 1996–July 1996, PIPSC Joint Management/Executive Committee Meeting Minutes, March 21, 1996. This wasn't the first time that PIPSC supported another union in their strike activities. In the late 1990s, the Ontario Public Service Employee Union was looking for a $1 million interest free-loan in support of striking members. Rather than loan them the money, PIPSC unconditionally gave them $100,000.

8. Eddie Gillis interview, 12 July 2018.

9. PIPSC Storage Cage, Box Office of the President Correspondence Michèle Demers, Michèle Demers to Maureen Harper, 19 September 2005.

10. Gary Corbett interview, 13 December 2018.

11. Corbett interview.

12. Steve Hindle and Bob McIntosh interview, 18 December 2017.

13. Corbett interview.

14. Hindle and McIntosh interview.

15. Richard Rice interview, 17 November 2017.

16. Robert Bowie-Reed interview, 29 August 2018.

17. Danielle Auclair interview, 13 March 2019.

18. PIPSC Storage Room, Financial Statements, 31 May 2000, 1.

19. Advisory Committee on Labour Management Relations in the Federal Public Service, *Identifying the Issues: Final Report, May 2000* (Ottawa: Government of Canada, 2000), 4, 42, https://www.tbs-sct.gc.ca/.

20. *Identifying the Issues*, 42.

21. PIPSC, *The Big Chill: Silencing Public Interest Science* [2013], https://www.pipsc.ca/.

22. PIPSC Storage Room, Binder Constitutional Challenge, press release, 5 May 2008; Larry Savage and Charles W. Smith, *Unions in Court: Organized Labour and the Charter of Rights and Freedoms* (Vancouver: University of British Columbia Press, 2017), 3–4.

23. Savage and Smith, 167–71.

24. *Agreement Between the House of Commons and the Professional Institute of the Public Service Of Canada: Procedural Clerks and Analysis and Reference Bargaining Unit, 2003–2006,* 13–15, 24, https://www.sdc.gov.on.ca/.

25. *House of Commons and the Professional Institute,* Appendix A-1; Cost of living calculations are derived from the online Bank of Canada Inflation Calculator, https://www.bankofcanada.ca/.

26. PIPSC Collective Agreement Database, *Sunnybrook and Women's College Hospital and the Professional Institute of the Public Service of Canada in respect of the Sunnybrook & Women's Radiation Therapy (SW-RT) Group, 2004–2007,* 31–35; Bank of Canada Inflation Calculator, https://www.bankofcanada.ca/.

27. "Abuse of Authority," Federal Public Sector Labour Relations and Employment Board website (FPSLREB), accessed 19 June 2019, https://www.fpslreb-crtespf.gc.ca/; House of Commons v. Professional Institute of the Public Service of Canada et al., FPSLREB, accessed 19 June 2019, https://www.fpslreb-crtespf.gc.ca/.

28. Veillette v. Professional Institute of the Public Service of Canada and Rogers, FPSLREB, accessed 19 June 2019, https://www.fpslreb-crtespf.gc.ca/.

29. Dubuc v. Professional Institute of the Public Service of Canada and Sioui, FPSLREB, accessed 19 June 2019, https://www.fpslreb-crtespf.gc.ca/.

30. "Upstart Union Takes On the Mighty PSAC: PIPSC Targets Young Public Servants Who Think Unions Are Passe," *Ottawa Citizen,* 3 November 2002.

31. PIPSC Storage Cage, Box Office of the President Correspondence Michèle Demers, Michèle Demers to PIPSC Board of Directors and Stewards, 9 October 2008.

32. Waheed Khan interview, 13 December 2018; Carol Agócs, ed., *Employment Equity in Canada: The Legacy of the Abella Report* (Toronto: University of Toronto Press, 2014); Rosalie Abella, *Equality in Employment: A Royal Commission Report* (Ottawa: Government of Canada, 1984). Harris's characterization of Ontario's employment equity legislation is from "Harris Would Junk Equity-Hiring Law," *Globe and Mail,* 6 May 1995. On the election of the Conservative government in Ontario in 1995, see John Ibbitson, *Promised Land: Inside the Mike Harris Revolution* (Scarborough, ON: Prentice Hall, 1997).

33. Waheed Khan interview.

34. Glen Schjerning interview, 29 August 2018.

Chapter 6: Stepping Up to a Larger Union Stage, 2010–19

1. Wayne Lewchuk et al., *It's More Than Poverty: Employment Precarity and Household Well-Being* (Toronto and Hamilton: United Way Toronto and McMaster University, 2013); Guy Standing, *The Precariat: The Dangerous New Class* (London: Bloomsbury Academic, 2011).

2. "Union Status by Industry," Statistics Canada, accessed 22 August 2019, https://www150.statcan.gc.ca/; "Population of the Federal Public Service," Treasury Board Secretariat, Government of Canada, accessed 21 August 2019, https://www.canada.ca/.

3. Debi Daviau interview, 29 August 2018.

4. C. Wright Mills, *The New Men of Power: America's Labour Leaders* (Chicago: University of Illinois Press, 1948), 9.
5. Debi Daviau interview.
6. Eddie Gillis interview, 12 July 2018.
7. Nicholas Pernal interview, 13 March 2019.
8. Max Way interview, 14 March 2019.
9. International Association of Machinists and Aerospace Workers, TCU/IAM *Constitution/By-Laws* (July 2014), https://www.goiam.org/.
10. Unifor, *Constitution* (August 2016), https://www.unifor.org/; Canadian Union of Public Employees, *Constitution 2017*, https://cupe.azureedge.net/.
11. Eddie Gillis interview.
12. PIPSC Storage Cage, "Minutes of the 95th Annual General Meeting, November 7–8, 2014."
13. "Report on the Disposition of 2016 Carried Resolutions Presented to the 98th Annual General Meeting," PIPSC, accessed 1 January 2020, https://www.pipsc.ca/.
14. "Report on the Disposition of 2016 Carried Resolutions."
15. "Report on the Disposition of 2016 Carried Resolutions."
16. "2018 Member and Delegate Count," PIPSC, https://www.pipsc.ca/.
17. "Australian Payroll Fiasco Foreshadowed Phoenix's Failed Launch in Canada," CBC News, 26 February 2018, https://www.cbc.ca/.
18. "As Federal Phoenix Payroll Fiasco Hits 2-Year Mark, Families Continue to Bear Brunt of It," CBC News, 28 February 2018, https://www.cbc.ca/.
19. PIPSC, "PIPSC's Top 5 Frequently Asked Questions on Phoenix," Nix Phoenix Campaign Materials, Better Together website, PIPSC, accessed 1 January 2020, https://action.pipsc.ca/phoenixcampaignmaterial.
20. PIPSC, "Government of Canada and Public Service Unions Finalize Agreement to Compensate Federal Employees Impacted by the Phoenix Pay System," press release, 13 June 2019, https://www.pipsc.ca/.
21. "Federal Scientists Win Right to Be Unmuzzled in Tentative PIPSC Contract," *Ottawa Citizen*, 12 December 2016, https://ottawacitizen.com/; "President's New Year's Message, 2015," PIPSC, https://pipsc.ca/. The census was crucial because a range of groups across Canada—from social advocacy organizations to corporations—used it to gain accurate insights into the country's demographic changes.
22. Matthew MacLeod interview, 28 February 2019.
23. Mounted Police Association of Ontario v. Canada, 2015 SCC 1, [2015] 1 SCR 3, https://scc-csc.lexum.com/.
24. Larry Savage and Charles W. Smith, *Unions in Court: Organized Labour and the Charter of Rights and Freedoms* (Vancouver: University of British Columbia Press, 2017), 184.
25. "Central Table Negotiation Proposals 2019 Presented by PIPSC," PIPSC, https://pipsc.ca/.
26. *Applied Science and Patent Examination (SP) Agreement Between the Treasury Board and the Professional Institute of the Public Service of Canada* (Ottawa: Treasury Board of Canada Secretariat, 2017), 37, 57, https://www.tbs-sct.gc.ca/; *Research (RE) Agreement*

Between the Treasury Board and the Professional Institute of the Public Service of Canada (Ottawa: Treasury Board of Canada Secretariat, 2017), 39, 63, https://www.tbs-sct.gc.ca/. Reference in PIPSC contracts to NJC agreements had been standardized language since the 1980s. The full list of agreements included directives on bilingualism bonuses, commuting assistance, providing first aid to the general public, the foreign service, isolated posts and government housing, relocation, the definition of spouse, the public service health care plan, travel, uniforms, occupational health and safety, motor vehicle operations, and pesticide use.

27. *Research (RE) Agreement*, 79–80; *Applied Science and Patent Examination (SP) Agreement*, 96–97; Cost of living calculations are derived from the online Bank of Canada Inflation Calculator, accessed 30 July 2019, https://www.bankofcanada.ca/.

28. "Collective Bargaining Update," "Occupational Groups By Bargaining Unit Representation," and "Qualification Standards for the Core Public Administration by Occupational Group or Classification," Treasury Board Secretariat, Government of Canada, accessed 29 July 2019, https://www.canada.ca/.

29. Treasury Board v. Professional Institute of the Public Service of Canada, 2010 PSLRB 60 and Professional Institute of the Public Service of Canada v. Treasury Board, 2019 FPSLREB 7, Federal Public Sector Labour Relations and Employment Board, accessed 29 July 2019, https://www.fpslreb-crtespf.gc.ca/.

30. The full list of members included, on the union side, the Association of Canadian Financial Officers; the Association of Justice Counsels; the Canadian Air Traffic Control Association (Unifor Local 5454); the Canadian Association of Professional Employees; the Canadian Federal Pilots Association; the Canadian Merchant Service Guild; the Canadian Military Colleges Faculty Association; the Federal Government Dockyard Chargehands Association; the Federal Government Dockyard Trades and Labour Council (East); the Federal Government Dockyard Trades and Labour Council (West); the International Brotherhood of Electrical Workers, Local 2228; the Professional Association of Foreign Service Officers; PIPSC; PSAC; the Research Council Employees' Association; Unifor, Locals 2182 and 87-M; and the Union of Canadian Correctional Officers. The employer groups included the Canadian Food Inspection Agency; the Communications Security Establishment; the National Research Council; the Office of the Auditor General; and the Treasury Board Secretariat. See "NJC Membership," National Joint Council, accessed 29 July 2019, https://www.njc-cnm.gc.ca/.

31. *Union Coverage in Canada—2014* (Employment and Social Development Canada, 2015), http://publications.gc.ca/; Association of Justice Counsel, accessed 29 July 2019, https://ajc-ajj.net/; Laureen Allan, email message to author, 5 September 2019.

32. "Bilingualism Bonus Directive," National Joint Council, accessed 29 July 2019, https://www.njc-cnm.gc.ca/.

33. See CBC News, http://www.cbc.ca.

34. PIPSC, Board of Directors Meeting minutes, 26–27 April 2019.

35. Greg Scriver interview, 28 February 2019.

36. Sharon Trasatti interview, 13 March 2019.

37. Ginette Tardif interview, 28 February 2019.

38. Rob MacDonald interview, 28 February 2019.
39. Norma Domey interview, 28 February 2019.
40. Debi Daviau interview.
41. "More Public Servants Running for Office in 2015 Than Ever Before," CBC News, 8 October 2015, http://www.cbc.ca/news/.
42. "Political vs. Partisan," internal PIPSC policy paper, 2015, in author's possession.
43. "The International Civil Service Effectiveness (InCiSE) Index 2017," Institute for Government, https://www.bsg.ox.ac.uk/.
44. Madeleine Blais interview, 17 November 2017.
45. Andrew Wigmore interview, 14 March 2019.
46. Gordon Bulmer interview, 13 September 2018.

Conclusion

1. See Jason Russell, "Finding a Turn in Canadian Management Through Archival Sources," *Journal of Management History* 25, no. 4 (2019): 550–64.
2. For background, see John Maynard Keyes, *The General Theory of Employment, Interest, and Money* (London: MacMillan, 1936) and Friedrich von Hayek, *The Road to Serfdom* (Chicago: University of Chicago Press, 1944).
3. Donald Savoie, *Governing From The Centre: The Concentration of Power in Canadian Politics* (Toronto: University of Toronto Press, 1999), 43–45; Prime Minister's Office, Government of Canada, accessed 21 August 2019, https://pm.gc.ca/en/cabinet.
4. Stephanie Ross, "Varieties of Social Unionism: Toward a Framework for Comparison," *Just Labour* 11 (Autumn 2007): 16.
5. Daphne Taras, "Why Nonunion Representation is Legal in Canada," *Industrial Relations/Relations Industrielles* 53, no. 4 (1997): 763–86. Taras's article is one of the few available works that references the influence of Whitley in Canada.
6. Larry Savage and Michelle Webber, "The Paradox of Professionalism: Unions of Professionals in the Public Sector," in *Public Sector Unions in the Age of Austerity*, edited by Stephanie Ross and Larry Savage (Halifax: Fernwood, 2014), 114–26.
7. By-laws and Regulations, PIPSC, accessed 7 September 2019, https://pipsc.ca/.
8. Laureen Allan, email message to author, 6 September 2019.
9. See Harry Braverman, *Labour and Monopoly Capital: The Degradation of Work in the Twentieth Century* (New York: Monthly Review Press, 1974) and James Rinehart, *The Tyranny of Work: Alienation and the Labour Process*, 5th ed. (Toronto: Nelson, 2006).
10. Thomas Landry interview, 17 November 2017.
11. Glenn Maxwell interview, 17 November 2017.
12. Susan O'Donnell interview, 17 November 2017.
13. Terry Peters interview, 17 November 2017.
14. Bonnie Pratt interview, 17 November 2017.
15. Terry Sing interview, 17 November 2017.
16. Barrie Wickware interview, 17 November 2017.
17. Steve Hindle and Bob McIntosh interview, 18 December 2017.

Index